'WORLD'S GREATEST AUTO SHOW"

Celebrating a Century in *Chicago*

James M. Flammang and Mitchel J. Frumkin

Foreword by Mayor Richard M. Daley

Published by

**krause
publications**

700 E. State Street • Iola, WI 54990-0001
Telephone: 715/445-2214

Please call or write for our free catalog of automotive publications.
Our toll-free number to place an order or obtain a free catalog is 800-258-0929 or please use our regular business
telephone 715-445-2214 for editorial comment
and further information.

Library of Congress Catalog Number: 98-87293
ISBN: 0-87341-6961
Printed in the United States of America

CONTENTS

ACKNOWLEDGMENTS

No books of consequence are written without help, and this one is definitely no exception. Without the ceaseless cooperation and encouragement of the officers and staff of the Chicago Automobile Trade Association, this book could not have been written. Very special thanks go to CATA President Jerry H. Cizek III, Executive Vice-President David Sloan, Dealer Relations Director Jack Gallagher, and Communications Director Paul Brian.

We also extend special thanks to long-time Krause Publications contributor Phil Hall for providing detailed information on concept vehicles, and to Dan Kirchner of the American Automobile Manufacturers Association for his research efforts. Mark Patrick of the National Automotive History Collection, in Detroit, generously allowed access to his files to search for historic Chicago Auto Show photos.

Chicago's top automotive journalists, Jim Mateja of the C[ ]cago Tribune and Dan Jedlicka of the Chicago Sun-Times, c[ ]tributed both recollections of the auto show and encouragem[ ] about the project.

Another vote of thanks goes to the people who agreed to [ ] interviewed for the book, including: Bill Wilt; Victor Callewa[ ] Richard Bishop; Cal MacRitchie; Julia (Kazlauskis) Bartosch; J[ ] Marie (O'Connell) Platenka; and James Sawyer.

This book could not have been successfully written with[ ] the efforts of two staff members at Krause Publications: J[ ] Gunnell, who proposed the original idea; and Ron Kowalke, w[ ] provided expert editorial guidance.

PHOTOGRAPHY

The authors gratefully acknowledge the cooperation of the following people who supplied photography and memorabilia, to help make this book possible. Our greatest appreciation goes to Tom Poliak, who supplied dozens of photos. We also wish to thank: Daniel F. Kirchner (American Automobile Manufacturers Association); Sandra Spikes and Walter Wojtowicz (Chicago Tribune); Helen J. Early (Oldsmobile); Fred R. Egloff; Mark Patrick (National Automotive History Collection); Richard Bishop; Richard T. Quinn; Rennie Heath (Commonwealth Edison); JoAnn K. Bongiorno (Drake Hotel); Gregg J. Buttermore (Auburn Cord Duesenberg Museum); Joan M. Taffe (Conrad Hilton); Jim Benjaminson; Pat Baknaus (University of Illinois at Chicago);

Mary Kay Marquisos (Metropolitan Pier and Expositi[ ] Authority); Dan Jedlicka; Hugh Edfors; Julia (Kazlausl[ ] Bartosch; June Marie (O'Connell) Platenka; Col. Eugene [ ] Scott, Ret. (Chicago Daily Defender); Victor Callewa[ ] (Ryba's Fudge); James Sawyer (SVT); Frank Opalka; G[ ] Povalish; George Drolet; Dale Livingston; Howard S. Solotr[ ] and Ray Barnowski.

Special thanks go to: Sam Griffith (Griffith Studio, In[ ] Jim Frenak and Marty Engel (Frenak Photo and Imaging); B[ ] Hofgren Literature; Nicky Wright (Wright, Inc.); Lee R[ ] Hartung (Hartung's Automotive Museum); Bob Whal[ ] Photo Ideas, Inc.; Stan Hurd Auto Literature; Peggy VaGen[ ] (Photo Ops); and Ken Jackson.

PHOTO CREDITS

Chicago Tribune: 12, 43, 45, 46, 50, 52, 53, 59, 60, 61, 64, 66, 67, 76, 79, 84, 86, 87, 98; **Oldsmobile History Center:** 18, 89, 119, 132, 143, 162, 164, 202, 212; **Mitchel J. Frumkin:** 19, 205, 284; **Fred R. Egloff:** 33, 44; **The National Automobile History Collection of the Detroit Public Library:** 36, 42, 43, 44, 50, 51, 52, 60, 74, 75, 77, 78, 80, 82, 178, 285, 286, 287; **American Automobile Manufacturers Association:** 37, 40, 41, 62, 77, 134, 135; **Richard Bishop:** 39; **Commonwealth Edison Incorporated:** 40; **Chicago Historical Society:** 46, 47, 53, 55, 76; **Library of Congress:** 49; **Richard T. Quinn:** 58, 75, 88, 91, 169, 184; **The Drake Hotel, Chicago:** 62; **Auburn Cord Duesenberg Museum:** 70, 75, 85, 178; **Conrad Hilton Hotel and Towers, Chicago:** 77; **Jim Benjaminson:** 78; **University of Illinois at Chicago (University Library Dept. of Special Collections):** 79; **Metropolitan Pier and Exposition Authority:** 128, 154; **Hugh Edfors:** 129; **Dan Jedlicka:** 130; **Ju[ ] Kazlauskis Bartosch:** 205; **June Marie (O'Connell) Platen[ ]** 209; **Tom Poliak:** 186, 188, 220, 221, 222, 223, 224, 225, 2[ ] 227, 228, 229, 231, 232, 233, 234, 238, 239, 240, 241, 2[ ] 243, 244, 245, 246, 247, 248, 249, 250, 251, 252, 254, 2[ ] 256, 257, 258, 259, 260, 261, 263, 264, 265, 266, 267, 2[ ] 269, 270, 271, 272, 273, 274, 275, 276, 277; **Chicago Da[ ] Defender:** 230; **Ryba's Fudge:** 288; **SVT (Ford Special Vehi[ ] Team):** 295; **Opalka Vintage Autos:** 177, 180; **Gary Povali[ ]** 186; **George Drolet:** 187; **Dale Livingston:** 183, 185; **Howa[ ] S. Solotroff:** 184, 185; **Ray Barnowski:** 183, 184.

All other photos were supplied by the **Chicago Automob[ ] Trade Association (CATA)**.

FOREWORD

Richard M. Daley
Mayor of Chicago

Americans, all Americans, love their cars. It doesn't matter if they are rich or poor. It doesn't matter what their background may be or how much money they earn. It doesn't even matter what kind of car they can afford to buy—they still love their cars and treat them like they were their children.

When people see a new car, they begin to dream. They think about what it would be like to drive that car—and what it would take to buy it.

That is why the Chicago Auto Show is always one of the most exciting events in Chicago each year. It is an event that brings people together, everyone wanting to look at the newest, the most luxurious and the fastest.

As a child, I was amazed by the enthusiasm of the people who went to the auto shows. The cars seemed like they were built for a different era, for a future we were waiting to enter. And people looked over these cars like they were looking at a flying saucer or a jet pack.

Some of the cars deserved that kind of admiration. Cars like the Thunderbird really captured my imagination. I remember the incredible quality of the cars—and I thought about all the hard work that must have gone into the design and manufacture of these huge steel machines.

To see a new car—especially a concept car—is to get a glimpse of the future and the very best in human ingenuity.

Today, people are just as fascinated by cars—maybe even more so. Cars come from around the world and are a symbol of the strong world economy. This competition has inspired even more creativity and quality. That is why people turn out year after year, to see what is coming next.

As we approach the new millennium, most people are expecting to enter a new world with new possibilities. Cars help ignite that curiosity and those dreams. The Auto Show has always been a great benefit to Chicago, to our economy, and to our vision of the future.

INTRODUCTION

Ever since the dawn of the 20th century, the American public has taken the annual auto shows to heart. From the very beginning, too, Chicago has enjoyed a reputation as the center of attention in that thrilling automobile world.

Chicago's annual event can lay claim to being the longest consecutive running auto show in the United States—and one of the oldest overall. With a colorful history that dates all the way back to 1898, the Chicago show parallels and reflects aspects of *all* of the auto shows held throughout the world, during the past century.

Through all those years, annual auto shows have been the place where manufacturers invite the public to gather and celebrate exciting innovations in automotive transportation. Held in a pleasant and clean environment, auto shows allow entire families to wander happily and view fabulous new designs, marvel at the engineering genius that emanates from the automakers, debate the latest fashions (and fads), and enjoy an inspiring glimpse into the future.

Having attended the Chicago Auto Show since the mid-1950s, the authors bring personal touches and insights to this book, to augment their thorough historical research. They take you behind the scenes of the annual event, and introduce you to a variety of personalities who have been involved with the show's success.

Informative timelines highlight dates and events for each year—in the industry and at the auto show itself. Here, you'll find quick rundowns of the car models that were new or reworked for that model year, special vehicles that appeared at the show, and historical events that were reshaping the automotive world.

An introduction to each chapter summarizes the evolution of the auto industry during that period, and chronicles the changes that took place at the auto show. It also traces the development of the Chicago Automobile Trade Association, from its inception in 1904 to its role today as auto-show organizer and valued adjunct to Chicagoland auto dealerships.

Words tell the auto-show story in detail, while accompanying pictures enhance the sensation of "being there." More than a thousand carefully-selected photographs let the reader visually relive aspects of nearly one hundred years of the Chicago Auto Show, providing a sense of all the pageantry and glamour that made ea[ch] event so special, and so memorable. These photos b[e] illustrate the ever-evolving automobile, the grandeur of t[he] musical stage revues that began in 1935, and the appeal the "beauty queens" who graced the show from 1935 1960. They also provide a close look at intrigui[ng] memorabilia, printed material that a visitor might ha[ve] picked up at the show, and much more.

Paging through the photos and reading the text lets see many of the changes that have taken place in t[he] world around us, as well as the automotive element of th[e] world. In the early days, for example, the auto show w[as] far more than a gathering of the latest automobile Attending the show was an all-out event, one th[at] warranted dressing for the occasion. Men were likely wear suits, ties, and hats; women dressed in their mo[st] stylish attire. Auto-show buildings were bedecked wi[th] ornate and colorful decorations, typically intended remind visitors of European palaces and exotic locales.

Even in the 1950s, we'll see, it was common f[or] families to visit the auto show garbed as if they we[re] attending a wedding or ceremony. This was a fami[ly] focused occasion, and looking "proper" was part of t[he] preparation. All this, of course, is in stark contrast today's casual style, when those who head on down McCormick Place each winter are far more likely to [be] wearing jeans than suitcoats.

Today's auto-show visitor is likely to be armed wi[th] plenty of knowledge about the cars on display, and wh[at] he or she might wish to buy. In the early years of t[he] century, as we'll discover, people had yet to be convinc[ed] of the worth of the automobile, and persuaded that the[y] might indeed want to have one themselves.

We'll see how automobiles—and the auto show—changed as America faced the Great Depression of t[he] 1930s. Why, for instance, did the auto-show organize[rs] turn to intense showmanship at this time, planning a[n] elaborate stage revue for each year's event—comple[te] with "beauty queens," no less? What happened to t[he] auto show during World War II? Why was there no au[to] show in Chicago in the late 1940s? Why did the popu[lar] stage revues cease after the Fifties? What did subseque[nt] auto shows have, to attract comparable attention fro[m] people on the show floor?

Perusing these pages will give answers to all of those estions, and many more.

Chicago's auto show has taken place at only three ations since 1901. From that year to 1935, the show ened at the Coliseum—a castle-like structure built from remains of Libby Prison, a Civil War institution that had en moved to Chicago to serve as a tourist attraction. The ernational Amphitheatre, at 42nd and Halsted, hosted auto show from 1936 to 1961—and again from 1967 1970, following the disastrous fire that destroyed cCormick Place.

Those who attended the auto show at the nphitheatre, in particular, are likely to have vivid emories of the occasion, partly because the building was ated near the legendary—but long-ago departed—nicago Stockyards. As CATA President Jerry Cizek curately describes it, the air in that part of the city nded to be "ripe" much of the time. But that did not ssuade Chicagoans and Midwesterners from attending—d fully enjoying—their yearly auto show.

The modern-day Chicago Auto Show has actually set shop in three different McCormick Places: the original ilding (1961–66); its replacement at the same lakefront ation (1971–96); and the new McCormick Place South nce 1997).

Until the 1990s, Chicago's role as the greatest auto ow in America was hardly threatened. New York's show, nich also got underway at the beginning of the century, as long considered to be a mere exhibition of what was w. Chicago, in contrast, had the "selling" show—the e that caused people to dash over to a dealership and tually buy some of those automobiles, after the show osed its doors.

Not until Detroit decided to expand its own show, lling it the North American International Auto Show, did rious competition emerge. And even when Detroit could ast of having more new-model introductions than nicago, it couldn't even begin to approach the endance figures of the Chicago event.

Every winter in Chicago, tens of thousands of motor-nded folks—entire families and groups of friends—rolled down to the auto show to look over the new models. In e days before "everyone" owned an automobile, they rived by streetcar or took the train. Today, they're more ely to drive, facing frightful traffic along the Outer Drive get an opportunity to survey all the latest vehicle odels, and a lot more, in one convenient location.

Raging blizzards and Chicago's famed winds failed to ep them away. Tales abound of long lines of people aiting to get into the Coliseum or Amphitheatre, even en the weather was dismal outside. Residents of Carl andburg's "city of big shoulders" are tough, after all. A

few snowflakes weren't about to keep them from gazing upon the latest dreams out of Detroit.

Speaking of dreams, it was the long series of "dream cars," especially those of the Fifties, that might have exerted the strongest grasp on the attention of showgoers. Only rarely did anything similar to the show cars created by such styling legends as Harley Earl at General Motors and Virgil Exner at Chrysler make it into production. But that didn't matter. Americans love to dream, and the long series of concept vehicles gave them an opportunity to imagine what might lie ahead in the automotive future.

Engineers, too, lent their talents to the dream cars, turning out a long series of one-of-a-kind models that leaped well ahead of the latest technology. Most of their forward-thinking ideas faded out of the limelight, along with the fantastic body shapes that were created. But before they did, auto-show visitors were permitted to ponder what it might be like to drive a car without a steering wheel, for instance; or pilot a turbine-engine automobile. Better yet, some of those seemingly-fantastic ideas turned out to be workable in real life. And when that happened, visitors to the auto show could claim, correctly, that they'd seen it first.

Unlike any other book in existence, this one gives the reader a unique opportunity to view, once again, hundreds of those one-of-a-kind vehicles. In addition to the well-known "dream cars" that have become an integral part of automotive history, manufacturers would often bring last-minute design exercises to the show, to tease and tantalize the public. Some of these were basically stock vehicles with special names, custom paint jobs, and distinctive interiors and wheels. These cars might have appeared at just a few of the larger auto shows during the year, then disappeared forever, with few (if any) published photos and facts to mark their existence.

Fortunately, many such vehicles were photographed at their displays during the Chicago Auto Show. These cars are identified and featured in this book.

Not every vehicle that appeared at the Chicago show at one time or another could be included in this book, of course. We've picked the very best examples from the thousands of photographs that were available to us. Then too, if one of your favorite production or dream cars has been omitted from these pages, the photographer of that day might simply have missed it.

Thankfully, from 1950 to the present day, the Chicago Automobile Trade Association has assigned photographers to shoot hundreds of scenes from each annual show. These rare photos provide the foundation of this treasure trove of images that helps each of us, author and reader alike, relive the glorious past of the Chicago Auto Show—arguably, through so many marvelous years, the "World's Greatest Auto Show."

The Golden Years
(1950-54)
Part 1

As the decade of the Fifties opened, Chicagoans were ready, willing—and eager—to look over some cars. After all, Chicago had not seen an auto show since late 1940—a year before Pearl Harbor sent the United States full-bore into World War II.

Through the war years, no automobiles had been produced for civilian consumption. Every vehicle that rolled out of an American assembly plant went to the military, or to government officials. No point having an auto show when there are no vehicles to be purchased and millions of potential buyers were serving their country overseas.

The only cars on sale were *used* cars. Between 1942 and 1945, dealers struggled to gather enough secondhand merchandise to resell, in an attempt to keep their dealerships alive.

After the war ended in August 1945, production started up slowly. Ford was first with 1946 models, which were essentially warmed-over '42s. Most automakers followed that same pattern, touching up their final prewar models to make them look a little different, but changing little underneath the skin.

As wartime veterans returned to civilian life, a new car typically topped the list of things they wanted right away. Most of the veterans, and most people who'd spent the war toiling in factories at home, had money in their pockets. But there were few cars to be found. In what quickly became known as a "seller's market," dealers were easily able to sell every car they could lay their hands on, for an impressive profit. Car-hungry Americans put their names on waiting lists, and knew they might have to pay a premium price if they were offered a car.

Not all cars were sold in the normal way, either. A "gray market" in cars developed in the early postwar years, as customers expressed willingness to bend the rules somewhat if the end result was a new car in the driveway. Many returning veterans had been moving into new suburbs, and millions more would do so through the 1950s, as farmland surrounding most major cities turned into residential subdivisions. Suburbia was beginning to develop, and those freshly-paved driveways looked almost naked without a 1947 or '48 automobile resting its rubber on the surface.

A 1949 car might be better yet. Studebaker and Hudson had introduced brand-new models with modern styling for

1947 and '48, respectively. Studes had what some called a "Is it coming or going?" profile, while Hudson turned to the "Step-down" design. The all-new Kaisers and Frazers had debuted as 1947 models. For most automakers, though, 1949 was the year for introducing fresh postwar design, which handily captured the attention of the motoring public.

Production was building, and the industry was poised for a record production year in 1950. By mid-1949, members of the Chicago Automobile Trade Association (CATA) realized the time was ripe for a revived auto show. Though the "seller's market" still ruled, availability of cars was beginning to ease. Soon, they knew, Midwesterners would no longer grab up every automobile that went on sale.

No, they would have to be "sold," just as they had in the prewar era. And what better way to sell than to hold a show—an extravaganza on the order of the auto show before the war, but with some decidedly modern touches thrown in. Ever since 1935, the CATA had been operating the Chicago Auto Show, and its members were enthusiastic about getting the postwar ball rolling.

For its first auto show after World War II, the Chicago Automobile Trade Association revived the stage revues that had been used to introduce the new car models. Shown is a 1950 Nash on stage at this year's "Wheels of Freedom" revue. Nash's "upside-down bathtub" design had been introduced in 1949.

Planning began with the appointment by the CATA board of directors of an executive show committee. Members then considered the best dates for a show, and decided on a location. No reason not to use the International Amphitheatre at 42nd and Halsted, near the famed Chicago stockyards. After all, the Amphitheatre had served as the site of each Chicago Auto Show since 1935, and it could be made ready in a reasonable time.

Instead of holding the show late in the year, though—as they'd done before the war—they decided to have it shortly after the *beginning* of the year. That's how it had been in the early years of the Chicago show. Dating back to the turn of the century, the Chicago Automobile Show had opened somewhere between January and March. That schedule had changed in 1935, as the government sought to equalize auto-industry production schedules. But now, it seemed wiser to go back to the original idea. A late-winter show revived interest in automobiles, paving the way for a strong selling season in the spring.

Show planners then had to enlist the support of dealers and manufacturers. They needed to hold drawings for exhibit spaces in the car and truck sections, so everyone would feel the selection process was fair and random. Spaces also had to be allotted for accessory exhibits and special educational displays.

Showmanship had become a big part of the auto-show picture, ever since the CATA had taken over the reins in 1935. People needed more than a bunch of cars sitting on display. They needed a gala, an extravaganza, some colorful hoopla. A bevy of beautiful young women participating in the event wouldn't hurt, either.

Therefore, the twice-daily stage revues that had drawn thousands of spectators into the Amphitheatre's central arena would be revived for the 1950 auto show. Instead of the "nationality queens" who had assisted with prewar presentations, however, the CATA decided to feature "neighborhood and community queens." Contests were held throughout the city and suburban neighborhoods. Several hundred young women entered. From that total, 19 were selected to participate in the 1950 auto show, helping to present the new car models and adding a large dash of glamour to the production. The stage-show area had 10,000 seats, plus standing room. As many as 15,000 people watched the show at one time.

As the program described it, "an ultra-feminine feature of the stage show will be a galaxy of 'gorgeously gowned glamor girls' chosen as queens in Chicago communities and suburbs, who will appear in a 'Pageant of Pulchritude' number." The women would be followed by "another impressive array of 'Beauties on Wheels,'" the cars themselves, presented on a special elevated stage. Appropriate one-minute comments about the outstanding features of each car will be told as the car is driven slowly into a turntable stage and revolves before the audience." Each "queen" sponsored one car.

In cooperation with the Chicago Safety Information Committee, chaired by Mayor Martin H. Kennelly, the CATA sponsored a safety slogan contest in Chicago-area schools.

Jack Gallagher —from auto show usher to CATA executive

Not many people can boast of a history with the Chicago Auto Show that reaches anywhere close to Jack Gallagher's. Currently serving as the auto show's exhibit coordinator (and director of dealer relations for the Chicago Automobile Trade Association), Gallagher began his career as an usher with the Andy Frain organization, way back in 1949. By 1954, he headed the troop of ushers that performed their duties at the show.

His own tasks at that event included assisting each community "beauty queen" as she pointed out the merits of a car model on the stage. That included opening the car door as it arrived onstage, and formally tipping his hat to the young woman. During the performance, Gallagher was dressed in a handsome usher's uniform.

Although his onstage duties varied little from one automobile to the next, and one year's show to the next, an occasional mishap did occur. Gallagher recalls, for instance, how a door handle once came off in his hand, as he attempted to let the young woman out.

During the Sixties, after the move to McCormick Place, Gallagher "never did the stage show, because they'd done away with the neighborhood queens." Therefore, "I wasn't nervous anymore."

Winners got U.S. Savings Bonds. The mayor designated the auto-show period as Traffic Safety Week.

Some 10,000 CATA members, employees and families, and guests previewed the exhibits and the stage show on the night before the show's opening. Earlier that day, out-of-town media people had arrived on special planes to attend a Kaiser-Frazer program, along with company President Edgar F. Kaiser, to debut Kaiser's new low-priced car (to be called the Henry J).

Automotive News, the trade paper, reported that everything at the Chicago Auto Show was "on a big scale." Paintings of George Washington and Abraham Lincoln, for instance, stood 24 feet high—said to be the biggest such portraits ever. The stage had what *Ward's Automobile Topics* called the "largest proscenium in the middle west," measuring 200 feet wide.

Billed as a "momentous musical melange," the "Wheels of Freedom" stage spectacle presented the story of transportation, accompanied by folklore, music, singing, and dancing. Naturally, the revue—produced by Will J. Harris—culminated with presentations of the 1950 automobiles.

"The audience will thrill to the arrival of immigrants through the Seat [of the United States]," the program promised, "as the stirring episodical extravaganza goes into action." Flashing back first to covered-wagon days, the revue moved into the Iron Horse era and beyond as "dramatic, eye-filling scenes portray[ed] the evolution of motive power in America."

Commentator and soloist Alexander Gray had starred in such productions as "Desert Song" and "Student Prince." Gray was joined by the Frank Bennett Singers, and the Melba Cordes Dancers. John C. Becker, head of Becker Brothers Studios, again oversaw the stage-revue set design and production, as he'd done since 1935.

Because most cars had been redesigned in 1949 (if not before), the 1950 models were largely carryovers with modest facelifts. That didn't keep the spectators from paying close attention. Visitors had plenty of special vehicles to gaze at, too. For starters, many exhibits that had been seen at GM's "MidCentury Motorama" in New York's Waldorf-Astoria Hotel, in January, came to the Chicago show. GM's exhibit included mechanized exhibits as well as cutaways of new automatic transmissions. Some cars were painted in special spring colors, establishing a trend for the Chicago show, which would often feature "spring specials."

Cadillac exhibited a posh $35,000 Debutante, with upholstery and floors partly covered in leopard skins. Visitors were asked to examine the little red Nash N-X-I and give an opinion. That car evolved into the Nash Metropolitan, which went on sale in 1954. Nash also displayed the new compact Rambler convertible and station wagon.

Chevrolet and Pontiac promoted their new pillarless hardtop body styles, introduced a year earlier on other GM makes. Cadillac continued its tailfins of 1948-49, as well as the modern overhead-valve V-8 engine that had debuted in '49 Cadillac and Oldsmobile models. Introduction of that modern V-8 engine had helped Cadillac earn *Motor Trend* magazine's very first "Car of the Year" award, in 1949. A special Oldsmobile Palm Beach coupe featured door panels trimmed in alligator skin.

In addition to the then-unnamed Henry J, the Kaiser-Frazer company exhibited the dramatically redesigned Kaiser sedan, both intended for sale as '51 models.

Chicago's event was the only major automobile show in the nation this year. Bad weather during all but three days of the 1950 show failed to keep the crowds away. At 478,000, attendance beat the 1940 record by 84,000. James F. McManus, chairman of the executive show committee, noted that "it just seemed as if nothing could keep people away from the show."

An estimated 10,000 cars and trucks were sold at the show and at dealerships, as a direct result. McManus predicted that sales volume would reach $65 million, and orders taken at the show itself ran 35 percent ahead of the pace in 1940.

How much did the new cars cost? Well, a 1950 Chevrolet Styleline DeLuxe sedan went for $1,529, and the average worker earned $3,851 per year. Despite the fact that the Korean War broke out during 1950, prosperity was

the watchword. Nearly everyone expected to do better th year than last—and better yet next year. Buying on cre was expanding rapidly, and automobiles topped the list items to be purchased through "time payments."

Attendance at the 1951 Chicago Auto Show dipped bit, to 457,000. This was a season of more facelifts, and n so many truly fresh models. Chrysler introduced its pote "Hemi" V-8 engine this year, and showgoers could study cutaway of its operation. Chrysler was named *Motor Tre* "Car of the Year" in 1951, largely on the basis of that V design. Oldsmobile used the Chicago show as a launch p for its new Super 88 model, with an updated "Rocket" V engine.

Auto-show planners had another elaborate and color revue in mind for 1951. Featuring a cast of one hundred, the music of Lew Diamond's orchestra, "Transportati U.S.A." placed the new cars "against a background dancing, gay songs, and gorgeously gowned glamor girls the hour-long extravaganza." Five musical selections in t stage revue culminated with the fitting tune: "Chicago, T City of Beautiful Girls." Chicago's well-known State Stre stores outfitted the 21 community and suburban "queen with the latest fashions for modern living and travel.

Car-shoppers feared shortages as a result of the Kore War. Despite production cutbacks, shortages did not occ but body trim pieces began to ebb in quality as precio metals went to the war effort.

Chicago was stepping tentatively into the expressw age. The Edens and Calumet parkways opened late in 195 Construction was underway on the Congress Expressw though delays moved its expected opening date into la 1953 or early '54.

"Motor Modes of 1952," directed by Dorothy Hild, w the title of the next year's stage revue. Once agai spectators learned the outstanding features of ea automobile as it revolved slowly on a turntable. This tim though, an off-stage voice described each car, over t public-address system.

Although the Chicago Auto Show was admittedly "selling show," the CATA explained in the program th salesmen "do not exert 'high pressure' methods. Th assignment is to explain features and answer questions fro visitors." The efforts of those salespeople at each exhib were supplemented by experts from the factories, equipp with information on technical and engineering details of t new models.

Attendance approached the record in 1952, w 474,000 visitors coming through the entrance gates. addition to viewing more than 150 production cars ar about 60 trucks, visitors had plenty of "dream cars" ar technical displays to ponder. A special Chrysler engineeri exhibit, called the "New Worlds in Engineering Show featured the Ghia-built K-310 concept car—one of ma that Chrysler designed in the Fifties.

Ford, Mercury, and Lincoln bodies were redesigned the modern mode. Showgoers got their first look at t redesigned Nash-Healey sports car, to go on sale in t spring. Cadillac exhibited a bright white Eldorado, with hea sisting glass in its curved windshield and in rectangular ings atop each door.

Once again, the attendance record was broken in 1953, 481,000 car-hungry visitors chose to visit the Chicago Auto Show. *Newsweek* reported that Chicago's show "has come the country's biggest." More than 87,000 people tended on the first Sunday alone.

Each year through the early Fifties, the International mphitheatre was decked out in a fresh color scheme. For 953, the choice of hues was marine blue and shell pink.

In the "Stars of Motordom" revue, twin turntables were ed to present the cars, modeled by another group of ommunity and suburban "queens." One revolving rntable provided dynamic scenic effects, while the other hibited cars from every angle.

The 1953 show opened at a later date than usual, said to e at the request of automakers. For one thing, a steel strike d been underway when plans began in summer of 1952. Some of the automakers," said show committee chairman ank H. Yarnall, had further "expressed the opinion the ter date would be closer to their good selling season."

Nash held a Fashion Salon five times daily to show off its designed Rambler, styled by Pinin Farina. Guests could even eet Miss America, Neva Jane Langley, at the Nash stand.

An even greater crop of "glamour" cars than usual reeted 1953 visitors to the Chicago show. They might ever be available at any dealership, but "dream cars" elped lure passersby into each make's exhibit area. Buick ad a fiberglass-bodied Wildcat, Cadillac a Le Mans, hrysler a Sports Special, and Lincoln-Mercury showed off s scarlet XL-500 with an all-glass roof. Oldsmobile isplayed a limited-production Fiesta coupe and an xperimental Starfire. Chrysler's Imperial Newport hardtop as shown for the first time anywhere.

Among production models, Hudson had a new compact t. Willys, well-known for its Jeep-based vehicles, had a new assenger car called the Aero. The new Kaiser-Darrin, soon to e available with unique sliding doors and a disappearing top, ould be seen in Chicago along with a "hardtop" Kaiser ragon sedan. Cadillac exhibited its limited-production dorado convertible, with a new panoramic windshield and etal top-well cover. Most General Motors vehicles had new odies. So did Chrysler products.

Studebaker just about stole the show with its dramatic ew coupe, designed to European principles by Raymond oewy and his team. Showgoers even got to see the first orvette sports car, months before its limited-production elease later in the year.

The Korean War ended in July, having had only a modest ffect on auto production over a three-year period. Manufacturers were worried about selling ever-greater umbers of cars. What became known as a sales "blitz" took lace in 1953-54, as automakers coerced dealers into pushing or higher sales, essentially by any means necessary. High-ressure sales practices that peaked during this period would ead to Congressional investigation later in the decade.

The Chicago Auto Show was a family affair, not just an xposition for Dad. "Visitors yesterday," the *Chicago*

Tribune noted in 1954, "included many father and son teams, as has been the case in the past."

A new Winners' Circle at the 1954 Chicago show featured famous American competition cars and race winners. The program advised that this section had been "added not to glorify speed, but to give due recognition to the great contribution to automotive advancement made by the courageous and inventive men of the roaring road." Motorsport fans could see Chuck Stevenson's Lincoln, Frank "Rebel" Mundy's Hudson, and other well-known competition vehicles of the day.

Ford Motor Company promoted its new "Y-Block" V-8 engine, taking over from the legendary but outdated "flathead" V-8 that had powered Ford products since 1932.

"Wheels of Progress" was the title of the 1954 stage revue, in a setting that included a live flower garden, working fountain, and an on-stage orchestra. Copper and white hues decorated the interior of the Amphitheatre.

Despite record-setting production in 1950, and impressive totals over the next few years, the industry stood ready for even more motoring thrills in '55. Chicago was ready to take a hard look at what some considered the greatest crop of new models ever. The auto show's "golden years" had barely begun, it seemed.

Before surveying the rest of the "golden years," though, we need to look back at how the Chicago Auto Show began.

Bill Wilt's gift at the auto show

Bill Wilt had a plan in mind for the 1953 Chicago Auto Show. He intended to present a car—a tan/brown DeSoto station wagon—to his father. But he wanted to keep that car in top shape until he turned over the keys. Not an easy matter, when the car is to be displayed every day at the Amphitheatre.

Bill was a Chicagoland district sales manager for DeSoto at the time, so he was able to influence the choice of a station wagon to be on the rotating turntable, instead of a specially-painted convertible. His dad's wagon was now in view of, but not easily touched by, the auto-show crowd.

"My dad had a great time during the show," Bill recalls, "bringing various friends and relatives to admire his new car on display." The show went well, but a long delay came at the end, when it was time to bring the car down from the second-floor display area. "We did not realize that there was but one elevator that would transport a single vehicle at a time to the main level. We waited to the wee hours of the morning before we were able to finally drive the new car out of the building, but it was worth it."

1950

42nd annual Chicago Automobile Show

(February 18-26, 1950)

- First Chicago show since 1940
- Preparations begin in mid-1949, months before show opens
- Held at International Amphitheatre—site of final prewar shows
- "Wheels of Freedom" stage show, like pre-war extravaganzas, draws enthusiastic audiences twice a day ... revue includes neighborhood "beauty queens"
- 478,000 visitors attend auto show's 9-day run, despite bad weather
- Most new models are face lifts of major 1948-49 redesigns
- Radically restyled '51 Kaiser seen at 1950 show, along with Kaiser compact
- Chevrolet and Pontiac introduce hardtop (pillarless) coupes
- Cadillac and Buick continue OHV V-8, introduced for 1949
- Ford, Mercury, and Lincoln models still use flathead V-8 engines
- Studebaker keeps "coming-or-going" profile, introduced in 1947
- Nash Rambler debuts; other Nash models retain "bathtub" look of 1949
- Experimental N-X-I unveiled (will become Nash Metropolitan)
- Auto industry is poised for a record-setting production year
- Seller's market still strong—dealers can easily sell every car they obtain
- Korean War is looming
- First members of "baby boom" generation approach school age

Planning for the 42nd annual Chicago Auto Show began in mid-1949.

Stage designer John Becker (left) and show producer Will J. Harris inspect a model of the "Wheels of Freedom" curtain.

Right: Posters and dozens—indeed, hundreds—of other items had to be approved and executed before the 1950 auto show could open.

Far Right: The Chicago Tribune put the auto show's opening day on the front page, as a banner headline. Newspaper publicity helped to draw visitors to each year's show.

Attendance at the 1950 Chicago Auto Show beat the 1940 record by 84,000. A total of 62,000 people arrived on the first Sunday alone.

The Amphitheatre had 15 acres of guarded, free parking space for auto-show visitors. Families could arrive easily by streetcar or elevated line, too.

Paintings of George Washington and Abraham Lincoln, each 24 feet high, were said to be the biggest-ever pictures of those Presidents. They served as a backdrop curtain for the "Wheels of Freedom" spectacle.

Fords still had the flathead V-8 engine that had been introduced in 1932, but that didn't prevent eager buyers from looking hard at the '50 models.

Lincoln attempted to draw gapers with a stripped chassis, revealing the car's old-fashioned flathead V-8 engine.

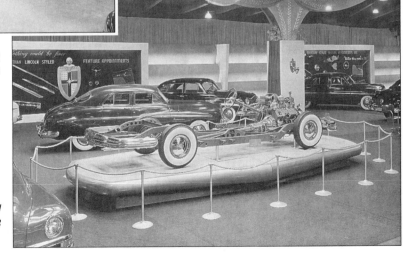

Nash exhibited an experimental red N-X-I car, designed to use little gas and sell for une
$1,000 (if produced). Ads asked readers to examine the N-X-I and fill out questionnaires w
their opinions. A few years later, the N-X-I evolved into the British-built Nash Metropolitan.

Kukla and Ollie—puppet membe
of the popular Kukla, Fran, ar
Ollie children's TV show—visit tf
auto show with puppeteer Bı
Tillstrom. Fran Allison (not show.
was the third member of the o.
screen trio.

Right: Olympic star Jesse Owens
(fifth from left) joins radio
personality Vince Garrity at one of
the auto-show events.

Left: Manufacturers ran their own
newspaper ads to entice auto-
show visitors—or those who
weren't sure they wanted to
attend.

Many people considered the Studebaker somewhat strange in styling—perhaps matched by the apparel worn by the woman who gave the rundown at the auto show.

dillac exhibited this $35,000 car
h upholstery and floor partly
vered in leopard skin. Instrument
nels and fittings were plated with
-karat gold. Named Debutante, it
s called "the most luxurious car
er built by Cadillac."

Like most American cars, Chevrolets had received new bodies for 1949, facelifted a bit for '50. A Powerglide automatic transmission was new this year.

Auto-show planners had to be pleased by the crowds that turned out for the 1950 Chicago Auto Show.

Kaiser used the 1950 Chicago Auto Show to show off its forthcoming, radically restyled sedan, scheduled to go on sale as a '51 model.

Frazers, produced by the same company that made the Kaiser, also were reworked for 1951; but that make would not last much longer.

Performers in the "Wheels of Freedom" revue included the Melba Cordes dancers and the Frank Bennett singers. Along with the show and neighborhood "queens" came beauties of another stripe: the 1950 automobiles.

Skits were part of the entertainment at this year's "Wheels of Freedom" revue. Note the old touring car and tandem bicycle.

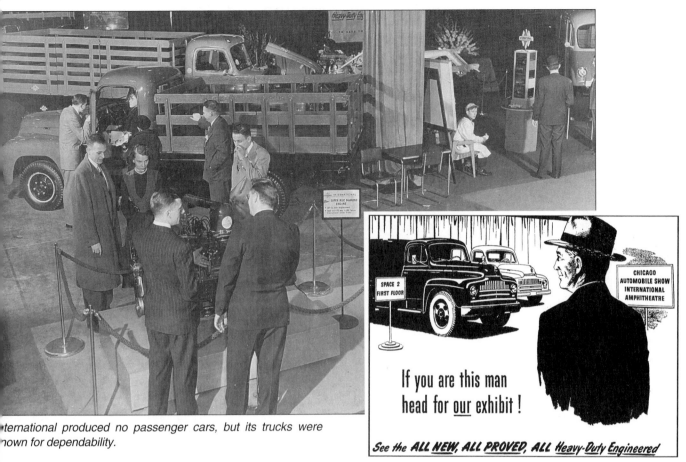

ternational produced no passenger cars, but its trucks were
nown for dependability.

What sort of man buys an International truck? In 1950, it would
be a man who ran a business that required hauling of some sort.

transparent side gives onlookers an excellent view of the
orkings of this Chevrolet panel van.

In the Fifties, trucks were sought for their practical utility, not as a
fashion statement. Chevrolets were popular in both passenger-car
and truck guise.

1951

43rd annual Chicago Automobile Show

(February 17-25, 1951)

- International Amphitheatre again is site for Chicago show
- 457,000 visitors attend the show during its 9-day run
- "Transportation U.S.A." stage show features Lew Diamond's orchestra
- 21 neighborhood "beauty queens" model State Street fashions, assist with new-car presentations
- Chrysler launches "Hemi" V-8 engine
- Hudson introduces hot Hornet
- Ford and Plymouth add hardtop body style
- Oldsmobile Super 88 seen for first time at Chicago Automobile Show
- Compact Henry J debuts
- British-built Nash-Healey is imported
- Packards get all-new, squarish bodies
- Production cutbacks ordered, due to Korean War—feared shortages do not appear, but brightwork on new cars gets thinner and weaker

To participate in the auto show, neighborhood "queens" had to be 17 to 21 ye of age. Each area held a contest to select a "queen."

Oldsmobile had introduced Rocket V-8 engine for 19 setting off the "horsepo race." For 1951, a ho version powered the n Super 88.

New for 1951 was Oldsmobile's Super 88, packing the strongest "Rocket" V-8 engine into the lightweight 88 body.

arl "Mad Man" Muntz (inset), best known for building TV sets,
*so turned out a sports car in the early Fifties. The Muntz Jet held
Lincoln flathead V-8 engine.

Marian Heinz, Miss North Cook County, extols the virtues of a steel-
bodied Willys Jeep station wagon at the 1951 auto show.

*MC had been building trucks—including fire and emergency
*hicles—since before World War I.

19

Built in England, the Nash-Healey sports car debuted as a 1951 model. Most presenters were not so bizarrely attired.

Hudson launched the potent Hornet for 1951—a step beyond the company's modern "Step-down" body that had debuted for 1948.

Chrysler introduced its "Hemi" V-8 engine for 1951. Note the engine, mounted on a pedestal, at the rear.

Grace Quinn, Miss Brighton Park, wears western garb to show off the Crosley convertible. Crosley introduced its minicar in 1939.

Ford's new hardtop (pillarless) coupe draws plenty of attention at the 1951 auto show.

Cadillac had introduced tailfins with its 1948 models, refining—or enlarging—them regularly through the Fifties. Most upwardly-mobile strivers of that day considered Cadillac the car of their dreams—the car they "deserved" at a certain point in their lives.

Planning for each auto-show revue began with scale models of the stage.

Lavishly-costumed performers and a full orchestra helped focus audience attention on the new automobiles.

Cars were the stars of the "Transportation U.S.A." stage revue, following the musical selection: "Chicago, The City of Beautiful Girls." This Mercury got a smooth facelift for '51.

1952

44th annual Chicago Automobile Show

(February 16-24, 1952)

- "Motor Modes of '52" stage show draws visitors at International Amphitheatre
- Stage show starts with Cinderella, features dancers, singers, "beauty queens" and 1952 cars
- Auto-show attendance totals 474,000 visitors
- 19 car makes, 9 truck makes, and 42 other exhibits at show
- Ford, Mercury, and Lincoln get modern, all-new bodies ... Lincolns get OHV V-8
- "Hemi" V-8 goes into DeSotos
- Studebaker adds hardtop body style
- Willys Aero debuts, joining the company's Jeep models
- Hudsons can have "Twin-H Power"
- Full-size Nash models restyled in part by Pinin Farina, lose their "bathtub" look
- Cadillacs have built-in dual exhaust tips
- Compact Allstate debuts—but sold at Sears, Roebuck stores
- One-third of cars have V-8 engine
- Korean War continues
- International Amphitheatre also used to host Democratic and Republican political conventions, later in year

Chicagoans and out-of-towners loved each year's auto show, as shown by the crowds that turned up at the Amphitheatre.

Studebaker promoted its V-8 engine, introduced in 1950, at this year's auto show.

In convertible form, the once-stodgy Packard cut quite a dashing figure for '52.

Cutaway of the all-new Ford revealed its overhead-valve "Y-Block" V-8 engine and coil-spring front suspension—vital steps forward for Ford—as well as the spacious interior.

Below: W.K. Edmund and Ray Heure discuss the new Ford. Auto-show visitors had always been drawn to cutaway vehicles that revealed new features.

Right: Chrysler gained a reputation for stylish and innovative concept cars in the 1950s, many penned by design chief Virgil Exner and built by Ghia in Italy. One of the first was the K-310, seen at the Chicago Auto Show in '52.

Ramblers had debuted in 1950, produced by Nash. Few other manufacturers held much hope for sales of compact cars.

Left: Rolling a Hudson onto its side allowed observers to study the "Step-down" design close-up. Note the twin carburetors, called "Twin H-Power" by Hudson.

Below: Hoping to attract interest in a compact model, the Kaiser company had launched an economy-oriented Henry J for 1951.

Some cars had design features that were virtual trademarks. For DeSoto, it was the bold grille "teeth."

25

A brand-new, modern-styled Lincoln debuted for 1952, complete with overhead-valve V-8 engine. For the next few years, Lincolns brought home trophies from the Carrera Panamericana race in Baja, Mexico.

A display of scale models highlighted the International Truck exhibit at the auto show.

Pontiacs stuck with the san body they'd received in 1949, b changes were about to happen

1953
45th annual Chicago Automobile Show
(March 14-22, 1953)

- International Amphitheatre again is site
- Later dates than usual were requested by manufacturers
- Attendance sets another record, at 481,000 visitors
- "Stars of Freedom" stage show has astronomical theme, spotlights all the 1953 models
- Buicks get V-8 engines, losing familiar straight-eights
- Limited-edition Cadillac Eldorado and Buick Skylark convertibles debut ... so does Oldsmobile Fiesta
- Chevrolets and Pontiacs wear fresh bodies
- Chrysler products get bigger, squarer bodies—Dodge adopts Red Ram V-8
- Stylish, European-inspired Studebaker coupe "wows" auto show audience
- First fiberglass-bodied Corvette seen at Chicago show, goes into production late in 1953 model year; only 315 are sold
- Kaiser-Darrin seen at Chicago show
- Hudson introduces compact Jet
- Korean War ends in July
- Sales "blitz" underway, as factories push dealers to sell more cars
- Half of new cars have automatic transmission
- Hugh Hefner starts *Playboy* magazine in Chicago ... first *TV Guide* is published

Sprayed in white lacquer, with a sharply curved windshield and "jetlike" rear-fender air scoops, the Cadillac Eldorado convertible captured the imaginations of showgoers. A year later, Eldorados would go on sale—in different form, as a limited edition.

Well-known for its Jeep-based vehicles, Willys followed the lead of Nash and introduced the compact Aero sedan for 1953.

Conventional in structure, the Willys Aero had appealing styling and might have benefited from a reputation for durability earned by the Jeeps. Sales never really took off, and the Aero did not last long.

Months before the first Corvettes came off the line, visitors to the Chicago Au Show got to see Chevrolet's startling fiberglass-bodied two-seater. Chevro announced that the car was "planned for limited production late in 1953."

Like Pontiac and Buick, Chevrolet got a fresh body for 1953—more squared than before, but with neatly rounded edges. Underneath the hood sat the familiar "Stovebolt Six" engine.

For 1953, the Nash-Healey sports car adopted a different appearance. Visitors to the Chicago Auto Show get a first look at the car, which went on sale in the spring.

Scooters were growing popular on the streets Chicago, but an electric-powered machine w seldom seen.

Crowds swarmed around the 1953 Studebaker—and with good reason. No one had ever seen a shape like this on an American coupe: European-inspired, low, rakish, penned by Raymond Loewy and his team. Even more surprising, Studebaker was a moderately-priced car.

Like other Chrysler products, Dodge got an all-new body for 1953, as well as a new "Ram" V-8 engine.

Buick introduced a limited-edition Skylark convertible in 1953, with fully exposed wheels and a wraparound windshield. A V-8 engine was installed in all Buicks except the Special this year.

Trucks were a major part of Studebaker's annual sales totals, even if they could never approach the rakish appeal of the company's sport coupe.

Ford's F-1 series trucks had gone on sale in 1948, but 1953 brought a brand-new, sleeker model: the F-150. Not every auto-show guest paid attention to pickups, unless one was needed for business purposes.

1954
46th annual Chicago Automobile Show
(March 13-21, 1954)

- "Wheels of Progress" stage show takes place in "Autotown, U.S.A."
- Jimmy Richards Orchestra provides music for stage extravaganza
- 467,000 visitors attend auto show during its 9-day run
- New "winner's circle" at show displays competition cars ... management advises that exhibit does not endorse speed
- Panoramic windshields appear on Buicks and Cadillacs
- Ford and Mercury get new "Y-block" V-8 engines; flathead V-8 is history
- Ford and Mercury models with Plexiglas roof panels debut
- New Buick Century mixes Roadmaster engine with lightweight Special body
- Hudson Italia seen at Chicago show—built in Italy for limited sale
- Nash-Kelvinator and Hudson merge to form American Motors Corporation, later in year
- Studebaker and Packard meld into Studebaker-Packard Corporation

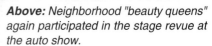

Above: Neighborhood "beauty queens" again participated in the stage revue at the auto show.

Left: The Chicago Automobile Trade Association (CATA), sponsor of the Chicago Auto Show, celebrated its 50th anniversary in 1954.

Seen at the Chicago Auto Show four years earlier, as the N-X-I, the Nash Metropolitan went on sale this year. Built in England, the little Metro held an Austin engine and seated three.

All Buicks, including the Special, had V-8 engines in 1954. Note the wire wheels and textured roof on the Century (right), a new model this year, which melded a Roadmaster engine into a lighter Special body.

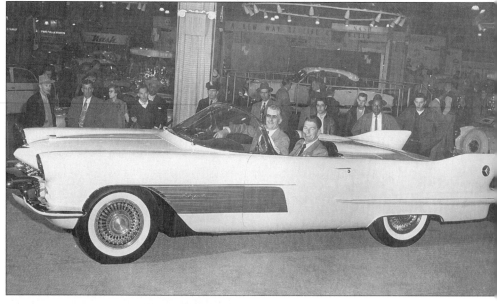

Ronald Reagan, then a popular movie actor and TV personality, slipped behind the wheel of a Cadillac La Espada convertible at the 1954 Chicago Auto Show. Tall tailfins on this concept car suggested the shape of fins to come on Cadillacs—and other American automobiles.

Entertainer Cab Calloway waves from a stylis Ford Thunderbird. Ford showed its new tw seater at the 1954 Chicago Auto Show, but would go on sale as a '55 model.

Neighborhood newspapers, such as the Southtown Economist, were closely involved with the auto show in the 1950s. U.S. Senator Joseph McCarthy (R-Wis.), standing next to flag, appeared at this banquet.

Once considered dowdy, Packards earned a gaudier reputation by 1954, courtesy of such colorful vehicles as the Caribbean convertible.

Fred R. Egloff slipped behind the wheel of this Excalibur with his friend, Kevin Moran, in the passenger seat. Egloff assisted at the Excalibur exhibit during the 1954 auto show. The car had raced at Sebring, in 1953.

or its second season on the market, Studebaker merely gave its dramatically-shaped coupe a fresh grille and a few touch-ups. The newy-styled Studebaker was considered one of the sharpest designs of the century, so why tamper with success?

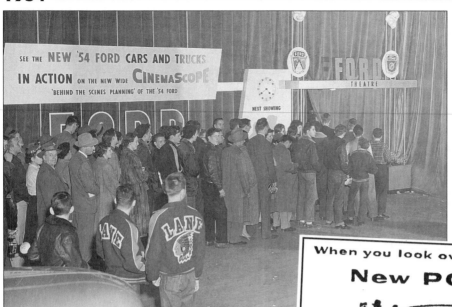

Cinemascope was luring moviegoers in[to] theaters—but auto-show visitors could se[e] Ford promotions in the wide-screen proces[s]. Lane Technical High School on the North Si[de] was the city's largest school for boys.

Gadgetry continued to capture automobile buyers, just as it had in prewar years. GM cars could be equipped with an Autronic Eye headlight dimmer.

As part of its last gasp in the marketplace, Kaiser launched the Kaiser-Darrin sports car in 1954, complete with unique forward-sliding doors.

Willys promoted the great versatility of its Jeep, born in wartime but able to handle demanding tasks anywhere— even on the farm.

ight: Small newspaper ads uld trigger interest in trucks at e show, even if the actual ehicle details were never entioned or explained.

ar Right: In real life at the auto how, the Dodge truck that had een advertised did look like it at in a fancy, opened box.

Families made a visit to the auto show a special occasion in the Fifties, each member dressed neatly and tidily—far different from today's sartorial standards.

2
Early Years of the Auto Show
(1898-1929)

When the first automobile show opened, "horseless carriages" weren't completely new to Chicago. As early as 1893, one of them was exhibited at the Columbian Exposition—the first world's fair in the city. Not many people paid any attention.

Two years later, the Times-Herald Race took place. Despite ample publicity in the newspaper that sponsored the grueling 54-mile trek through snow-covered streets, not many Chicago residents turned out to watch. Only the most farsighted people could envision the vast automotive industry that was beginning to blossom.

By the turn of the century, then, Chicagoans might have *seen* one of those newfangled automobiles parading down one of the city's streets. Yet, few folks had ever driven one—or even *sat* in one.

Would people who lacked direct experience with a motor vehicle turn up at an auto exposition? Even the promoters of the first auto shows in Chicago weren't sure whether they would flop or succeed.

So, when *was* the first Chicago auto show? Like many historical questions, this one has no single answer. The first "official" show—and the first one to be held indoors—happened in 1901. But at least three events took place earlier. Whether each qualifies as the first true auto show is a matter of dispute.

Motorcars were exhibited in the city late in 1898, but they were essentially tucked into a corner at a bicycle-oriented event, drawing no huge crowds. According to the *Chicago Tribune*, in a story written a decade later, automobiles were formally placed on exhibition for the first time in Chicago 1898, when N.H. Van Sicklen promoted a bicycle show in the Edson Keith building, at Wabash Avenue and Monroe Street. Van Sicklen exhibited a group of motorcars on the third floor. In that 1909 issue, the *Tribune* recalled that a Woods electric made its first appearance at Tattersall's bicycle meet, during the fall festival. "Each evening during the week a section of the indoor track was removed and two electric rigs were run into the inclosure for the inspection of the public."

"Chicago's first motor vehicle show," declared the October 1899 issue of *The Motor Vehicle Review*, "is now in progress at Tattersall's and considerable enthusiasm is being worked up over the exhibition." On opening night, only three Woods electric vehicles were on hand. But by Saturday, the magazine reported 25 machines on display, including a maroon phaeton that came all the way from Kansas. For half an hour each evening, drivers demonstrated stopping short, backing, and sharp cornering. The *Chicago Tribune* counted 28 vehicles on exhibition or running around the track. Promoters blamed short preparation time for the lack of visitors.

Moving past the turn of the century, during September of 1900, thousands of folks took advantage of the opportunity to study—and even ride in—an automobile at Washington Park, on the south side. Held under the auspices of Chicago's *Inter-Ocean* newspaper, this was basically a race meet, which opened with an automobile parade. *The Automobile* magazine in October 1900 called the event "very successful in point of contestants entered and records made," but faulted management for failing to keep spectators informed about the scheduled events.

"Practical utility" tests at Washington Park, such as draw-bar pull, assured skeptical audiences that motor vehicles could perform. Tests demonstrated friction, economy, speed

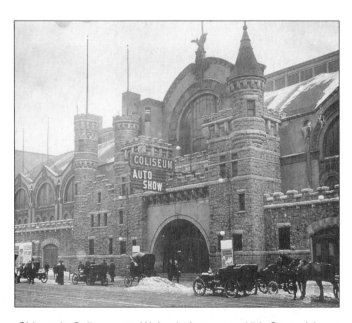

Chicago's Coliseum on Wabash Avenue at 15th Street (shown as it appeared in 1903) was the site of the auto show from 1901 to 1935. Reconstructed from the shell of Libby prison, the building had been used for the Columbian Exposition of 1893.

ll climbing, safety devices, noiselessness, and accessibility of akes for repairs. Races were held separately for steam, ectric, and gasoline vehicles.

According to *The Horseless Age* magazine, "attendance as rather light" at this First International Automobile xhibition and Tournament, though the opening-day crowd as estimated at 4,000, and the show was extended for two xtra days. Principal exhibitors included the Woods electric bout 20 vehicles), Mobile steam (with a dozen runabouts), veral gasoline cars from The Chicago Motor Vehicle ompany, plus scattered entrants from Waverly, Rambler, ewitt Lindstrom, Locomobile, De Dion-Bouton, Olds, and a w others. Accessory makers also demonstrated their wares.

Mr. Jack Worth put his Chicago gasoline delivery wagon rough a see-saw display, in which an egg was cracked but ot crushed as his car rocked back and forth. Participants in an ostacle race encountered dummy figures, tree trunks, large ones—obstructions that "might be met with in a journey ross country or in the mazes of a large city." A mail race was pervised by postal officials, duplicating a portion of a rural ail route.

Special Illinois Central express trains brought visitors to the ounds. According to the *Daily Times-Herald*, Chicago sued licenses to all visiting automobilists, so they could run eir vehicles anywhere in the city "without fear of arrest." omen participated, too. "Little Janette Lindstrom, in her ell automobile," said *Horseless Age*, beat Miss M.A. Ryan a women's race. The *Chicago Tribune* later called the ashington Park event "the first auto show in America."

Later in 1900, New Yorkers visited that city's first utomobile show, which featured 40 makers and some 300 rs, as well as demonstrations of driving skill.

To produce a great show on the proper scale, Chicago eeded a great promoter. Samuel Miles (see sidebar) met that andard. A former promoter of bicycle shows, Miles took the ins of the first auto show at the Coliseum. Located on a uare block between Wabash and Michigan Avenues, and 5th and 16th Streets, the huge Coliseum had been constructed from the shell of Libby prison—one of Chicago's tractions during the Columbian Exposition of 1893.

"Chicago has had an automobile show before," noted *e Motor World* magazine in 1901; but that event "left a d taste in the mouth." No comparable criticism attacked the 901 gala at the Coliseum.

How big a show was it? Contemporary reports vary idely, but more than fifty makers had exhibits—though not were actual automobiles. Many were motor bicycles, otorboats, and accessories. Chris Sinsabaugh, press agent of e 1901 Chicago show, wrote in his biography that there ere 31 exhibits of complete cars and 20 of parts and cessories. *The Motor World* listed 56 exhibitors, while the hicago Tribune reported that 65 firms had displays. *The Gas ngine* estimated that 102 exhibit spaces were filled by the cond night, representing 70 firms; and that opening-night tendance totaled 6,000.

Demonstrations took place on an improvised track that cled the exhibit area. According to *Motor Age* magazine, he track was always full."

Samuel A. Miles
Show manager, 1901 to 1932

Without the herculean efforts of Samuel Miles, the Chicago Auto Show might never have gotten off the ground in 1901. Without his continued guidance for the next three decades, it surely would have taken a different form. "Under Miles' hand," wrote *Automobile Topics* magazine in 1932, "the shows prospered greatly and became the envy of all other industries."

Born in Bristol, England, Miles began his career as a promoter and official of bicycle races in Chicago, after arriving in 1883. He'd immigrated to New York three years earlier, at age 18, soon becoming a silent partner in a Pierce-Arrow dealership.

In Chicago, Miles became a writer, then later editor, for the *Sporting and Theatrical Journal*. Active in many sports, he promoted his first bicycle show and race meet in 1887. By 1896, when the Coliseum was built, the bicycle show had outgrown its prior quarters. Miles signed up for two years, but the building's roof caved in and that year saw no bicycle show.

After a year back in England, Miles returned to Chicago. His *Cycling Age* magazine evolved into *Motor Age*. In 1901, he staged what was later termed the "first Chicago automobile show." It included a 20-foot track, built around the arena. The next year, as exhibits became more numerous, Miles eliminated the track in favor of a treadmill-type display machine.

In 1903, the National Association of Automobile Manufacturers was organized, with Miles as general manager. He oversaw the production of the Chicago Auto Show until shortly before his death.

Many years later, in 1950, *Ward's Automobile Topics* referred to "a constant procession of vehicles on the track at night." Vehicles even carried visitors—without charge—from the corner of Wabash and Van Buren to the Coliseum, courtesy of the Mobile company.

At the Coliseum, an expert chauffeur demonstrated his skills by backing his vehicle onto a pocket watch that sat on the ground. As his rear wheel touched the watch, the crystal cracked; but, as *Ward's* later reported, "just as the vehicle was about to crush the dainty bit of jewelry, the lever was reversed, the automobile started ahead and the watch was saved."

The *Tribune* reported "many close calls" during the first night's race, due to people crossing the track when cars were coming. "A number had narrow escapes."

Riding in the cars could be just as frightful. "Speeding seems a favorite pastime of the show," the *Tribune* noted. One woman "almost fainted when whirled around the narrow turns," exclaiming that she would never again ride in one of "those things."

Samuel Miles later wrote that the first Chicago automobile show "was promoted without reference to any association other than the Chicago Automobile Club, whose officers refused to lend the club's sanction." Though not a financial success, it had proven to be "a bonanza for the automobile exhibitors."

The next show, in 1902, was held under the auspices of the Chicago Automobile Club and the National Association of Automobile Manufacturers—an organization that had been formed in 1900. *The Gas Engine* reported that 36 varieties of vehicles were exhibited (22 of them gasoline). The *Chicago Tribune* counted an even hundred exhibits, noting that Henry Ford of Detroit was expected to attend. "So great was the demand for space," according to the *Tribune*, "that the management abandoned the racing ring and devoted the space given to it last year to exhibits." Patrons were disappointed by the absence of races, which had been announced prior to the show's opening.

Already, the Chicago show was demonstrating its status as the event where cars were bought, not just studied idly. "Several manufacturers were compelled to cease taking orders," the *Tribune* advised, "the capacity of their factories being tested to the utmost." Manufacturers also used the shows to attract new dealers and agents.

Chicago's "show is declared to be more typical of America than was New York's," said the *Tribune* of the 1903 exposition, which featured 80 manufacturers and 325 machines—all but five American-built. Three-fourths of the automobiles were gasoline-powered; the remainder divided between steam and electric.

The *Tribune* offered similar praise in 1904, advising that Chicago's "show as a whole is said to be a more satisfying display than the recent exhibition in New York," where "exhibits were huddled together." At least 300 cars turned up this time, along with 70 exhibits of accessories: lamps, tires, goggles, cranks, sirens, and so forth. *The Gas Engine* called Chicago's event the "western show," in contrast to New York's eastern leaning.

In 1904, the Chicago Automobile Trade Association (CATA) was chartered by the State of Illinois as a non-profit corporation. Putting on shows was not part of the CATA's task. Those remained under the control of the auto manufacturers until the mid-Thirties (with an exception in 1919, when America was involved in The Great War).

Of the 1906 Chicago show, *Motor Age* proclaimed that it "deserves to go down in history as Miles' masterpiece, a grand affair which makes last year's effort, magnificent as it was, look like two-bits and a nickel." Each year, the decorations at the Coliseum were more lavish than the last. This season's color scheme, yellow with green, borrowed from nature. By now, the Coliseum itself was too small to hold all the exhibits, so organizers expanded into an Annex, and into the nearby Armory. At the Armory entrance, *Motor Age* reported, "automobiles are everywhere, lined up along the curb or dashing up to the door to unload their occupants." They also reported long lines at ticket offices.

Even an airship went on display at the 1907 show—just four years after the Wright brothers' successful flight at Kitty Hawk. Sam Miles and his staff had moved toward uniformity

of design in the display, rather than the hodgepodge that had characterized earlier events.

According to the *Chicago Tribune*, a long canopy stretched from the building entrance to the sidewalk's edge, and everyone entering the Wabash Avenue entrance was greeted by Mr. Miles himself. A tunnel permitted visitors to pass between the Coliseum and the Armory, but that was not a rewarding experience. One unhappy person called it a "sewer." A total of 105 spaces had been allotted to makers of automobiles, and 200 to manufacturers of accessories; but some of them doubled up, bringing the total to near 450.

In 1907, Miles put on a separate exhibition of commercial vehicles at Tattersall's, about a block from the Coliseum. Attendance was not great.

Instead of holding the show early in the year, as usual, promoters tried something different for the next event; they opened the show in late 1907, to reveal the 1908 models. That experiment failed, so they immediately reverted to a start-of-the-year schedule. Quite a few supplemental exhibitions could be found along Michigan Avenue, by makers who were unable to get space at the show—a trend that would continue for years to come.

Entering on Wabash Avenue, said the *Chicago Tribune* of the 1909 show, the visitor "finds himself set down beneath a bizarre firmament blocked out in yellow bordered green squares of bunting from the center of which descends an enormous white chandelier of a thousand lights." Stretching either way are "four red pillared arcades supporting clusters of ornate lamps and blooming with ivy, chrysanthemums, orchids and palms." Papier mâché arches and statuary were done in bronze tones this year. For those who appreciated mechanical details more than the grand milieu of the Coliseum, engines could be started, allowing the visitor to enjoy "all the sensations save that of the scenery racing by." Motorcycles occupied a separate section of the hall.

"Chicago is the natural buying centre for the great Western territory," said *The Horseless Age* in 1910. Chicago Coliseum "represents a [rural] landscape so closely as to cause the entering visitor to pause for a moment before he is sure that he has not chanced on a bit of summer landscape tucked away in the midst of the chill winter night." Real trees had "breeze stirring their branches."

Most exhibits were from members of the National Association of Licensed Automobile Manufacturers—companies that had agreed to pay royalties to the holders of the Selden Patent. Henry Ford and others refused to acknowledge the patent's validity, and either participated in their own, separate association or, in the case of Ford, shunned the manufacturers' groups altogether.

Prior shows also featured trucks, but not this time. Miles preferred to focus on pleasure cars, whose makers clamored for space.

A French motif greeted visitors to the 1911 auto show, featuring four gigantic fountains and a massive painting—plus close to 400 vehicles. A separate show for commercial vehicles was held during the second week.

The Supreme Court had ruled the Selden Patent valid, but not infringed, allowing non-licensed automakers back into the fold. But Henry Ford continued to avoid the manufacturers' association, keeping his company independent.

Miles tried an experiment in 1912: Society Day. According to the *Tribune*, he sought an affair "on a par with the horse show and grand opera premiers." But an increased admission he failed to keep out non-society folks.

"Cyclecars" were sprinkled among the 500 vehicles exhibited at the 1914 automobile show. Blending the attributes of the motorcycle and the low-priced car, the cyclecar craze lasted barely two seasons. No truck show was held this year.

By 1915, the auto show was under the auspices of the national Automobile Chamber of Commerce, formed in 1913. Gasoline-powered automobiles had dominated the field for years, but eight makers of electrics exhibited.

Expensive and exotic makes got their own show, starting in 1916—separate from the one at the Coliseum. Automobile salons at the Congress Hotel exhibited such makes as Locomobile and Cunningham.

Opening to a crowd of 40,000, the 1917 auto show at the Coliseum set an industry record for start-up attendance. "In Chicago," said *Automobile Topics* magazine, "business is the chief matter of interest. It is to Chicago that the car makers look for the real test" of their products.

War had been raging in Europe since 1914, but not until 1917 did the United States become involved. *Motor Age* described the Coliseum's "distinctly wartime appearance" for the 1918 auto show, its decorating scheme suggesting "a spirit of warlike patriotism." War or not, the Automobile Salon in the Elizabethan Room of the Congress Hotel was described as "a concentration of the aristocracy of motordom." *The Accessory and Garage Journal* described the Coliseum show as "the greatest dealers' show in the world."

Although the Chicago Automobile Trade Association was not responsible for each year's auto show, in 1917 and 1918 it operated a Used Automobile and Truck Show at the Coliseum, later in the season. That experience doubtless helped pave the way for the CATA's takeover of the 1919 auto show, at a time when manufacturers were more concerned with the last days of the war effort. According to the *Tribune*, the National Automobile Chamber of Commerce had voted not to hold either a New York or Chicago exhibit, "under the impression that this was the government's desire." But "with the armistice signed, there was no disposition at Washington to frown further on industrial displays." For the first time in years, a truck show followed the car event, a week later.

Automakers resumed control of the 1920 show at the Coliseum, as well as a national motor truck show at the Amphitheatre, several miles to the west. The truck event began with a parade of commercial vehicles through downtown streets.

The Fifth Automobile Salon moved to the grand ballroom and adjoining French restaurant of the new Drake Hotel in 1921, again held as an event separate from the auto show at the Coliseum. *Automobile Topics* magazine suggested that Chicago offered a "more cheering exhibition than that at New York," with brightly-colored show cars adding to the "gala effect."

In the words of *Motor World*, the Coliseum's "unsightly rafters and girders [were] completely hidden behind trimmings and trappings of Moorish and Flemish grandeur" for the 1922 auto show. Special events included a parade of more than 200 cars behind racing pioneer Barney Oldfield, at the helm of an

1899 Locomobile. Of the 81 car makes exhibited, 77 were gasoline-powered and three were electric—plus the ever-present Stanley Steamer.

Auto-show attendance figures showed constant growth, as Midwesterners adopted the automobile. The largest opening-day crowds ever turned up at the 1924 show. Far more Americans drove Model T Fords than any other make, but Ford continued to skip the auto-show circuit.

Officially viewed as having begun in 1901, the Chicago Automobile Show celebrated its Silver Jubilee in 1925. The number of passenger-car manufacturers was beginning to dwindle by this time, but 200 cars from 54 makers went on exhibit—not to mention five taxicabs and nearly 250 displays of accessories and parts. Except for the Stanley Steamer, all cars exhibited had gasoline engines.

Selling had always been a big part of the Chicago show, and 1926 was no exception. Cadillac salesmen, for example, were eager to give demonstration rides between the Coliseum and their salesroom. Lincoln offered demonstrations, too, offering to take a person to his home or hotel. Some makers issued a flood of literature, though others offered none, and certain ones made printed pieces available only upon request.

The *Chicago Daily News* called the 1928 show, with more than 300 cars exhibited, a "riot of color and price-cutting." The Twenties had been an era of unabashed prosperity for unprecedented numbers of Americans, but a handful of observers were beginning to wonder if the "good times" could last forever.

As in prior years, the 1929 Chicago Automobile Show at the Coliseum was only one of the places where potential customers could get a look at products. In addition to the Automobile Salon at the Drake Hotel, there were auxiliary shows by General Motors at the Stevens Hotel, by Ford at the 131st Armory, by Chrysler at the Congress Hotel, by Willys-Overland at the Sherman, by Graham-Paige at the Blackstone—and even more at other sites. Manufacturers weren't about to miss out on any prospects. Few foresaw the dark days of autumn in 1929, after the stock market crashed and burned. The Great Depression was underway. What would that mean to the industry—and to the promoters of the Chicago Automobile Show?

1925 Acorn truck bought at Chicago show

William Bishop (center) bought this Acorn truck—produced by the American Ice Company—at the Chicago Automobile Show in 1925. According to his grandson, Richard, Mr. Bishop bought three other trucks that day, as well as a Moon sedan. Also pictured at this July 4th gathering are Harry Bishop (left) and John Hartung.

1898-99

- Four Woods vehicles exhibited at Edson Keith building downtown, in late 1898
- Small auto show held at Tattersall's, September 26 to October 3, 1899, under auspices of Arena Athletic Club
- Famed traction magnate Samuel Insull, president of Chicago Edison Co., declines to bring electric vehicle to 1899 program
- 25 vehicles show up on Saturday night at 1899 event
- Drivers at 1899 event demonstrate stopping short, backing up, cornering

Samuel Insull chose not to enter his elect[ric] vehicle at the 1899 show. Like many indus[try] leaders at the time, Insull doubted that t[he] "horseless carriage" had any future.

Electric vehicles, such as the Chicago-built Woods, dominated the earliest automobile shows.

WOODS MOTOR VEHICLE COMPANY,

110-112 East 20th St.,   547-49 Wabash Ave.,
CHICAGO, ILL.

Manufacturers of high class Coach and Carriage Work in electrically propelled vehicles. Over 30 styles to select from. Prompt deliveries from 30 to 90 days. Order your private Broughams and Cabs now for Winter use and consider your wants for next year in order to insure early deliveries in Spring. Guaranteed in every particular.

Drop us a card and Representative will call with vehicle, or will mail catalogue as requested.

BICYCLE RACES

The Greatest Ever Held in Chicago,
At Tattersall's, 16th and Clark-sts.

Every Prominent Rider in America.

The professionals include COOPER, KISER, MAC-FARLAND, FISHER and others. Among the Amatures are EARL PEABODY and FRANK KRAMER, the Amateur Champions of the world.

SPECIAL PROGRAM FOR TONIGHT.

One Mile Handicap—Professional.

Match race between EARL PEABODY of Chicago and FRANK L. KRAMER of New York for Amateur Championship of the U. S. One mile heat, best 2 in 3.
One Mile Open for Professionals. Special middle distance match race between BURNS PIERCE of Boston and FRANK STARBUCK of Philadelphia. Purse $500.

Automobile Exhibit opens at 7 p. m.
Parade at 9:30 p. m.

Prices 25c, 50c, 75c, $1.00.

Above: *Bicycles might have been the ma[in] attraction at Tattersall's in 1899, but automobile exhibit opened in the evening.*

1900

- Autos exhibited at Washington Park as adjunct to bicycle and automobile races
- 1900 show runs September 18-25, under auspices of *Inter-Ocean* newspaper
- Auto parade leads off the show, which includes "practical utility" tests
- Demonstrations run on improvised track that circles exhibit area
- Show is called "First International Automobile Exhibition and Tournament"
- Opening-day attendance claimed to be 4,000 ... 11 manufacturers exhibit automobiles—accessories also displayed
- New York's first auto show opens late in 1900—considered first indoor show

Not all early vehicles had four wheels—and not all went into actual production. This Lawson Motor Wheel appeared at the Washington Park event in 1900.

Demonstrations of vehicle capabilities were an important part of the 1900 show at Washington Park.

To the surprise of many onlookers, vehicles at the 1900 show were able to climb a 35-percent grade.

THE EVENT OF THE PERIOD

First
International
Exhibition
and

AUTOMOBILE RACE MEET

OF AMERICA

Washington Park Club Grounds
Sept. 18, 19, 20, 21, 22

DAILY CONCERTS
BY BROOKE'S
MARINE BAND.

ELABORATE PROGRAMME. GENERAL ADMISSION, 50 CENTS

Promoters extended the run of the 1900 show past its announced closing date.

Several massive test devices put vehicles through grueling trials at the 1900 show.

Seen at the 1900 exhibition, the Rambler—equipped with left-hand steering and a front engine—was produced by a well-known bicycle company. Thomas Jeffery, a partner in the firm, sold the bike business to the American Bicycle Company and turned to automobile production.

1901
1st annual Chicago Automobile Show
(March 23-30, 1901)

- First "official" Chicago show held inside Coliseum, located at 15th and Wabash
- Samuel Miles manages 1901 show—he will continue in that capacity for the next three decades
- As many as 65 firms reportedly display vehicles or accessories at Chicago's first indoor automobile show
- Vehicles can be driven on circular track that surrounds exhibits
- Spectators have opportunities to ride in vehicles
- First-night attendance estimated between 2,000 and 6,000
- Several "narrow escapes" reported where visitors cross track
- "Home-trainer" setup lets two vehicles "race" while standing still, using rollers

Left: Chicago's Coliseum seemed to have plenty of space for exhibits in 1901, but future shows would spill over into nearby buildings.

Below: Although most De Dion-Bouton vehicles were French-built, the Motorette—displayed at the 1901 show—was produced in Brooklyn.

WHO'LL BE THERE
AND WHAT THEY'LL SHOW

What better figurehead for the first "official" Chicago Auto Show than "Miss I Will," at the wheel of one of those newfangled machines?

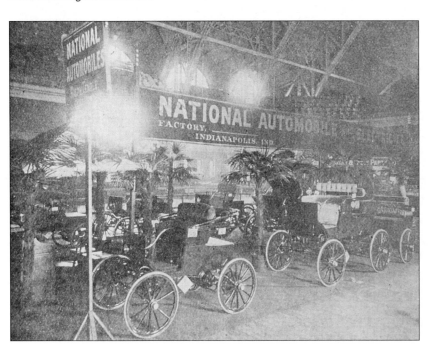

COLISEUM.
MARCH 23 - 30,
10 a. m. to 10:30 p. m.

AUTOMOBILE SHOW.

Vehicles always running on the track for the use of visitors.
Motors and accessories.

Above: For most visitors, the 1901 show was the first opportunity to ride in an automobile. A track circled the Coliseum's exhibit area.

Left: Most vehicles were steered by tiller in 1901, including the Indiana-built National Electric.

1902
2nd annual Chicago Automobile Show
(March 1-8, 1902)

- Chicago Automobile Show again held at Coliseum—destined to be site for more than three decades
- Show opens under auspices of Chicago Automobile Club and National Association of Automobile Manufacturers
- 50-cent admission is charged
- 36 varieties of vehicles exhibited (22 of them gasoline-powered)
- Total of 100 vehicles exhibited
- Show runs until 10:30 p.m. each day—but closed on Sunday
- Morning sessions open only to trade
- Nearly 800 vehicles sold to dealers during show—majority are runabouts
- Due to demand for exhibit space, no races are run this year

Above: *Two cars at a time could be tested on treadmills at the 1902 show. Red and blue hands above the chauffeurs indicated the speeds achieved.*

Left: *Several trade magazines ran extensive reports on early auto shows, often including promotional artwork.*

Showgoers looked forward to seeing Henri Fournier, who'd traveled a mile in record time (51.6 seconds) on Coney Island Boulevard. His "mud-spattered" $8,000 machine made an appearance, but Fournier did not have an opportunity to try a repeat run in Chicago.

1903

3rd annual Chicago Automobile Show

(February 14-21, 1903)

- Despite bad weather, Coliseum is said to be "filled all day long"
- Vehicle exhibitors include Olds, Peerless, Pierce, Cadillac, Packard, Locomobile, Winton, Franklin, Woods, Stearns, Haynes-Apperson, Cleveland, Rambler, and Chicago Motor Vehicle Company
- Only four foreign makes are exhibited
- Chicago show has 26 exhibits that were not already seen in New York
- Show consists of 325 vehicles from 80 manufacturers ... 75 percent are gasoline

Most automakers offered either an electric or a gasoline automobile. The Columbia came either way.

All of the automobiles at the 1903 Chicago show were exhibited on one floor the Coliseum.

The February 21, 1903, issue of The Automobile *magazine promoted the Chicago Automobile Show right on its cover. The chauffeur and lady appear to be in a runabout near the shore of Lake Michigan—perhaps near the Coliseum.*

After a hard day of studying the vehicles displayed, a restaurant beckoned at the end of the Coliseum's show floor.

1904
4th annual Chicago Automobile Show
(February 6-13, 1904)

- Show open 10 a.m. to 10:30 p.m., Saturday to Saturday—but closed on Sunday
- VIPs get private viewing and dinner, held by National Association of Automobile Manufacturers on Friday before public opening
- Admission is 50 cents
- Vehicles priced from $500 to $10,000
- 70 accessory exhibits seen at show
- Show has total of 252 exhibits
- Part of show is in Coliseum Annex
- Chicago Automobile Trade Association formed in 1904, with Howard Tucker (a Winton dealer) as president ... chartered as non-profit corporation in Illinois

Chicago's Coliseum was quite an imposing and sizable structure, but it soon proved to have insufficient space to hold all the new models at the automobile show.

This formal-looking Columbia held a record for traveling from New York to Chicago—where show visitors could see it.

THE STAR ATTRACTION AT THE SHOW.

**THE THOMAS "FLYER," $2,500
THOMASINE (Limousine), $2,750**

*th models exhibited by the Thomas company of Buffalo,
"Flyer" and the limousine, had three-cylinder engines.*

*1904, Winton had been in the automobile business for half a dozen years. Two-
d four-cylinder models could be ordered.*

Newspaper ads beckoned Chicagoans—and out-of-towners—to come to the Coliseum in 1904.

1905

5th annual Chicago Automobile Show

(February 4-11, 1905)

- Show visitors see more full-size cars with weather protection
- Runabouts are giving way to vehicles that carry more than two occupants
- Chicago show is gaining reputation for elaborate, artistic decorations
- Demonstration cars are available outside exhibit area, for prospective customers
- Ford display includes new four-cylinder chassis
- Exhibits that were not seen at New York show include Holsman high-wheel buggy, Adams-Farwell with radial engine, Tincher semi-racing car, Gale runabout, Moline runabout and touring car, dual-cylinder Auburn, and Bartholomew made in Peoria
- Second floor of Annex is added to display area

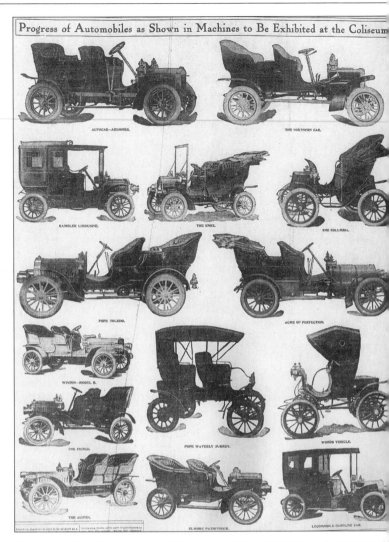

A variety of vehicle types could be seen at the 1905 show. An "automob row" of dealerships was beginning to develop along Michigan Avenue, clo to the Coliseum and adjoining Armory.

Exhibitors were becoming too numerous for the Coliseum, so show promoters began to prepare the adjoining Armory building (shown) to handle the overflow.

Showgoers had an opportunity to study various types of engines, including the unique air-cooled design used by Knox.

1905   MODEL F TONNEAU

WATERLESS

KNOX

The Famous Patented Air-Cooling System

SEE THEM AT THE CHICAGO SHOW.

Chicago Salesroom, KNOX AUTO COMPANY, 1251 Michigan-av.   GEO. A. CRANE, Mgr.
'PHONE SOUTH 1189.

THE

ROYAL

NOT A SENSATION,

But a Car of Real Merit!

Don't overlook it at the Auto Show, Coliseum, stands 83, 84, 85.

SOLD BY

HARRY BRANSTETTER

1468 MICHIGAN-AV.

Made in Cleveland.

Royal Motor Car Co.

TOURIST $3000.00

Introduced to the market a year earlier, Royal Tourist mod came to the Chicago show in 1905. Despite modest advertis claims, the cars were relatively advanced in design.

1906

6th annual Chicago Automobile Show

(February 3-10, 1906)

- Show occupies Coliseum and adjoining First Regiment Armory building
- Board-covered passage between the two buildings is known as "bridge of sparks"
- Coliseum is lavishly decorated ... yellow/green color scheme borrows from nature
- Waltz and march music greets visitors
- Most cars still have solid rubber tires
- Famed race driver Barney Oldfield attends
- 97 makers show at least 400 autos
- Foreign section is in the Armory
- Show is described as "Miles' masterpiece, a grand affair"
- Exhibits include Ford, Glide (from Peoria), White steamer, Pierce Great Arrow, Royal, Franklin, Winton, Corbin, Baker electric, Studebaker electric, Stearns, St. Louis
- During 1906, CATA sponsors Reliability Run, Hill Climb, and Economy Test

The Baby REO

Parents and children alike were drawn to the Baby Reo, an exact replica called the "smallest perfect working automobile ever produced," exhibited at the Coliseum.

Above: *Before long, the Coliseum's vacant floor would be filled with 1906 automobiles.*

Right: *European-built automobiles attracted affluent visitors to the Chicago show.*

Left: *Rivaling Pierce-Arrow and Packard in the luxury market, Peerless produced two four-cylinder series in 1906.*

1907
7th annual Chicago Automobile Show
(February 2-9, 1907)

- Show expands again: occupies Coliseum plus First and Second Regiment Armories
- 300 exhibitors on hand—twice the number as at previous shows ... 105 spaces allotted to vehicle manufacturers
- *Chicago Tribune* claims 1907 is first time in history that "every American-made machine is exhibited under one roof"
- Exhibits even include an airship
- Coliseum is filled with long lanes of red and green carpet ... artistic plaster casts above represent automobiles
- Armory decorated in white and light green
- Observers praise Chicago show's uniformity of design
- Samuel Miles greets visitors at Wabash Avenue entrance
- Cafe is new—built specially for show

Right: Prospective buyers faced a bewildering selection of makes, including the racy but short-lived Dragon—extinct after 1908.

Left: Simple ads in the Amusements section of the newspaper gave no hint of the lavish displays waiting at the Coliseum and Armory.

Below: Like many competitors, the Matheson advertised the fact that it was licensed under the Selden patent. Four-cylinder Matheson cars excelled in competition.

Any Queens at the 1907 Chicago show were likely to be leftovers, as the company had recently moved to Detroit and begun to produce a different make—the Blomstrom.

1908

8th annual Chicago Automobile Show

(November 30-December 7, 1907)

- For one year only, Chicago show is held at end of the previous year instead of at beginning of calendar year
- Show area expands: occupies Coliseum and Annex basement, plus First and Seventh Regiment Armories
- More than a dozen six-cylinder cars are exhibited
- Several automakers exhibit at nearby showrooms on Michigan Avenue
- Ad promotes automobiles that are licensed under Selden patent ... most automakers have agreed to pay royalties, with the notable exception of Ford (which fights Selden forces in court)
- Demand for closed cars is growing
- Bouncers oust man who tries to re-enter show ... he turns out to be president of city civil service commission

Right: Many Chicago-area dealers handled a variety of car makes in 1908. Auto show exhibits were generally set up by the manufacturers.

Above: Early in the century, far-sighted manufacturers set their sights on the preferences of women concerning motorcars.

Names of the vehicle makes, displayed along interior walls of the elaborately-decorated Coliseum, made it easier for a visitor to the 1908 show to spot a particular example for closer scrutiny.

Nearly every car at the Chicago show was promoted as special in some way—though the claims often had little foundation. Four- and six-cylinder Stearns models were costly.

1909
9th annual Chicago Automobile Show
(February 6-13, 1909)

- Show is in Coliseum and First Regiment Armory
- About 20 makes at Chicago show were not seen in New York previously
- Show has 270 exhibitors, showing 92 different automobile makes
- 47 exhibitors are on main floor of Coliseum; 35 in Armory (including trucks)
- 10,000 visitors arrive for opening night, breaking all records ... Samuel Miles predicts attendance of 200,000
- Arches and statuary are bronze papier-mâché ... 170,000 feet of bunting used
- Colonnade arches are filled with bronze reliefs depicting the modern race—and autos manned by muscled humans
- Car engines can be started at show
- 19 motorcycle makes in separate area

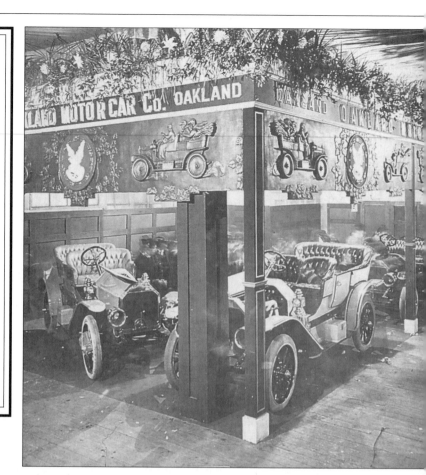

Eye-catching displays were arranged around the vehicles, complementing th elaborate Coliseum decorations.

Plenty of cars in 1909 were driven by chauffeurs. This cartoon shows owners being offered a selection.

Drivers and passengers in 1909 vehicles had to be properly attired for the occasion. People also dressed up to visit the auto show.

Automobiles that did not find space in the Coliseum c Armory might be viewed at auxiliary exhibits. Not man 1909 cars pushed top speed this hard.

An intricate display area helped attract prospects to the Glide cars, produced in Peoria, Illinois, by the Bartholomew Company.

All over the Coliseum, visitors to the 1909 auto show could see this intricate symbol of the event—not unlike Hermes, the mythical messenger, but clutching an automobile steering wheel.

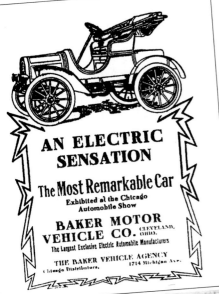

AN ELECTRIC SENSATION

The Most Remarkable Car

Exhibited at the Chicago Automobile Show

BAKER MOTOR VEHICLE CO. CLEVELAND, OHIO.

The Largest Exclusive Electric Automobile Manufacturers

THE BAKER VEHICLE AGENCY
Chicago Distributors, 1714 Michigan Ave.

Electric vehicles continued to attract attention at the show. Women, in particular, were thought to appreciate their quietness.

By 1909, Cadillac had existed for six years. A year earlier, Cadillac won the coveted DeWar Trophy for the use of precise, interchangeable parts. Note the ornate decorations above the cars.

1910

10th annual Chicago Automobile Show

(February 5-12, 1910)

- 123 makes of pleasure cars and commercial vehicles on display ... 267 exhibitors in all
- Attendance of 300,000 predicted
- Green is dominant decorator color, for English Garden look—with real trees
- Some cars are positioned over mirrors
- Waiting list for space held 130 names

1911

11th annual Chicago Automobile Show

(January 28-February 11, 1911)

- First show week is for pleasure cars; second week for commercial vehicles
- Decor simulates time of Louis XV, including four fountains and huge painting
- Close to 400 cars on display
- Many auxiliary "shows" take place at hotels and auto showrooms

THE HEAVENLY BODIES.
They Will Be Visible at the Coliseum Next Week.

Left: *While many folk dreamed of the "heavenly" bodies, visitors to the 191_ show could survey the ware_ of 101 automobile maker_ enticingly displayed.*

Below: *Lecturers often de_ scribed the technical dis_ plays and exhibits of chassi_ and engines at the 191_ show, including a revolvin_ chassis at the Thomas area_*

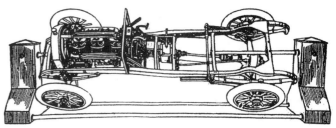

THE SENSATION OF THE NEW YORK SHOW—
IT WILL BE THE TALK OF THE CHICAGO SHOW—
DON'T FAIL TO SEE IT.

The Thomas Revolving Chassis

Above: *Even in 1911, Chicago vied to have new models seen first at its auto show. Hupmobile expanded its line this year.*

Right: *Almost 400 automobiles sought the eye of showgoers at the 1911 auto show, in the Coliseum and Armory.*

1912

12th annual Chicago Automobile Show

(January 27-February 3, 1912)

- Coliseum and First Regiment Armory hold pleasure cars
- Separate commercial vehicle exhibit opens on February 5, for one week
- Coliseum is decorated with hundreds of columns and large mural paintings ... huge canvas gives effect of a blue sky
- 13 companies show electric vehicles
- Franklin has the only air-cooled engine
- More than 70 makes have self-starter
- Left-hand steering and central gearshift said to be "gaining in leaps and bounds"
- Admission is doubled for Society Night, but high attendance surprises officials
- Many makes have demountable rims ... more equipment is one of the year's trends
- Knight sleeve-valve engine is found in several makes

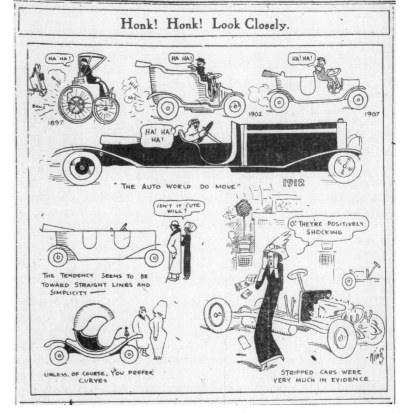

Above: Cartoonists capitalized on the humor in Americans' growing devotion to the automobile.

Below: Electric lights, columns, flags, and paintings decorated the Coliseum for the 1912 Chicago Auto Show.

Above: Shoppers in 1912 tended to be intrigued by innovations, such as the "Silent-Knight" sleeve-valve engine, installed in Stearns-Knight cars.

1913

13th annual Chicago Automobile Show

(February 1-8, 1913)

- 102 makes exhibit cars in three buildings: Coliseum, First Regiment Armory, and Wilson Building ... only 70 of those makes had been seen at New York show
- Some cars are displayed at Greer Building
- Separate commercial vehicle show held from February 10-15
- Most makes now offer at least one six-cylinder model
- 30,000 "first nighters" visit auto show
- Imitation stained glass highlights this year's decorating theme ... side walls, dropping from glass-like dome, resemble panels in ruins of Grecian or Roman homes
- Greater number of "foredoor" (four-door) cars seen this year
- Speedwell Six has rotary-valve motor—shown for first time

Which Shall It Be? Gasoline Car or Woods Electric? Work or Play?

IF YOU LOVE YOUR WIFE, GIVE HER A WOODS

WOODS EXHIBIT IS JUST INSIDE MICHIGAN AVENUE ENTRANCE TO ARMORY

Woods Motor Vehicle Co.

Factory and Salesrooms—25th Street, Calumet and Cottage Grove Avenues
OUR OWN GARAGES AT HIGHLAND PARK AND EVANSTON

At the Coliseum Automobile Show Do Not Fail to See the Aristocratic

Premier Little Six

Above: By 1913, most people already knew whether they preferred a gasoline- or electric-powered automobile.

Right: Since 1906, National had been producing only gasoline automobiles. Four-cylinder engines powered all 1913 models.

Left: Starting in 1913, only six-cylinder Premiers were produced.

STOCK CHAMPION   INTERNATIONAL CHAMPION

National

BULLETIN

Resilient springs.

Deep, comfortable upholstery.

Latest and most comfortable body designs.

FIVE MODELS
$2750 to $3400

See the
NATIONAL
at Auto Show

National Motor Car Co.
Chicago
2430 Michigan Avenue

Electrically Lighted   **AMERICAN** UNDERSLUNG   Electrically Started

The "American Tourist" (Type 34-A) $2350—Complete

Bigger Road Clearance

See the "American Underslung" exhibit at the Coliseum Show—Space N-1, Annex.

The "American Scout" $1475 Complete
The "American Traveler" $4500 Complete
(Improved Electric Starter with Tourist $150 extra)

American Traveler-Coey Co.
1424 Michigan Avenue
American Motors Company, Indianapolis, Indiana

Right: American Underslung models were aptly named for their frames, which hung below the axles. Early in 1914, the company went bankrupt.

1914

14th annual Chicago Automobile Show

(January 24-31, 1914)

- Coliseum is fitted to resemble palaces of Louis XIV, highlighted by gold scrollwork
- Thousands of tiny electric lights show off detailed mechanisms of automobiles
- First Regiment Armory again contains portion of exhibit space
- 85 manufacturers display 75 gasoline automobiles and 10 electrics ... total of 500 "machines" on exhibit
- Show includes several exhibits of cyclecars—low-priced vehicles that mix attributes of full-size car and motorcycle
- 215 accessory exhibitors on hand
- Society Day has double admission price
- Telephones in some cars let riders communicate with chauffeur
- No truck show takes place this year

Lavish decorations helped make the 1914 cars at the show look special. Note the stripped chassis in the foreground.

1915 Woods Electrics

At the Automobile Show (in the Armory)

The 1915 Woods is a full year ahead of other Electric cars in Exterior Beauty, Interior Roominess and Comfortable Seating. As usual the Woods has many exclusive features that make for greater convenience, safety and ease of handling.

Woods Motor Vehicle Co.

Factory and Sales Room: 25th St., Calumet, and Cottage Grove Ave., Chicago, Ill.

AMERICA'S MOST DISTINCTIVE MOTOR CAR **The New "Six-48" Keeton**

By the time the 1914 Keeton "Six-48" appeared at the Chicago Auto Show, the company was being absorbed, and soon would face liquidation.

Above: *Advance showings weren't yet common, but Woods displayed its 1915 model at the '14 auto show.*

Right: *Lozier was one of many near-luxury makes to be seen at the 1914 Chicago show, but the company also produced a new, lower-priced four-cylinder model.*

"The Choice of Men Who Know"

1915
15th annual Chicago Automobile Show
(January 23-30, 1915)

- Well over 500 cars occupy Coliseum, Coliseum Annex, and First Regiment Armory
- Show is open to public until 10:30 p.m.
- 87 automakers have cars on display—all gasoline-powered, except 8 electrics
- 215 accessory manufacturers display at auto show ... 302 exhibits in all
- Background decor simulates interior of conservatory, with sky effect, in colors of white, gold, and green ... scheme is duplicated in Armory and Annex
- No foreign automobiles are exhibited
- Grant and Twombly cars are new this year; Saxon shown for first time
- Dodge exhibit features twisted engine parts, to flaunt their durability
- Makers unable to get space at Coliseum or Armory can again show their wares at Greer Building
- Auto show brings at least 20,000 out-of-town visitors and 3,000 dealers to Chicago, according to manager Miles
- Show cars valued at $3.5 million ... prices range from $295 to $6,000

PREMIER SPACE 0 2
Coliseum Annex

COMPARE IT!
The New Premier
Six Cylinders—50-90 H. P.
$1985

Chicago's auto show still had two purposes in 1915: to display cars to prospective customers, and to welcome dealers for that make.

Advertisements had to be clever to induce prospects to stop and look at particular vehicles. Starting in 1915, all Chalmers engines were six-cylinder.

ARGO
MOTORVIQUE

4-cylinder, shaft drive, sliding-gear transmission, 2-passenger.

$295
f. o. b. Factory

See it at the Auto Show
Space 3, Coliseum Basement.
Argo Motor Co., Inc.   Jackson, Mich.

Few conventional cars sold for anything near the price advertised for the Argo—one of the cyclecars that were a short-lived trend in 1914-15.

1916
16th annual Chicago Automobile Show
(January 22-29, 1916)

- 85 gasoline-powered makes and 7 electric cars find space in Coliseum, Annex, First Regiment Armory, or Greer Building—94,000 square feet in all
- Of the 300 accessory exhibits, 48 are new this year
- All automobiles exhibited at 1916 show are American-made
- "Twin Six" (V-12) engines are seen at show for first time
- Show is open daily except Sunday, 10 a.m. to 10:30 p.m.
- Society Night is on Wednesday, but with no increase in admission price this year—well-to-do Chicagoans pay same entry fee as everyone else
- Coliseum described as stately and colorful "Indoor Tokio," complete with bugles and crash of orchestral music
- Exhibition is valued at $3 million
- Car prices range from $295 to $6,000—same as in 1915

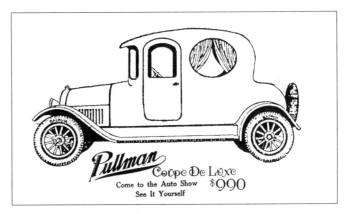

First showing of the new
PEERLESS EIGHT
at The National Automobile Show, The Coliseum
January 22nd to January 29th

Premieres of brand-new models helped cement the Chicago Auto Show's reputation as an event where actual business was done. Previously, Peerless used six-cylinder engines.

Pullman Coupe De Luxe $990
Come to the Auto Show
See It Yourself

Billed as "Palace Cars of the Road," Pullman models came with four- or six-cylinder engines. Shown is a Junior coupe sedan.

The Auto Show Favorite

National Highway
12 $1990

"HIGHWAY" SIX $1690	"HIGHWAY" TWELVE $1990	"NEWPORT" SIX $2375

NATIONAL MOTOR VEHICLE CO., Manufacturers, Indianapolis, 16th Year
PEARSON-BUCK MOTORS CO.
2515 Michigan Avenue

Above: National was one manufacturer with a V-12 engine, dubbed the "Highway Twelve" and considerably cheaper than Packard's Twin Six.

Price cuts were important to buyers of mid-priced models in 1916.

Lexington Six $1075

The Paradox of the Auto Show
Quality Raised— but Price Lowered

Everybody is asking—"How can Lexington create such a roomy, beautiful, and efficient car for so modest a price?" Are you acquainted with this remarkable new Lexington "Minute Man Six?" Don't fail to "get hep!"

Lexington Auto Show Exhibit A-5 (Armory)

If you can't come to the show write for illustrated folder, free

Lexington Motors Chicago Co.
1842 Michigan Avenue. 'Phone Calumet 5789

The Lexington-Howard Co., Mfrs., Connersville, Ind.

1917
17th annual Chicago Automobile Show
(January 27-February 3, 1917)

- Coliseum and three neighboring buildings again are site of Chicago show
- Stately pillars, topped with illuminated globes, outline floor space as hundreds of lamps twinkle from ceiling ... effect is called "that of an English cathedral"
- Decorations are amber, green, rose, black
- 400 vehicles go on exhibit
- Opening-day crowd of 40,000 sets record for the industry
- Innovations are few this year
- Pathfinder features disappearing top
- 1917 cars unveiled at Chicago show, unseen in New York, include Classic, Cummins-Monitor, Dixie, Chicago, Glide, Hassler, Maibohm, Stevens Six, Woods.
- America enters "The Great War" (World War I) on April 6, 1917

At auto-show time, the Coliseum and nearby buildings became like a miniature city, devoted to the automobile.

The Feature of the Show
The Studebaker GOLD CAR
At the Automobile Show

Complete car designed and manufactured in Studebaker factories.
Body, Top and Upholstery from Studebaker Custom Body Departments.
Gold plating by Yale & Towne, Stamford, Conn.

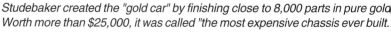

Studebaker created the "gold car" by finishing close to 8,000 parts in pure gold. Worth more than $25,000, it was called "the most expensive chassis ever built."

Above: Auto-show visitors appeared to have an over-abundance of choices in 1917, but the number of makes on the market was beginning to shrink—a "shake-out" trend that would escalate in the Twenties.

Right: Within a few months, the United States would enter the war that was raging in Europe. Early in 1917, however, concerns about conflict did not keep people from attending the automobile show.

1918

18th annual Chicago Automobile Show

(January 26–February 2, 1918)

- Show opens during a blizzard
- Coliseum ceiling is studded with stars, with French Colonial motif
- Shields along balcony hold clusters of flags from Allied nations
- Annex, Greer Building, and Armory have nearly-identical decorations
- Service flags, seen at nearly every booth, mark a company's defense contribution
- About 400 car models, in 92 makes, appear at show ... at least 250 accessory makers have exhibit space
- Comet, Maibohm, and Pan-American cars seen in Chicago—but not New York
- Automobile Salon with exotic cars is at Elizabethan Room of Congress Hotel
- Henry Ford shuns auto show, as usual, but local dealer sets up his own exhibit
- World War I ends on November 11

An Entz electromagnetic transmission, used in the Owen Magnetic, operated without gearshifting of any kind.

Automobiles had changed a lot since the first official Chicago Automobile Show, in 1901.

Left: Steam cars seemed old-fashioned to most 1918 shoppers, but the Stanley still had its fans.

Right: Showgoers loved to see innovations: (clockwise, from top left) air-cooled Holmes; National with built-in kitchen; low-priced Overland; cut-down doors; Marmon's gearshift-mounted lock; the Studebaker's beveled-edge body.

1919

19th annual Chicago Automobile Show

(January 25-February 1, 1919)

- For this year only, auto show is under auspices of Chicago Automobile Trade Association
- Because of war, National Automobile Chamber of Commerce had voted not to hold a New York or Chicago show
- Dealers step in at last minute, and Chicago leads off the auto-show season for the first time
- Most cars are actually 1918 models, with few revisions
- Four-cylinder Essex, built by Hudson, makes its debut at Chicago auto show
- About 300 cars are on display, from 50 manufacturers—only 3 are electrics
- Show contains total of 252 exhibits, including 182 accessory makers
- Admission is 50 cents, plus "war tax"

1919 Wrinkles in Automobile Body Design

With Engines About as Good as They Can Make Them, the Builders Turn to Refinements Elsewhere.

Consumers took a growing interest in automotive design through the Teens and into the Twenties.

Above: *A separate show was held for trucks in 1919.*

Right: *An Oldsmobile was General Motors' millionth car.*

Left: *Bill Adair stops in Chicago's Loop while undergoing an endurance run with an air-cooled Holmes—its hood sealed shut. At the Coliseum Annex, the car's hood was to be opened, allegedly to demonstrate why its airplane-derived engine ran so quietly.*

1920

20th annual Chicago Automobile Show

(January 24-31, 1920)

- Auto show occupies Coliseum and Annex, First Infantry Armory, and Greer Building
- Trucks are exhibited separately, at International Amphitheatre, starting with parade through downtown streets
- 84 vehicle exhibitors turn up at auto show, along with 163 accessory firms
- Fourth Automobile Salon is in Elizabethan Room of Congress Hotel, displaying high-priced and exotic marques
- All attendance records are broken at automobile show, but truck show draws smaller crowds
- 250 wounded men are guests of management on Friday, arriving from Fort Sheridan and Public Health Service Hospital

The National Sextet At the Show

A new and finer National is on exhibition at the Coliseum—the Sextet, a car which we believe to be the best we have ever produced.

We urge that you set aside definitely a few minutes of your time, sufficient to learn the merits and see the beauty of this new car.

THE NATIONAL SEXTET IS BUILT IN FIVE CUSTOM BODY STYLES

NATIONAL MOTOR CAR & VEHICLE CORP., INDIANAPOLIS
Twentieth Successful Year

National Motor Sales Company

Chicago Distributor   2515 Michigan Avenue

NATIONAL SEXTET SEVEN-PASSENGER TOURING CAR

"Sextet" denoted all National models for 1920, as the company's prior V-12 engine disappeared.

You Won't See the Show Unless You View the Jackson

Round out your visit to the Automobile Show by inspecting the three beautiful models of the Jackson on display. As a distinctly new standard in moderate priced sixes the Jackson is the hit of the show!

Smith-Sauer Motor Co.
2250 South Michigan Avenue
Calumet 163

Touring Car, $1987
Sport Car - $2500
Sedan - - $2850

Unlike most companies, Jackson had produced no 1919 models at all, turning instead to war work. For 1920, it was back with a six-cylinder series.

GASOLINE ALLEY—SAMPLING THE NEW MODELS.

Gasoline Alley was one of the first comic strips to focus on the automobile in American life.

1921
21st annual Chicago Automobile Show
(January 29-February 5, 1921)

- At least 80 vehicle makes and 256 accessory exhibits greet visitors to show
- Car prices range from $750 to $12,000
- Coliseum decorated in white, faint tints
- Nash exhibits new four-cylinder car
- Marmon features quarter-scale models
- Ace features disc-valve engine
- Mercer display has bare chassis
- Oldsmobile Light Four debuts at Chicago
- Automobile Salon is now at Drake Hotel, in grand ballroom and French restaurant
- Country is attempting to recover from Depression that broke out in late 1920

1922
22nd annual Chicago Automobile Show
(January 28-February 4, 1922)

- Coliseum, Annex, and First Regiment Armory are used for auto show
- Start-off parade covers most of Chicago's boulevard system
- 81 car makes are exhibited: 77 gasoline-powered, 3 electrics, and Stanley Steamer
- Show walls and roof are hidden under curtains of carmine, green, white, gold
- Automobile Salon has cars from England, France, Italy, Belgium, and America
- Many cars have taillight "Stop" signals
- Jackson is the only car at Chicago that was not also seen in New York

First Place at the Show for the Fourth Consecutive Year

For the fourth consecutive year Buick has been awarded first choice of space at the National Automobile Shows. This honor is conferred each year by the automobile manufacturers who are members of the National Automobile Chamber of Commerce, upon the member having done the greatest volume of business during the previous year. The figures on which this 1922 award was made proved Buick to be the largest builder of six-cylinder cars in the world.

See the New Model

BUICK MOTOR COMPANY, Chicago Branch

Left: When Rolls-Royce brought cars to Chicago, they went to the Salon rather than the Coliseum.

ROLLS-ROYCE
EXHIBIT AT THE SALON HOTEL DRAKE
JANUARY TWENTY-NINTH TO FEBRUARY FIFTH
ROLLS-ROYCE BRANCH 900 Michigan Ave.

Drake Hotel, site of the 1921 Automobile Salon, overlooked Oak Street Beach. This scene was shot several months after auto-show week.

By 1921, women drivers were becoming common. This is an Apperson V-8 wearing an Illinois dealer's license plate.

Getting first choice for auto-show space could make quite a difference in sales totals for the season.

1923
23rd annual Chicago Automobile Show
(January 27-February 3, 1923)

- 350 cars go on exhibit, from 79 manufacturers
- 74 makes are gasoline-powered, 3 are electric—plus the inevitable Stanley Steamer, which continues to attract a modest following
- 300 accessory exhibits occupy Coliseum's balcony
- Exhibits are in Coliseum, Annex, and First Regiment Armory
- Admission is 75 cents (including "war tax")
- Closed bodies are the rage in 1923—seen at every exhibit on the show floor
- Innovations and novelties run the gamut, from built-in trunk to vanity case
- Eighth Annual Automobile Salon, at Drake Hotel, has cars from five nations: England, Belgium, Italy, Germany, America
- 100,000 visitors said to overflow Chicago's Loop hotels

Showgoers might well have talked about the Davis, because the make was produced for more than two decades.

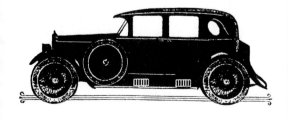
Fabric-covered bodies turned out to be a short-lived fad, used only by a few manufacturers.

Introduced just three years earlier, the Gardner sold well.

1924
24th annual Chicago Automobile Show
(January 26-February 2, 1924)

- 470 cars (all gasoline-powered) are exhibited by 74 manufacturers
- Show draws record opening-day crowd
- Decorative art is reminiscent of Louis VIII and Louis XIV periods
- More than 200,000 sq. ft. of muslin used ... lampshades are 8-1/2 feet in diameter ... 13 paintings measure 165 x 25 feet
- Balloon tires are promoted this year
- Four-wheel brakes coming into use
- Ninth Annual Automobile Salon is at Drake Hotel; includes Isotta Fraschini, Minerva, and two fabric-bodied cars
- Pullman company displays all-steel body at Automotive Salon
- New Haynes models seen for first time at an auto show

THE THINKER—1924 MODEL

Many of the refinements of the previous five years, and nearly all closed-car developments, were attributed to meeting the requirements of women.

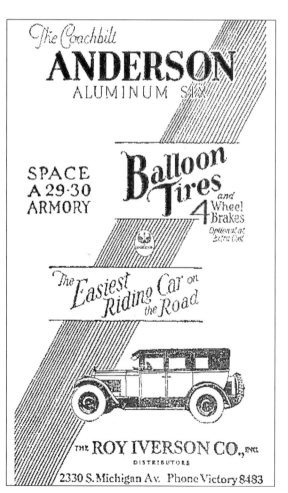

The Coachbuilt
ANDERSON
ALUMINUM SIX

SPACE A 29-30 ARMORY

Balloon Tires and 4 Wheel Brakes
Optional at Extra Cost

The Easiest Riding Car on the Road

THE ROY IVERSON CO., INC.
DISTRIBUTORS
2330 S. Michigan Av. Phone Victory 8483

Not too many automobiles were available with balloon tires or four-wheel brakes in 1924.

NASH
At the Show
The Business Coupe

Of all the body styles available, the business coupe tended to be the cheapest. Nashes did not change for '24.

Automotive stunts and feats still were promoted by manufacturers to trigger interest in their products among auto-show visitors.

You're Right—
it's the car that "Cannon Ball Baker" drove across continent in high gear!

a SIX at $750

See this wonderful Oldsmobile Six at the Show or at our showroom

OLDSMOBILE SIX
PRODUCT OF GENERAL MOTORS

1925
25th annual Chicago Automobile Show
(January 24-31, 1925)

- Chicago show celebrates its Silver Jubilee
- 200 cars from 54 makers go on display, along with 5 taxicabs
- Nearly 250 accessory and parts companies have exhibits
- All cars are gasoline-powered, except for Stanley Steamer
- Jubilee Tower dominates show floor, flashing 360 multi-colored floodlights
- Hidden chamber in Tower contains an orchestra that broadcasts to all parts of the building
- 1925 models said to spell "stabilization" in engineering and body building
- Balloon tires and four-wheel brakes common among popular-priced cars
- Many cars now have front/rear bumpers
- 37 automobiles have rear signals

Above: *By 1925, Chevrolet was beginning to approach Ford's lead in sales. Being at the auto show helped, since Ford shunned such events.*

John North Willys headed the company that produced Willys, Willys-Knight, and Overland models in 1925.

Left: *After a quarter-century, Sam Miles was still in charge of Chicago's lavish auto show.*

Left: *Produced in Moline, Illinois, the mid-priced Velie lasted for two decades (1909-29).*

Right: *Many of Chicago's most notable auto dealers were on "automobile row," on or near South Michigan Avenue, near the Coliseum.*

1926

26th annual Chicago Automobile Show

(January 30–February 6, 1926)

- 49 car makes exhibited this year—number of auto companies is gradually declining
- Balloon tires now are the rule, and closed cars dominate the exhibit
- Open cars are displayed with tops down, to make them look sporty
- Show opens on mild, sunny afternoon
- Pontiac is new name this year
- Decoration theme at Coliseum is Spanish garden
- Many salesmen are prepared to give demonstration rides to showgoers
- Automobile Salon at Drake Hotel has larger number of cars, in brighter colors
- National Automobile Dealers Association holds annual convention at LaSalle hotel, at same time as auto show at Coliseum
- 64 percent of new cars bought on time

Right: Manufactured since 1899, the posh Packard was inevitably one of the stars of the Automobile Salon.

CONQUERING NEW MARKETS

PACKARD

Ask the man who owns one

Below: Speed had been attracting a certain breed of buyer since the early days. This make bore the name of World War I flying ace, Eddie Rickenbacker.

The Chicago Tribune *called the auto show a "mecca for automobile industry." As usual, record crowds were anticipated for the week-long event.*

PERFORMANCE

100 H. P.
90 M. P. H.

¶ In the Rickenbacker booth at the Automobile Show you will see the fastest stock model exhibited this year.

¶ This model has a 100 Horse Power motor that will develop better than 90 miles per hour.

Rickenbacker
A · CAR · WORTHY · OF · ITS · NAME

Not only was Pontiac a new make for 1926, but one example was the five-millionth car built by General Motors.

1927
27th annual Chicago Automobile Show
(January 29-February 5, 1927)

- 300 new models exhibited in Coliseum, from 44 manufacturers
- Chicago show often is referred to as "National Automobile Show"
- 200,000 visitors expected to see Chicago Auto Show in 1927
- Decorative scheme in Coliseum includes murals taken from the age of Darius, King of Persia, plus 40,000 yards of golden-colored fabric
- 12th Annual Automobile Salon, at Drake Hotel, is said to function as "arbiter of fashion" ... Salon is biggest ever
- Several fabric-covered bodies are displayed at Salon—a design trend that never caught hold
- Ford halts production of long-lived Model T, and plans launch of Model A ... but Ford remains a non-participant in auto show

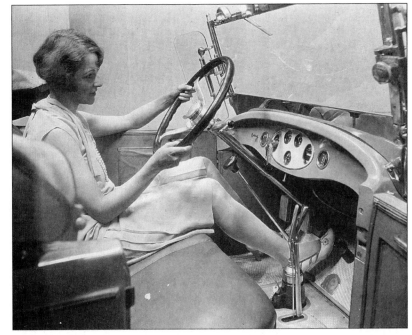

New for 1927, the moderately-priced Falcon-Knight was one of many manufacturers that tried to make its cars more appealing to women.

"Recognition of the economic advantages of automobile ownership is inspiring the two-cars-to-a-family trend enveloping America. There are two automobiles operating for every three families in the United States and the time is not far distant when the average well-to-do family will have two cars."

1927—R.H. Grant, general sales manager, Chevrolet Motor Co.

Chicago's Automobile Show had a variety of new cars suitable for middle-class and affluent families, but some folks were hard to please, as this cartoon suggested. Working-class Americans generally bought used cars, not new ones.

Ads in Chicago-area newspapers, prior to and during the auto show, tried in many ways to induce car-hungry customers to visit the Coliseum.

1928
28th annual Chicago Automobile Show
(January 28-February 4, 1928)

- More than 300 cars are exhibited, including large number of new models and new lines
- Cars that are new for 1928 include Erskine, Falcon, LaSalle, Wolverine, Durant, Graham-Paige, and Plymouth
- Majority of cars have six-cylinder engines
- Show open from 10 a.m. to 10:30 p.m. daily, except Sunday
- Four-wheel brakes now standard in all automobiles
- Coliseum gets an outdoors-like setting, including sky with twinkling stars, plus ample quantity of plants and greenery
- Show is described as a "riot of color and price-cutting"
- Style is stressed by most manufacturers

Gardner Motor Sales, Inc.
Chicago Factory Branch   Phone Michigan 1166   2530 S. Michigan Ave.

Interested parties were invited to see the new models either at the Coliseum or in a local showroom.

Again the stage belongs to **HUDSON-ESSEX**

Above: *If a Hudson was a little too rich for one's blood, how about a lower-priced Essex, built by the same company?*

Ads for more costly makes, such as the Stearns-Knight, did not hesitate to appeal to class-consciousness.

JUDGE THE CAR
BY THE PEOPLE AROUND IT

CHEVROLET

Bigger and Better

Reduced Prices!
The COACH
$585
The Roadster . $495
The Touring . $495
The Coupe . $595
The 4-Door Sedan . $675
The Sport Cabriolet . $665
The Imperial Landau . $715
Utility Truck . $495
Light Delivery . $375
All prices f.o.b. Flint, Mich.

Everywhere—a tremendous, enthusiastic reception for Chevrolet! 9,000,000 saw it the first three days! Bigger—better—smoother — more powerful — more beautiful — and reduced in price! Everyone says it's the greatest motor car sensation of the year!

See this Great New Car at the Auto Show or Grand Showing General Motors Cars—Stevens Hotel

January 28th to February 4th (Inclusive)

Price cuts helped Chevrolet in its joust against Ford, which introduced the Model A this season. Ford still did not participate in the auto show.

1929
29th annual Chicago Automobile Show
(January 26-February 2, 1929)

- Show occupies north and south halls of Coliseum
- More than 300 cars and chassis are exhibited
- Three taxicab makes are seen at show
- 150 accessory exhibits can be viewed, along with 82 exhibits of shop equipment
- DeSotos now are on sale
- Roster of American automobiles has shrunk by half in past six years
- As usual, many auxiliary shows draw visitors to hotels and showrooms ... Ford hosts its own show at Armory
- Year begins with continued expectation of prosperity, in auto industry and in all of American life
- Stock market crashes on October 29 ... Great Depression begins

Prosperity was presumed to be permanent when the 1929 auto show opened. Note the exposed chassis at several displays—a popular attraction in the Twenties.

Left: *Few automobiles in the late 1920s looked anything like the Auburn Cabin Speedster. Copywriters knew that promoting the "scientific" aspects of a product captured consumers' attention.*

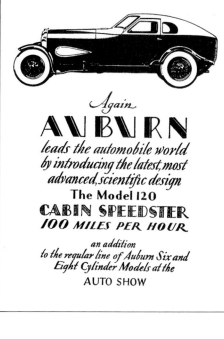

Ever since the Teens, an annual Automobile Salon had been held at a downtown hotel, separate from the auto show at the Coliseum. Elegant surroundings showcased the exotic machinery.

A Buick was General Motors' 10-millionth car.

3

Surviving the Great Depression (1930-41)

As the first auto show after the "crash" opened its doors, in January of 1930, the American mood was one of uncertainty. Would economic disaster be with us for years to come, perhaps with rampant unemployment and crushing poverty? Or would the stock market find its way back to normalcy, bringing the nation back to—or at least closer to—the "boom" times of the Twenties?

For the first time ever, in 1930, the auto show was open on Sunday. More than 300 cars, taxicabs and chassis of at least 44 makes were seen, along with 83 exhibits of accessories and 32 of shop equipment.

Visitors could see everything from an Auburn, Black Hawk, and Cunningham, to a Moon and Pierce-Arrow, a Willys-Knight and a Windsor. One Cadillac model, an Imperial Cabriolet with Fisher Madame X body, even held a V-16 engine, predicting a modest trend in the Thirties. Even as ordinary families found themselves unable to consider buying a new car of any sort, magnificent classic machines with powerful engines rolled out of the shops of custom coachbuilders.

Cars and taxis were found on the main floor of the Coliseum, as well as the north hall and south annex. Accessories stood on the mezzanine floor, and second floor of the south annex. As in the Twenties, a host of auxiliary shows drew interested parties. In addition to the Coliseum exhibits, General Motors displayed its vehicles at the Stevens Hotel; Chrysler at the Congress; Graham-Paige at the Palmer House; and Packard at the Drake. Ford cars (and a tri-motor Ford airplane) could be seen at the 131st Armory building; Lincolns at 2440 South Michigan Avenue; and Reos at Michigan and 15th Street.

Automobile Topics magazine reported that "the old Coliseum never was adorned to greater advantage. Merrie England furnished the inspiration ... a panorama of hill and dale with a cloud effect achieved by an overhead canopy." Illuminated exhibit names stood above gates in low brick walls. Several cars at the show even had radios, "demonstrated in quiet tones."

As the Great Depression deepened, auto production began to sink. After a peak in 1929, at 5,621,715 vehicles, output dipped close to 3.5 million in 1930, then to 2,465,000 in '31.

GM's auxiliary show at the Stevens Hotel, supplementing the 1931 auto show, featured no fewer than 99 cars and trucks. A concert orchestra entertained, afternoons and evenings. Admission to the auxiliary event was free, in contrast to the usual charge at the Coliseum. (Even at the low point of the Depression, in 1933, auto-show patrons paid 50 cents to enter.)

Opening-day attendance sagged in 1931, but rebounded a bit the next year, signaling what the *Chicago Tribune* called "a revival of interest." Part of the increase was deemed due to the show "introducing more new models than ever before in pursuance of an agreement on announcement dates arranged by" the National Automobile Chamber of Commerce.

At the annual dinner of the Chicago Automobile Trade Association (CATA), Paul G. Hoffman, president of Studebaker Sales Corporation, told 1,400 dealers and salesmen that their 1932 business would depend upon how intelligently and aggressively they went after it.

In 1932, the CATA sponsored the 17th annual salon of custom-built cars, at the Drake Hotel. Close to 60 automobiles were exhibited, from 11 makers.

To draw attention to the main event at the Coliseum, banners and flags were displayed not only along Michigan Avenue's "auto row," but in Chicago community centers. Several thousand Yellow Cabs carried auto show flags, too.

Even during the depths of the Depression, Americans bought cars at every price level. These are Auburns, pictured at Chicago's 1933-34 Century of Progress exposition.

As reported by the *Automotive Daily News*, the number of dealers attending stood "far in excess of anything in a number of years." Furthermore, "despite adverse weather conditions crowds have constantly filled the big building comfortably and at times have even jammed it.... Wise crackers and curiosity seekers are far less numerous than for some years past and in their stead are men and women seriously interested in the new models apparently from a buying viewpoint."

Samuel Miles passed away in 1932, after three decades at the helm of the Chicago Automobile Show. Miles earned credit for continuous growth of Chicago's annual event, both in terms of attendance and importance to the auto industry. Detroit's leaders knew that Chicago remained the "selling show," where the results of their development and production efforts either sank or swam.

The national economy hit bottom in 1933, as unemployment reached its dismal peak. Americans needed diversion, whether at the movies, from cumbersome radios in the living room—or as an all-day outing at the Coliseum's auto show, where more than 250 cars, taxicabs, and chassis of 25 makes could be scrutinized.

"Gone are the formal rows of vehicles," declared the *Chicago Tribune*, "with little more than the carpet to distinguish the place from a storage garage. The new show has action, color, movies, pretty girls and dissected engines."

GM's free-admission exhibit at the Stevens Hotel stayed open until midnight. Chrysler products could be found at the Congress Hotel, as well as the Coliseum; Packards at the Edgewater Beach Hotel on the north-side lakefront; Lincolns at the Drake Hotel; Studebaker and Rockne at the Auditorium Hotel downtown.

Three years before the opening of the Century of Progress, in 1933, CATA President J.R. Histed had sent a letter to the event's manager, Major L.R. Lohr. Histed offered the CATA's assistance in setting up the automotive portion of the world's fair, noting that "more motor cars are sold [in Chicago] than in any other one community in the world." Experience in that endeavor laid the background for the CATA's ability to step in and take over the running of the annual auto show, not long afterward.

Fan-dancer Sally Rand and her cohorts along the "Streets of Paris" at Chicago's Century of Progress drew eager, massive audiences. So did dozens—hundreds—of exhibitors of more mundane products and services. Avid visitors wandered through a host of automotive exhibits, in separate buildings constructed by General Motors, Ford, and other companies. They could even watch a GM car being assembled, at a mini-factory built right on the show grounds. The Century of Progress had proven so popular in 1933 that a second season was arranged.

Back at the auto show and the Coliseum, the number of cars on display dipped a little in 1934—no great surprise, as the crop of automakers was gradually declining in the Thirties. Even so, Midwesterners looked forward to their day at the Coliseum, Depression notwithstanding.

Officers of the CATA got a shock later in 1934, learning that both the New York and Chicago shows were to be abandoned by the National Automobile Chamber of Commerce. As reported in a letter from CATA President Lafayette Markle, "the burden will fall upon this Association for the Chicago show."

So it did, but the CATA was ready for this responsibility—and destined to carry it out from that point forward. The trade association had taken over during the First World War, when auto manufacturers had dropped out as sponsors, but that was only for a single season.

As usual, the 1935 show took place early that year, in late January. Some 300 models of 24 makes moved into the show, along with 61 displays of accessories and equipment.

Said CATA President M.J. Lanahan at the association's banquet, at the Stevens Hotel: "The public is buying cars, 45 percent more in 1934 than in 1933 and 100 percent more last year than in '32." Henry Ford was officially at the show "for the first time," according to the *Chicago Tribune*, "exercising his knowledge of showmanship gained at the 1934 World's Fair."

Long lines of people waited to enter the Coliseum on opening day, "disregarding the heavily falling snow." A.C. Faeh, now the show manager, noted that "the significant thing is that it was a buying as well as a sightseeing crowd.... People not only are buying, but they are buying expensive cars."

Innovations for this show included a slogan and essay contest, with cash prizes, based on what individuals could do to promote auto safety.

Early in 1935, President Roosevelt announced that manufacturers had agreed to alter their production schedules, so new models would be produced in the autumn, not at the first of each year. "The decision to set the automobile show dates ahead some two months," said Show Committee Chairman H.T. Hollingshead, "was made by the motor car manufacturers, through the desire to cooperate with the federal administration in an effort to spread employment" more evenly. Doing so, analysts thought, would help alleviate the unwanted economic impact of the seasonal nature of automobile production.

Therefore, Chicago had two auto shows in 1935: one in January to promote the 1935 models, and another in November to push the '36 models. No less significant was a move out of the Coliseum at 15th and Wabash, over to the recently-completed International Amphitheatre, at 43rd and Halsted. Promoters claimed that the Amphitheatre and Coliseum were just eight minutes apart, but in this era of slow-moving traffic and no expressways that might have been an exaggeration.

Whereas the first 1935 show drew 125,000 visitors to the Coliseum, the one that fall attracted 225,000 to the Amphitheatre. Available floor space "multiplied four times," according to the *Chicago Tribune*, "giving Chicago the largest automobile show in the world." Protected parking for 5,500 cars was free.

A new age of showmanship emerged at the fall 1935 show, said to be "inspired by the optimism in the industry." Not only could visitors see about 300 models of cars, trucks, trailers, and motor coaches (29 vehicle makes in all), they could enjoy a revue featuring some lovely ladies. Twenty "manikins" were hired to take part in a fur fashion parade, seen twice daily, at 4:30 and 9:30. Wearing a million dollars worth of furs, the women rode into the Amphitheatre's arena in twenty-one 1936 automobiles, accompanied by the music of Peter Cavallo's symphonic orchestra.

Decorations at the Amphitheatre were arranged by J.C. Becker, a noted Chicago artist and exposition builder, building on a "Hall of Stars" motif with rich blue and silver colors. The show floor adopted a "follow the arrow" plan, so visitors could see it all in what the CATA called "a systematic manner." How did they bill this more showmanlike event? Immodestly—as "The World's Greatest Automobile Show." Declared show manager A.C. Faeh: At the Amphitheatre, "the visitor may see an event packed with dreams."

A trend toward showmanship actually had begun to evolve a few years earlier, with such things as cutaway exhibits, Faeh explained. Those "demonstrated to show committees that the motorist loves to see 'what makes the wheels go 'round.'" Next, someone came up with the idea of showing chassis in operation, under glass, driven by electricity. Lecturers were introduced, to extol the merits of the motorcars and explain the technical workings. And for this 1935 event, 40 attractive "usherettes" were selected and trained by the Andy Frain organization.

No outside hotel exhibits took place this year. Everything was at the Amphitheatre. As one promotional effort, the Keep Chicago Safe Committee sponsored a safety poster and slogan contest in the city's high schools.

By the mid-1930s, the economy was improving a bit—though another severe downturn was waiting in the wings. "Optimism is traditional with us in this industry," said CATA President K.K. Kenderdine, "and it seems to me that our perennially high hopes are better founded than at any time during the past six years."

Autumn auto shows continued for the rest of the decade, with the level of entertainment escalating each year, even if the number of exhibits sometimes declined. Only 130 exhibits were set up at the show in late 1936 (promoting the '37 car models), but visitors had another form of excitement to observe. A new "Brides of the Nations" Revue featured women of 22 nationalities.

This year's educational display, sponsored by the Keep Chicago Safe Committee, fell under the charge of William A. Sears, an auto technician at Lane Technical High School on the north side. A course on traffic safety, considered to be the first in the nation, had just begun at the all-boys public school.

The *Chicago Tribune* called the late-1937 show (for '38 models) "an educational exhibit," noting that "companies display bisected sedan bodies, cutaway engines, stripped wheel suspension, and dismembered clutches, transmissions and brakes. Labels and lecturers give men and women without a mechanical background an easy understanding of the latest advancements in automotive engineering." The Amphitheatre was decorated with peach-colored ceilings and walled columns of red and black, with white trim.

Instead of "Brides of the Nations," the featured attraction at the previous year's event, this show offered a "Fashions of the World" performance each afternoon and evening. As the *Tribune* described it, the presentation consisted of "pretty girls with the latest styles in gowns and furs."

According to the show program, the women wore "beautiful native costumes, evening gowns and furs." Nineteen women selected on the basis of their ethnicity (and beauty) were joined by Miss Chicago, Miss Hollywood, Miss Miami, and Miss New York.

Of the twenty-five 1938 vehicle makes exhibited, just one was foreign. The model count rose sharply, to 220.

About 64 accessory exhibitors added to the intrigue, including Zenith Radio, Encyclopedia Britannica, Coleman Lamp, Quaker State oil, *Motor* magazine, Simoniz, Vogue Rubber Company, Hartford insurance, and the Hoof Products Company. (What products that latter firm produced is lost to history.)

After the auto show, a person might stop at the Empire Room of the Palmer House to see the "magic music" of Wayne King and his orchestra. Seekers after something more risqué could make a stop at Harry's New York Cabaret on North Wabash, with its "Whirl of Girls" and an eight-course dinner for $1.25. The Chez Paree nightclub featured "minstrel man" Benny Fields and the vocals of Gracie Barrie, plus the "Chez Paree Dancing Ensemble." Rates at the Hotel Chicagoan, at 67 West Madison in the "heart of the Loop," started at $2.50 a day.

A different sort of twice-daily pageant helped draw visitors to the next auto show, late in 1938, featuring the '39 models. Called "An Age of Wheel Prints," the revue depicted the evolution of transportation since the Civil War. "During the intermission," declared the *Chicago Tribune*, "there is a promenade of eleven pretty girls, each a 'nationality queen' selected for pulchritude typical of the country she is representing."

Admission was reduced this year, to 40 cents until 4 p.m., or 55 cents thereafter. Perhaps that helped attendance swell to an estimated 316,000—a record figure. Something new this year was a used-car section, finally acknowledging

After the Chicago Automobile Trade Association took over sponsorship in 1935, a big dose of showmanship turned the annual auto show into a major spectacle.

e fact that for many Depression-burdened Americans, condhand (if not thirdhand) was the only way to go.

"Dame Fashion" was the title of the 1939 stage revue, led as a "musical melange" with a cast of one hundred d presented at 3:30 and 9 p.m. Performances ran the mut from opera to jitterbug, with 19 "nationality queens" help keep the entertainment intriguing.

In addition to having an opportunity to survey the 1940 r models, showgoers could get a look at demonstrations of levision. TV had been seen at the New York World's Fair, plenty of Chicagoans took advantage of the opportunity the Amphitheatre.

The auto show's run was extended to nine days, from e usual eight. This year's used-car section, returning cause it had resulted in strong sales in 1938, contained 95 aces—50 percent larger than before.

As 1940 approached its close, war was on the minds of ost Americans. Conflict was building in Europe, and many lieved it was only a matter of time until America would ter the battle against Hitler.

"The auto industry's role in national defense will be essed in [the 1940] show," advised the *Chicago Tribune*, with the army, navy and marine corps displaying some of ncle Sam's latest fighting equipment." Several anufacturers had dropped out of the picture in recent ars, including Pierce-Arrow and Cord. As a result, only 19 akes of 1941 vehicles made the lineup. Eight truck makes ppeared in the south wing, along with seven station agons—a body style that was far from common at this int.

"Non-Stop America" was the title of the stage spectacle, escribed as a "music and girl melange dramatizing the story of motor cars." Something new attracted showgoers. stead of "nationality queens," 20 community and uburban "queens," chosen by contests in their own areas, ppeared at the auto show.

On a more mundane level, the Amphitheatre boasted 96 aces for late-model used cars in the north wing, as well as accessories/parts/educational exhibits in both wings. All ld, there were 164 exhibits and more than 400 vehicles to studied.

Chris Sinsabaugh, an auto-show press agent since the rly days, and later a major auto editor, wrote in 1940 that e New York show started the season and got more ublicity. Nevertheless, "Chicago is different—it's the aler's show, attracting more retailers than New York and fording manufacturers a better opportunity to get in touch ith their customers than they have in New York."

Another Chicago Auto Show was tentatively scheduled r October 1941, to feature the '42 models, then canceled. t was the strong consensus of opinion," explained CATA esident Ben T. Wright, "that because of the needs of the fense program and because of curtailed production, a otor vehicle exposition is not feasible this year."

Automotive events didn't stop in the Forties, of course. eston Tucker, for example, used the International mphitheatre soon after the war to display his futuristic new tomobile. One of the authors of this book recalls, as a

small child, sitting on his father's shoulders at that presentation, mesmerized by the Tucker's centrally-mounted "cyclops" third headlight, which rotated along with the front wheels.

Automotive News reported on October 29, 1945, that an automobile-industry Golden Jubilee was to open on November 1, at the Museum of Science and Industry. A Parade of Cars was scheduled on Thanksgiving Day, headed by six early models. J. Frank Duryea planned to attend, to drive an 1896 Duryea.

The CATA remained active through the war years and into the postwar era, handling issues of importance to its dealer members. One of the programs initiated after the war was a drive to rid Chicago of jalopies, deemed eyesores by some. That effort proved to be only partially successful. After all, many Chicagoans wanted—or needed—their jalopies. A seemingly worn-out prewar automobile was their only mode of transportation. Even those who had the money to purchase a new vehicle couldn't do so readily, as cars were in short supply after the war and for several years afterward.

As we've already seen in Chapter 1, the early postwar years ushered in a "golden age" at the auto show, setting the stage for even more excitement by the mid-Fifties.

Automobiles during World War II

When the CATA decided to omit an auto show for October 1941, Pearl Harbor was still two months off. Even so, most Americans realized that the country's entry into World War II was imminent—and wondered how that would affect motoring.

After a brief flurry of turning out 1942 models, civilian production ground to a halt, and would not resume until July 1945, led by Ford. In the meantime, auto plants were hurriedly converted to wartime output. Factories that had issued passenger cars now turned to tanks and military trucks, bombs and aircraft. A handful of passenger vehicles were built between 1942 and 1945, but strictly for military and essential applications.

With no new cars to be sold, dealers focused on used cars and servicing for the duration. Gasoline was rationed, and pleasure driving discouraged. Many people put their cars up on blocks, especially if the family head was serving overseas.

For several years after the war, car-starved motorists snapped up every vehicle that rolled off the assembly line, typically paying a premium price for the privilege of slipping behind the wheel.

The Great Depression had begun, but visitors to the 1930 Chicago Auto Sho[w] had more than 300 new car models to inspect—plus 83 exhibits [of] accessories, and 32 of shop equipment. England furnished the inspiration [for] the Coliseum's decorations. Names of the exhibits were in illuminated lette[rs] over grilled gates, while stone urns were set at intervals.

1930
30th annual Chicago Automobile Show
(January 25-February 1, 1930)

- More than 300 cars, taxis, and chassis at Coliseum, from at least 44 manufacturers
- Auto industry soon begins to feel impact of Great Depression
- Samuel Miles still manages Chicago show
- Auto show open on Sunday, for first time
- Cadillac model has V-16 engine
- Front-drive cars prominent at Coliseum: Cord, Ruxton, Gardner
- Several car models contain radios
- Coliseum is decorated with outdoor panorama; canopy adds cloud effect
- Auxiliary shows take place at downtown hotels ... Ford is at 131st Armory, with exhibit that includes tri-motor plane

1931
31st annual Chicago Automobile Show
(January 24-31, 1931)

- 300 cars displayed at Coliseum
- Auto show is open daily, including Sunday, from 10 a.m. to 10:30 p.m.
- Ford again has separate exhibition at Armory, but Lincoln is at Coliseum
- Separate GM show at Stevens Hotel

See

THE NEW OLDSMOBILE AT THE SHOW

Even during the Great Depression, visitors to exhibits at the auto show tend[ed] to be well-dressed. Cutaways and special displays continued to attract attenti[on] from Americans who wanted to know about the latest technology. This ad pr[o]moted the 1931 auto show.

Even if a family was facing economic troubles, a day at the auto show served as budget-priced entertainment. Lighting in the Coliseum consisted of a series of hanging candelabra, imitating old hammered copper candle holders. Accessories on display even included an Electric Doorman (garage door opener).

ourage and fortitude will be re-
rded in 1931. What you auto-
obile men need is a superiority
mplex like we drive into our
otball players."

—Knute Rockne, legendary Notre
Dame football coach, speaking at
the Chicago Automobile Trade Association annual dinner, January 23,
1931

e other automakers attempting
hang on through the early De-
ession years, Auburn adjusted
ces and promoted the compara-
e value of its automobiles.

1932

32nd annual Chicago Automobile Show

(January 30–February 6, 1932)

- More than 300 cars, taxis, and chassis exhibited at Coliseum, from at least 42 manufacturers
- Accessories section has 109 exhibits on mezzanine floor of Coliseum
- More new models introduced at 1932 auto show than ever before, though total list of manufacturers continues to thin out
- Cars said to be "safer, better, cheaper"
- Show promoters see increased opening-day attendance as sign of revived interest
- Automatic clutch standard in many cars
- Many models feature automatic starters, automatic chokes, adjustable shock absorbers
- CATA sponsors this year's Automobile Salon at Drake Hotel
- Samuel Miles dies, while in England

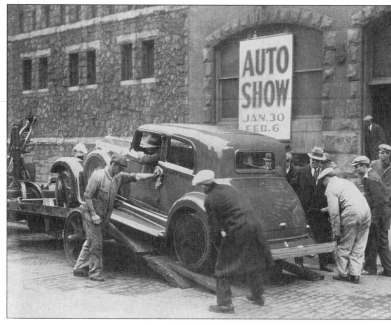

Workers unload a car at the Coliseum, for the 1932 auto show.

Cadillac presents Four New Cars

La Salle v-8 · *Cadillac* v-8 · *Cadillac* v-12 · *Cadillac* v-16

AT THE AUTOMOBILE SHOW AND THE HOTEL STEVENS

Right: *During the 1932 auto show, Chrysler set up its temporary "offices" at the Congress Hotel, a mile north of the Coliseum.*

Left: *Luxury cars continued to appear at a salon, separate from the auto show. Cadillac had proclaimed its cars the "standard of the world" in the early days.*

In 1932, the number of nameplates was diminishing, but showgoers still had plenty of cars to choose from. Pontiac launched a V-8 model this year—actually a continuation of the prior Oakland.

TAKING 'ER ON HIGH

Despite the realities of the growing Depression, optimi was the order of the day, especially in the auto tra Think positively, industry leaders insisted, and Amer really could send "Old Man Pessimism" to the sideline

ight: General Motors showed some of its 1932 wares at the evens Hotel (shown), but the Chicago Automobile Trade ssociation sponsored the annual Salon of custom-built cars, at the rake Hotel. Chevrolet and Graham were at the Palmer House; hrysler at the Congress; Willys-Overland at the Sherman Hotel; eVaux at the Auditorium Hotel. North side dealers had their own xhibit at the Edgewater Beach Hotel, and south side dealers were the Chicago Beach Hotel.

bove: Located a mile north of the Coliseum, the tevens Hotel hosted a separate General Motors xhibit in its Salon.

ight: Several automakers had exhibits in one of the owntown hotels, as well as at the regular show at e Coliseum.

elow: Outside exhibits might be free and fun, but ost prospective buyers—and tirekickers—went the full show at the Coliseum.

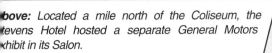

YOU'LL ENJOY IT

GRAND SHOWING OF GENERAL MOTORS CARS

STEVENS HOTEL

JAN. 23 to FEB. 8 — 10 A. M. to Midnight

MUSIC

ADMISSION FREE

Samuel A. Miles (1862-1932)

After three decades of managing the Chicago Auto Show, Samuel Arthur Miles died of an apoplectic seizure on April 25, 1932. Close to 70 years old, he was visiting his sister in Bristol, England. Miles had resigned as show manager for the National Automobile Chamber of Commerce, just three weeks earlier.

1933
33rd annual Chicago Automobile Show
(January 28-February 4, 1933)

- Great Depression sinks American economy to its lowest point in 1933
- More than 250 cars, taxicabs, and chassis appear at Coliseum, but come from only 25 manufacturers
- Cord, Durant, Peerless, and Willys-Knight automobiles no longer are produced
- Auto show admission is 50 cents—not a modest sum in this difficult year
- 75 exhibits occupy accessories section on mezzanine floor of Coliseum
- Trends of 1933 include sloping front radiator grilles, bigger fenders, tilted windshields, airplane-type gauges
- Several makes contain power brakes
- Shock absorbers finally are becoming standard, along with shatterproof glass
- Auxiliary exhibits, as usual, are located at various downtown hotels

Upper Right: *Even a new Plymouth was beyond the reach of most Americans in 1933, but families still enjoyed coming to the show—and dreaming of better times.*

Right: *More than 250 cars and chassis could be seen on the Coliseum's main floor, exhibited by 25 makers, from Auburn and Continental to Stutz and Willys.*

Despite the Great Depression, shoppers had plenty of flashy cars to choose from in '33, with sporty open bodies or practical closed bodies. The mezzanine held displays of accessories and shop equipment. Not everyone had fifty cents to spare in 1933, but automobile fans got a lot of entertainment for half a buck.

Century of Progress

- Century of Progress "world's fair" opens along Chicago's lakefront
- Exhibit area stretches from 12th Street to 39th Street
- First season's fair opens on May 27, 1933, and lasts until November 1—then extended until November 12
- Automobiles are a predominant feature of fair—even including GM assembly line
- Century of Progress begins with parade
- No free passes are issued; even politicians must pay 50 cents to enter
- Palwaukee World's Fair Airport, at 31st Street, opens on May 25
- Show promoters anticipate daily attendance of 350,000 people
- Second season of Century of Progress runs from April to end of October, 1934—includes new Ford exhibit

Above: At the Century of Progress, the Chrysler Building delighted the eye, according to this rendering.

Right: Three girls prepare to take a spin in a pint-sized automobile on Enchanted Island—a playground for youngsters at the Century of Progress.

Left: The Ford building looked particularly enchanting at night.

Above: Like nearly all the structures at the Century of Progress, the General Motors Building was meant to be temporary—torn down after the fair. At least 10 million visitors saw the General Motors and Chrysler buildings in 1933.

Left: Most Americans had never seen an automobile assembly line in action—but they could at the General Motors pavilion.

1934

34th annual Chicago Automobile Show

(January 27-February 3, 1934)

- 25 automakers present more than 200 cars, taxicabs, and chassis at Coliseum
- Admission is 50 cents, plus 5-cent tax
- 75 exhibits are in accessories division on mezzanine, which includes shop equipment
- Streamlined bodies and GM's "knee-action" independent front suspension are top trends of 1934
- Show open 10:30 a.m. until 11:00 p.m.
- Makes include Auburn, Buick, Cadillac, Chevrolet, Chrysler, Continental, DeSoto, Dodge, Franklin, Graham, Hudson, Hupmobile, Lafayette, LaSalle, Lincoln, Nash, Olds, Packard, Pierce-Arrow, Plymouth, Pontiac, Reo, Studebaker, Terraplane, Willys
- 125,000 people attend '34 auto show
- As in prior years, separate displays are held by manufacturers at Chicago hotels ... GM marks 25th birthday at Stevens Hotel

Manufacturers still operated the Chicago Auto Show in 1934, but the Chica Automobile Trade Association soon would be called upon to step in a sponsor future events.

Chicago's Mayor Edward Kelly was ready to speak over WGN radio, directly from the auto-show floor. Kelly had become mayor a year earlier, after his predecessor, Anton Cermak, was shot by an assassin who'd intended to kill President Roosevelt.

Like nearly all 1934 models, Dodges wore bodies that were even more streamlined than before. "Suicide doors" (rear-hinged) would not last much longer on American cars.

Chicago-area motorists and their counterparts across the country weren't ready for the advanced-design DeSoto Airflow, introduced in 1934, or for its Chrysler sibling. Both cars were deemed too revolutionary, and failed to sell, despite ultra-modern styling and impressive engineering.

e other General Motors cars, Oldsmobile and Pontiac got the "Knee-Action" front suspension for 1934. Despite ionwide economic Depression, automakers introduced a host otable innovations in the early Thirties.

1935
35th annual Chicago Automobile Show
(January 26-February 2, 1935)

- Chicago Automobile Trade Association takes over sponsorship of show—dealers step in at last minute
- Opening-day sees record attendance of 31,000 ... first-day visitors disregard heavy snow to wait in line
- 250,000 visitors expected to attend 35th auto show—final count claimed to approach that figure, helped by better weather
- Coliseum has new ramp entrance from Michigan Avenue, at 15th Street
- 24 automobile makes are on display—300 models in all, plus 61 displays of accessories and equipment
- Ford has official exhibit at Coliseum, for first time in many years
- Admission is 55 cents until 6:00 p.m.; 75 cents thereafter
- Show hours: 11 a.m. to 11 p.m.

Right: Now operated by the Chicago Automobile Trade Association (CATA), the 1935 auto show continued to use the old Coliseum—but change was in the works.

Model of area of the a show at the Coliseum, lo ing south down the cer aisle, depicts one of the 43-foot giant goddesses to at the ends of the build Also shown are two of the giant figures of transpo tion, towering 32 feet tall.

Photo of a portion of the actual show floor of the Coliseum reveals a few modifications from the model pictured on the preceding page, but the basic artistic theme was carried through.

eek lines of the 1935 models w attention, but coming up h the cash—or credit—to ve one home from a alership was no easy matter most families. Note the assis display, and the more odern appearance of the liseum's interior.

1936
36th annual Chicago Automobile Show
(November 16-23, 1935)

- For the first time since 1907, Chicago has two shows in a single year: one in February for the 1935 models, and then another in November for 1936 models
- November show moves to International Amphitheatre, 43rd and Halsted; no more auto shows will take place at Coliseum
- Amphitheatre boasts 255,000 square feet of space, versus 58,000 at Coliseum
- CATA continues as show sponsor
- Show attracts 225,000 visitors
- About 300 models of 29 makes are on display, including trailers, motor coaches
- 20 female "manikins" take part in fur fashion parade, twice daily ... women ride into arena in 1936 cars, accompanied by music from Cavallo's orchestra
- Radically-styled Cord seen for first time
- High school students participate in safety slogan contest

Above: Twenty "manikins" were to appear at the auto show, draped in a million dollars worth of furs as they helped introduce the 1936 cars.

Below: Artist's conception of the "Hall of Stars" suggests the level showmanship that might be coming to the auto show.

Above: Auto-show programs gave all the highlights of the performance that visitors were about to enjoy—plus details about the show itself.

Right: Planners believed a lushly-produced, free stage revue would put showgoers in a carefree frame of mind for visiting the auto display. Note the "stars" hanging from the ceiling—just part of the fancy decor that was planned.

Promotion for the move to the Amphitheatre began early. This is a 1934 rendering of the building, which had been used for truck display during auto shows of the distant past.

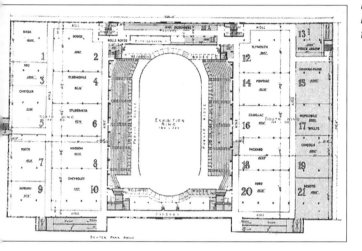

Above Left: Moving to the Amphitheatre gave exhibitors a lot more space for their products. It also helped give the CATA an opportunity to turn the auto show into a memorable spectacle.

Right: Readers of these simple ads were in for a treat if they took a streetcar or the "El" to the Amphitheatre. Plenty of parking was available for those who preferred to drive to 43rd and Halsted.

AUTO SHOW

at new location

INTERNATIONAL AMPHITHEATER

Halsted at 43rd St.

$3,000,000 exhibit of cars, trucks, trailers, accessories

FUR STYLE SHOW

4:00 and 9:00 P. M.

Cavallo's Symphonic Band

11 a. m to 11 p. m.

Free Parking for 8,000 Cars

Admission 55 cents including tax

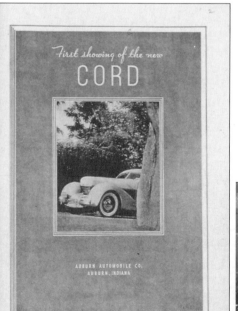

ove & Right: Chicagoans were among *e* first to see the dramatic new front-drive *rd,* with hidden headlights and "coffin-*se*" front end.

1937
37th annual Chicago Automobile Show
(November 14-21, 1936)

- 130 exhibits at Amphitheatre include 25 makes of cars, 11 trucks, 25 trailer coaches, and 66 accessories displays
- "Brides of the Nations" revue, seen twice daily, features women representing 22 nationalities
- Cavallo's Symphonic Band provides the musical accompaniment
- Admission is 55 cents; revue is free
- Final attendance count is 318,000
- Fisher has "door slam" exhibit to demonstrate new turret-top bodies
- Showgoers see cars from Auburn, Buick, Cadillac, Chevrolet, Chrysler, Cord, DeSoto, Dodge, Duesenberg, Ford, Graham, Hudson, Lafayette, LaSalle, Lincoln, Nash, Olds, Packard, Pierce-Arrow, Plymouth, Pontiac, Studebaker, Terraplane, Willys

Automobile Travel in 1936

The era of "auto-camping" had reached its peak in the Twenties, b[...] lot of people with cars still liked the idea of healthful, outdoor travel[...]

Americans who could afford an automobile just might want to purchase a vehicle equipped for camping.

Planning for the stage revue took plenty of effort on the part of show planners. H.T. Hollingshead served as the CATA's show committee chairman, while A.C. Faeh was show manager. Cavallo's Symphonic Band provided the musical accompaniment for the twice-daily "Brides of the Nations" revue.

After 1936, Reo—founded by Ransom E. Olds in 1904, a[...] he left the company that bore his name—decided to leave [...] passenger-car business to the competition, and focus so[...] on trucks.

1938
38th annual Chicago Automobile Show
(November 6-13, 1937)

- 220 separate vehicles are exhibited at Amphitheatre, from 25 makers (one of them foreign)
- Show is open 11 a.m. to 11 p.m., including Sunday
- Show manager A.C. Faeh estimates that attendance will top 300,000—total actually sets all-time record, at 416,000
- "Fashions of the World" revue takes place each afternoon and evening, with women wearing native costumes, evening gowns, and furs ... stage spectacle takes place beneath 40-foot revolving globe
- Central arena has seating for 12,000 visitors to watch the revue
- 64 accessory exhibits are part of show
- Amphitheatre is decorated with peach-colored ceiling and red/black columns

Left: Newspaper cartoons drew attention to the auto show, and also pointed out the importance of public enthusiasm in getting the economy rolling again.

Below: Ushers stood tall, ahead of the new cars, during the stage revue. Pictured are 1938 Oldsmobile, Plymouth, and Graham sedans.

Left: America could have used a few true economy cars in the Thirties—but not many buyers drove home a Bantam, which was far smaller than conventional vehicles.

Right: Clever ads continued to play a role in attracting visitors to the auto show each year.

Seats in the Amphitheatre's central arena held 12,000 revue-watchers.

1939
39th annual Chicago Automobile Show
(November 13-20, 1938)

- This year's revue is titled "An Age of Wheel Prints," depicting evolution of transportation since Civil War ... 1939 car models are introduced at climax
- 11 "nationality queens" promenade during revue's intermission
- Admission is reduced to 40 cents until 4 p.m., then 55 cents; children pay a quarter
- Show hours: 11 a.m. to 11 p.m.
- Used-car section is new this year; proves to be successful
- Most cars have column-mounted gearshift lever
- Sliding sunroof is seen on Cadillac and LaSalle models
- 310,000 people visit the 1939 auto show

Used cars got a special section at the auto show, on the main floor, along with trucks and accessories. The new 1939 cars occupied the second floor. Chevrolet's "OK" symbol for used cars was well-known by the public.

Eager crowds line up at the Amphitheatre entrance for this year's auto show.

Studebaker had a brand-new model to entice auto-show visitors: the lightweight, low-priced Champion. Even a budget-priced automobile warranted a lavish sendoff.

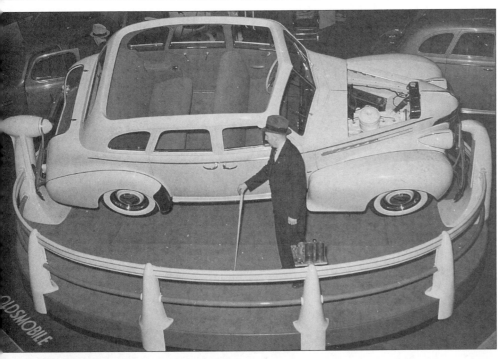

Oldsmobile snipped away the roof of this sedan and exposed the engine, to help attract the attention of potential customers.

Above: *Only one make in the moderately-priced field had a V-12 engine: the Lincoln Zephyr. Like Ford and the new Mercury, Lincoln got hydraulic brakes this year—far later than other automobiles.*

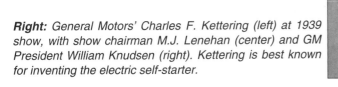

Right: *General Motors' Charles F. Kettering (left) at 1939 show, with show chairman M.J. Lenehan (center) and GM President William Knudsen (right). Kettering is best known for inventing the electric self-starter.*

1940
40th annual Chicago Automobile Show
(November 4-12, 1939)

- Show run is extended to nine days
- Showgoers can see free exhibition of television from RCA-Victor ... TV was seen earlier in 1939 at New York World's Fair
- "Dame Fashion" stage spectacle has cast of 100 ... the "Dame" stands 18 feet high, with cars emerging from her ruffled skirt
- "Nationality queens" are selected by their respective ethnic groups, to participate in auto show ... instead of stepping out of cars, the women are assigned different duties this year
- Orchestra is directed by Ralph Foote
- Stage for revue is the largest in Chicago; front curtain is 73 feet high
- No outside exhibits take place this year, accounting in part for strong show attendance
- Used-car section is enlarged this year

Top: "Dame Fashion" wore a ho skirt 16 feet wide, which concea the 1940 cars until they were rea to be introduced to the audience.

Middle: Quite a few makes had appeared through the Thirties, plenty of people managed to b cars. A Chevrolet was the 25-n lionth GM car built.

General sales manager L.D. Cos watches operation of Plymouth's po er top with "Miss Lithuania" (An Davis) and Lucille O'Connell (seate a "page" with the "Dame Fashi spectacle. Plymouth was first wit vacuum-operated top for conve ibles, installed on '39 models.

...ds got sealed-beam headlights for 1940, along with a ...umn-mounted gearshift—a year or two later than ...st makes.

Studebaker removed the doors from a sedan to promote the spaciousness of its back seat, at the 1940 auto show.

Exhibitors sought to dramatize the merits of their automobiles, at their own displays as well as during the revue. Stripped chassis had been popular auto-show features for decades.

1941
41st annual Chicago Automobile Show
(October 26-November 3, 1940)

- Final Chicago Auto Show before America enters World War II—turns out to be last one until 1950
- 18 manufacturers exhibit automobiles ... 7 makers have station wagons to show
- One wing of main floor is for trucks
- Stage spectacle is called "Non-Stop America," dramatizing history of cars in two acts (with change of scenery)
- 20 neighborhood and suburban "queens" participate in this year's pageant
- Exhibits from Army, Navy, and Marine Corps demonstrate fighting equipment available to American troops
- Close to 400,000 people attend this final show of the period
- Next show is tentatively scheduled for October 1941, but later canceled

Nothing was particularly surprising about the '41 Fords, but the resty bodies looked—and were—bigger than before. Fords had come w flathead V-8 engines since 1932.

Eagerness to view a Buick—or any other 1940 model—wasn't likely to give any showgoer license to speed. But ad writers liked to create witty ways to get their point across quickly to newspaper readers.

In addition to providing entertainment, the "Non-Stop America" musical revue had one specific purpose: to present coming year's cars—such as this '41 Plymouth—in an exciting setting.

the last three years before auto shows ceased in Chicago—due to the imminence of war—a separate used-car section was included at the Amphitheatre.

Air conditioning? In a 1941 automobile? That's right, Packard had it long before "air" became popular—or even available—in most cars.

SEE THE

MOTOR CAR THAT MAKES ICE CUBES

THE 1941 PACKARD has enough magic to astonish the Man from Mars! Special equipment for the Super-8 includes a cellarette, with service for six—including two trays of ice cubes! They freeze while you drive!

Again, there's real refrigerated Air Conditioning to rout the heat of Summer! Don't miss it! Ask the man who owns one!

PACKARD EXHIBIT
CHICAGO AUTO SHOW
INTERNATIONAL AMPHITHEATRE

A Pontiac gets its turn on the stage during the auto-show revue. Professional performers—including operatic prima donna Lola Fletcher, the Bennett singers, and the Virginia O'Brien ballet—were joined by the 20 neighborhood and suburban "queens" in what was described as a "music and girl melange."

4

The Golden Years
Part 2
(1955-62)

If all looked golden during the 1950-54 period at the Chicago Auto Show, the next few years took that golden hue and turned it into platinum. Modern-day car enthusiasts and collectors look back upon the mid- to late-Fifties as the apex of excess, and also the age when cars approached their limits in distinctiveness.

No one, then or now, is likely to mistake a 1959 Ford for a '59 Chevrolet; a Plymouth for a Studebaker. Each make had its own personality, its own set of characteristics—even if those differences were based on illusions and delusions, fancy and foolishness. Those who find this era silly, and its cars ugly, are invited to search for comparable distinctions among the various automobile makes and models on sale as the 21st century approaches.

Cadillac and Oldsmobile had issued the first modern overhead-valve V-8 engines in 1949, followed by Chrysler's "Hemi" V-8 two years later, and one from Ford in '54. A year later, Chevrolet and Plymouth had V-8 engines on tap, and the "horsepower race" (see sidebar) was in full swing.

Not everyone realized it at the time, but 1955 came to be viewed as a pivotal year—a turning point in the auto industry. No longer would automobiles be considered little more than ways to get from point A to point B. Now, they were becoming extensions of one's personality, movable demonstrations of status, and evidence of passion for the road.

Motivational researchers were busy, scrutinizing American behavior patterns and attitudes to see why they fell for certain kinds of vehicles. Automakers naturally took an interest in the results, attempting to remold their prod to attract the broadest possible audience.

Dowdy shapes were gone; dull colors disdained. 1955 Plymouths and Fords looked nothing like their ancestors; the 1957 Chevrolets and Dodges had little common with their workaday predecessors.

Bright pastels vied for attention with rich complemen hues, sometimes in three-tone paint jobs. Tailfins, seen on the 1948 Cadillac, blossomed in the late Fifties, stretch to startling heights on the 1959 Cadillac, as well Plymouths, Studebakers, and nearly every other make.

Meanwhile, a trend of another stripe was just beginr to emerge. Little by little, imported cars made their way public acceptance, led of course by the Volkswagen Beetle the end of the Fifties, Americans could hop down to import dealership and choose a Renault, Saab, Volvo, Aus MG, Jaguar, Borgward, Goliath, Citroën, Morris Minor, Llc Riley, Ford Taunus—even the first Toyotas, dubbed Toyop

Production set a record in 1955. So did that ye Chicago Auto Show, at the Amphitheatre in January, wh attendance approached the half-million mark.

Community "beauty queens" again appeared at "Motorevue" stage show, helping to introduce the r models as they were driven onto the stage to a mus accompaniment.

Several new models made their public debuts in Chica including the Studebaker Speedster and the Merc Montclair sedan. In years to come, many more would seen for the first time at the Chicago Auto Sh Manufacturers knew that the Chicago event continued to the "selling" show, the indisputable voice of the Midwest "heartland," just as it had been before World War Chicago was where new models earned either praise censure, as determined by sales totals at the dealerships.

General Motors exhibited its palette of "dream cars" separate wing, including the Chevrolet Nomad, Pon Bonneville, Oldsmobile F-88, and Buick Wildcat II. GM brought a pair of European-built cars to the 1955 sh (Vauxhall and Opel), as well as the Australian Holden.

Midwesterners who weren't able to get to the Chic Auto Show didn't have to do without a look at the r models. Once again, Chicago's station WGN-TV televi the auto show throughout the region.

Tailfins dominated the late Fifties automotive scene, as shown on the 1958 Dodge Custom Royal on display at the auto show. Note the women's fashionable attire.

Chevrolet showed its fully-redesigned models, now equipped with either six-cylinder or V-8 engines. Pontiac had similar lineup. Even Plymouth had a V-8 now.

Nash had a V-8 engine for its Ambassador, as well as for new Hudson Hornet, which looked more than a little like Nash. The distinctive "Step-down" that Hudson had launched just after World War II was gone, and Hudsons became little more than gaudy clones of Nash models. Movie fans didn't have to go to a regular theater to see a wide-screen Cinemascope film. Ford showed one of its own, a small theater on the Amphitheatre floor.

In their efforts to trigger ever-larger sales totals, automakers began—gradually—to recognize the impact of women on family auto purchases. Dodge chose an unfortunate route to address women's perceived needs, in the form of the La Femme: a pastel-hued hardtop equipped with color-coordinated personal accessories for milady, including an umbrella. Well, "milady" did not dash forward drive home the La Femme, which lasted only into 1956.

Four-door hardtops were the new body style of '56, introduced first on the bigger General Motors makes. Hardtop sedans were thought to mix the stylishness of a "hardtop convertible" (which is what the first hardtop coupes were called), with the practicality of a four-door body style. To a great extent, they succeeded in doing exactly that, becoming a popular choice.

A few months after the 1955 auto show, Richard J. Daley, previously a state legislator, was elected Mayor of Chicago. Daley would serve for almost two decades, much of that time tumultuous, becoming one of the most widely-recognized political figures in the country. Before long, if an American from elsewhere knew the name of just one big-city mayor, it was almost certain to be Daley's.

Instead of making use of two floors at the Amphitheatre, exhibits wound up on ground level in 1956, when auto-show attendance came within a few thousand of the half-million mark. That year's "Motorevue" featured a "College of Auto Knowledge," complemented by nearly a hundred musicians and entertainers. A new group of community "queens" participated in the festivities, assisting with the presentations of all the new American-built automobiles.

After introducing a V-8 engine a year earlier, Plymouth chose the Chicago Auto Show as a jumping-off point for its potent new Fury hardtop, packing 240 horsepower and a pair of little fins at the aft end. Gone were the days when Plymouth was known as a stodgy family car, suitable only for Mom and Dad, never for the young folks. Chrysler, meanwhile, unveiled its high-performance 300B coupe, after introducing the first "300" model a year earlier.

Three independent imported cars were exhibited in '56, but none of them appeared as part of the stage revue. Simca and Citroën (from France) and the inevitable Volkswagen had to rely on their own exhibit spaces to draw interested customers. Ford and Mercury, meanwhile, joined the list of automakers offering hardtop sedans.

Studebaker took its European-toned coupe of 1953-55 and cleverly transformed it into a series of Hawks. Top dog was the Golden Hawk, equipped with a huge (352 cubic-inch) Packard engine—a result of Studebaker and Packard joining forces in 1955.

Community "beauty queens" were back at the auto show in January of 1957: a different group of women, but performing the same service. Even more than its predecessors, this year's revue was said to offer the "pace and staging of a Broadway hit."

The lineup of imported makes kept growing, now including a big batch of British models (Austin, Singer, Humber, Hillman, Sunbeam, Jaguar, Morris Minor), as well as the French Renault and Swedish Volvo.

Organizers celebrated the auto show's Golden Jubilee in early January of 1958—the fiftieth official show to take place in Chicago. Providing a gift of sorts to the show planners, Midwesterners journeyed to the Amphitheatre in record numbers. For the first time, in fact, final attendance reached past the half-million barrier.

This year, 21 community "beauty queens" participated in the stage revue, which traced the history of the automobile while presenting the current models.

Even more imports found their way onto the show floor this year, from Berkeley to Bianchi and Bristol, Ferrari to Goggomobil, Panhard to Peugeot—even the tiny BMW-built Isetta with its single door up front. Antique and classic models might be viewed, too, in a separate "Motor Memories" section.

Ford's launch of the Edsel as a 1958 model might, in retrospect, be seen as a harbinger of bad tidings to come. Not

Cal MacRitchie — behind the scenes

Years before the Teamsters Union got into the trade-show business, the CATA relied on people like Cal MacRitchie to work the annual event. He worked full-time as a Chicago police officer.

"Each year I would take my vacation time to work for the trade association," MacRitchie recalls. "I started as an assistant at the show in 1955, and eventually became a floor manager. My responsibility was to make sure the truckers and exhibit services followed all rules and regulations. We also made sure that everything was set up for the stage show, including having a chain and tractor ready to pull a vehicle off stage if it stalled.

"My most vivid memories are of the huge crowds that attended, and especially the lines of people outside that stretched for blocks waiting to get into the show, in zero-degree weather. They were part of the reason we worked hard to make sure that the show ran smoothly."

only did the Edsel ultimately fail dismally in the sales charts, but America suffered a serious recession in '58, sending auto sales scurrying downward.

Only 18 community "queens" appeared at the 1959 auto show, where the "Motorevue" was again seen twice daily. Not many paid attention to the new Toyopet in a corner of the show floor, sent from Japan by Toyota. Far more folks doubtless turned to the new Wide-Track Pontiac Bonneville, or even to the smaller-than-compact Rambler American that debuted at the Chicago Auto Show.

Back in 1950, Nash had been the first American automaker to unleash a popular small car: the Rambler. Not until 1959 did other automakers follow suit, detecting an interest in economical driving by worried Americans. Many had been adversely affected by the 1958 recession, and were wary about spending money on a new automobile. While plenty of shoppers continued to lust after bigger-than-ever, increasingly potent "dream machines," others sought to apply their personal brakes and turn to more frugal vehicles.

Imported cars had their good points, and their zealous fans, but most of them were awfully small and puny-engined for Americans. Instead, the auto industry came up with the compact—smaller in dimensions than the familiar sedans, wagons and hardtops, but for the most part, roomier and more powerful than the foreign machines.

Studebaker was among the first, with its '59 Lark. A year later, Chevrolet introduced its amazingly radical Corvair, with a rear-mounted air-cooled engine, no less. That's what Volkswagens had, but few had imagined that a U.S. automaker would be so bold as to create anything out of kilter with the rest of the car crop.

Ford took a more conventional route with the Falcon, also in 1960, whereas Chrysler's Valiant fell somewhere in between: unorthodox in appearance, but clearly conservative in basic engineering.

One more time, in January 1960, the International Amphitheatre hosted the auto show, attracting more than 512,000 guests. This would be the final appearance of community "beauty queens," again part of the "Motorevue" as choreographed by Bob Frellson.

Deutsch-Bonnet? Fiat? Those were but two of the three dozen import makes to be seen at the 1960 auto show, along with Scarab and Bocar racing cars.

Chicago had a brand-new exposition center ready for the 1961 auto show, right along the city's magnificent lakefront at East 23rd Street. With more than 300,000 square feet of display space, constructed at a cost of $35 million, McCormick Place was bigger than a half-dozen football fields. Every American and imported vehicle could be seen in a single arena.

Midwesterners responded in droves, setting an attendance record at more than 789,000 visitors.

"Motorevues" didn't end with the move to McCormick Place. They took place in a new theater, later to be named the Arie Crown. Not unlike the revues at the Amphitheatre since the Thirties, cars were introduced via a series of musical vignettes.

Compact cars continued to gain favor. New modest-sized models at the 1961 auto show included the Buick Special, Oldsmobile F-85, Dodge Lancer, and Pontiac Tempest. All were conventional in basic design, with the exception of Tempest, which featured a radical drivetrain layout, unlike that of any other car on the market.

If rolling down the road wasn't good enough, visitors could even look over the Amphicar, a small car that also functioned as a boat when entering a waterway.

Manufacturer exhibits had been growing more imaginative each year. In 1961, a visitor might be excused for believing he or she was passing through a farm, a campground, a Hawaiian garden—or even Hong Kong's exotic waterfront. Automakers seemed to be realizing that while the "Motorevue" gave each new model a stirring introduction, extra attention was needed to attract as many people as possible into the exhibit area.

Adventurous souls could get a big "lift" at the '61 auto show: a 45-foot elevation, occupying the business end of a snorkel operated by the Chicago Fire Department. Quite an exciting way to get an overhead view of the show floor.

McCormick Place was fully completed when the 1961 auto show opened, ready to host more than 723,000 guests. One dollar let anyone see hundreds of new automobiles, trucks, and accessories, as well as the free "Motorevue" in the 5,000-seat Arie Crown Theater. Popular TV shows served as the revue's theme.

Tailfins finally had faded away, but engines were growing in size and power. Americans were thought to be demanding more and more comfort/convenience features—more electronic gadgetry and wizardry. Technology seemed to have an answer to every concern; but as America swept further into the Sixties, unforeseen challenges lay ahead for the auto industry.

The "horsepower" race

General Motors started it all, introducing a pair of overhead-valve V-8 engines in 1949. Chrysler upped the ante two years later, with its innovative "Hemi." Ford turned in its old flathead V-8 for a more modern OHV rendition in '54. A year later, Chevrolets, Plymouths, and Pontiacs had V-8s tucked under their hoods, and the notion of "power packs" emerged. The "horsepower race" was underway, destined to continue for some two decades.

Chrysler and DeSoto soon reached the near-mystical figure of one horsepower per cubic inch of engine displacement. So did Chevrolet in 1957, with its hottest fuel-injected V-8. Studebaker turned to superchargers to boost output. Turbochargers appeared in the Sixties. Engines grew bigger and more potent yearly. Not until the tightening of emissions regulations in the early Seventies did horsepower ratings finally begin to ebb.

1955

47th annual Chicago Automobile Show

(January 8–16, 1955)

- Auto industry ready for best year ever
- International Amphitheatre continues as auto-show site, with ultra-modern motif
- "Motorevue of 1955" stage show features 20 community "beauty queens" along with professional performers
- Attendance sets a record at 490,500 visitors for auto show's 9-day run ... first-Sunday attendance is record 72,000
- General Motors offers selection of "dream cars" in separate wing: Nomad, Bonneville, F-88, Wildcat II, El Camino
- Three foreign-made GM cars appear at show: Holden, Vauxhall, and Opel
- Show preview televised in Midwest
- Chevrolet introduces redesigned body and V-8 engine ... so does Pontiac
- All-new Nash and Hornet, with V-8 engines, have "special advance showing" in Chicago, "weeks ahead of the national announcement" ... Lee Ann Meriwether, Miss America, signs autographs
- Experimental Lincoln Futura makes world premiere at Chicago show ... so does new Mercury Montclair sedan
- Studebaker debuts Speedster in Chicago
- First public showing of latest Packard, including "Request" concept
- Importer S.H. Arnolt exhibits Arnolt-Bristol and Arnolt-MG sports cars
- Ford theater shows wide-screen movie
- Richard J. Daley is elected Mayor of Chicago this year; will serve for nearly two decades

As in 1950-54, a group of community "beauty queens" assisted with presentation of the new car models during the stage revue. Contests were held in Chicago-area neighborhoods and communities. Shown are (l-to-r): Constance Hodera (Miss Belmont), Nancy Freese (Miss Irving Park), Peggy Corcoran (Miss Logan Square), Faye Lindahl (Miss West Suburban), and Mary Lou Koeppe (Miss Portage Park).

Automakers ran their own newspaper advertisements, promoting both the Chicago show and their own new products. This would be a pivotal year for Chevrolet, which not only had an all-new body but a modern overhead-valve V-8 engine.

Eager crowds lined up to watch Ford's wide-screen movie—and ogle a new Thunderbird or two along the way. Chicagoans actually had seen a Thunderbird prototype a year earlier, at the 1954 auto show.

97

Plymouths wore brand-new bodies for '55, with their own brand of tailfins. Beneath the hood, shoppers might find either a familiar six-cylinder engine or the new V-8 (Plymouth's first). In foreground is a top-of-the-line Belvedere V-8 hardtop, with a Suburban V-8 station wagon at right rear.

Cartoonists might have found automobile shoppers amusing, but a healthy percentage of the hundreds of thousands of visitors to the Chicago Auto Show walked away ready to make a purchase—or at least were seriously thinking in that direction. Note the tailfin on the fish car—a tongue-in-cheek commentary on a growing industry trend.

Ever since 1952, when they got a new body and modern V-8 powe[r] Lincolns had been victorious in the demanding Carrera Panamerican[a] *annual race through the heart of Mexico. Motorsport victories made [a] difference in sales of a particular model, and many technic[al] improvements first saw the light of day on racing machines. This 195[4] winner appeared at the '55 Chicago show.*

Nothing like the experimental Lincoln Futura ever hit the road, but showgoers liked to look over the "dream" cars each year. The Futura predicted styling trends for the 1956 and '57 Lincolns, as well as the 1958-60 Ford Thunderbird.

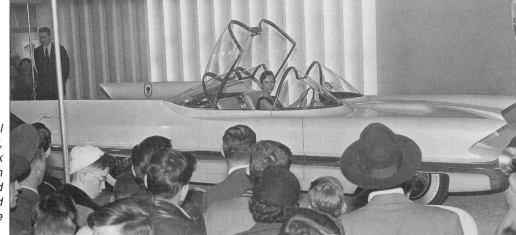

Auto-show officials had to be pleased by the enthusiastic crowds lined up at ticket windows. Close to half a million people visited the 1955 event.

Willys wouldn't be making its Aero hardtop much longer, but ou'd never know that from the glamorous presentation of the ar during the stage revue, by 20-year-old Ona Lee McDermott Miss Edgewater). Although Willys Jeeps and related vehicles ere highly regarded, the conventional passenger cars never uite caught on. Two-toning was popular.

In addition to gaining a "new look," Pontiacs finally lost their straight-eight engines, substituting an up-to-date V-8.

Sneak Preview of '55 Nash

at the Chicago Auto Show

AMERICAN MOTORS has chosen Chicago for the advance world showing of the completely new 1955 Nash cars, weeks ahead of the national announcement. We invite you to see them— with thrilling new V-8 power and performance. Cars built a new, better way with a new kind of ride. A new kind of steering. A new kind of seats. A new kind of Air Conditioning. A new standard of roominess. A whole new styling trend in the making, inspired by the famous Nash-Healey sports car. Don't buy any car until you see the new 1955 Nash Ambassador, Statesman, Rambler and Metropolitan at the Nash exhibit.

ke most of its competitors, Nash joined in the "horsepower race" in 1955, tucking a V-8 engine under the hoods of full-size models.

99

Buick and Oldsmobile introduced four-door hardtops this year. Judging by the crowd, the new body style must have been inviting.

After two years on the market with its luscious European-influenced coupes, Studebaker had something a little different for mid-year introduction: a Speedster hardtop. Assisting with the introduction is Carol Neumann (Miss Berwyn-Cicero), age 17. Only 2,215 Speedsters were built.

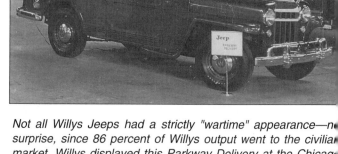

Not all Willys Jeeps had a strictly "wartime" appearance—no surprise, since 86 percent of Willys output went to the civilian market. Willys displayed this Parkway Delivery at the Chicago show.

Mercury adopted a completely new look for '55. Cars shown include a Montclair two-door hardtop and convertible (which sold for $2,631). Montclair was Mercury's most costly model.

1956
48th annual Chicago Automobile Show
(January 7–15, 1956)

- All exhibits on ground floor of International Amphitheatre, for the first time—new exposition hall is decorated like a park
- 493,143 visitors attend the show during its 9-day run
- "Motorevue of 1956" stage show features "College of Auto Knowledge" ... close to 100 musicians and entertainers work with community "queens"
- Plymouth launches Fury hardtop at Chicago show, with 240-horsepower V-8
- Three imported cars are exhibited, but not on stage: Simca, Volkswagen, Citroën
- "June in January" decor adds cheerful tone to Amphitheatre
- Chrysler unveils high-performance 300B and Plainsman station wagon ... Dodge premieres Town Wagon
- Ford Mystere dream car seen at show
- Dodge La Femme seeks female buyers
- Packard shows futuristic Predictor
- Mercury flaunts XM-Turnpike Cruiser
- Lincoln is most-changed '56 model
- Ford demonstrates development of X-1000 "idea car" from drawing to model
- Ford and Mercury add hardtop sedans
- New Studebaker Hawks keep Euro-look

Workmen still had a lot of work to do around the Hudson exhibit area when this photo was taken. Redesigned for 1955, Hudsons were back with a facelift this year. Pictured are a Hornet Custom four-door sedan (with "Continental" external spare tire) and a Rambler Custom Cross Country wagon. Note the 1956 Ford Sunliner far to the rear, with a protected convertible top.

Above: *Plymouth chose the Chicago Auto Show to introduce its new mid-year model: the aptly-named Fury hardtop, packing a 303-cubic-inch V-8 engine and sporting gold anodized trim on its white body. Using a metal jet fighter plane monolith as decoration at the as-yet-unfinished display seemed appropriate, in view of the aircraft-like styling touches on many American cars.*

Below: Bird's eye view of the 1956 Plymouth Belvedere convertible gives a great perspective on its dashboard and interior. Not many auto-show visitors got to see the vehicles from such a vantage point.

Packard showed the chassis of one of its 1956 models. This is considered the last year of "real" Packards. Final 1957-58 Packards were actually reworked Studebakers.

Cadillac's Eldorado Seville hardtop—and its Biarritz convertible companion—wore taller, sharper tailfins than other Cadillac models in 1956.

Below: Lincoln borrowed a legendary name from its past for an all-new luxury hardtop: the Continental Mark II. The first-generation Continental had been produced from 1940-48, with V-12 engines. This one got a modern overhead-valve V-8 and a larger hand-built body, plus a $10,000 price tag. Ford Motor Company lost money on each Continental that was sold.

Chrysler Corporation played on the lyrics of a Cole Porter tune to promote the 1956 DeSotos in radio and TV commercials.

DeSoto was one of several makes that added a four-door hardtop body style for 1956. Shown is a Fireflite Sportsman, with new push-button drive.

A Plexiglas hood shows off the powertrain of this Chevrolet Bel Air convertible. For 1956, the 265-cubic-inch V-8 engine, introduced a year earlier, produced as much as 225 horsepower.

Built in France, this Simca convertible was one of a handful of imported models to appear at the 1956 auto show. Customers could drive a Simca sedan home from a dealership for $1,695.

Above: Performance enthusiasts in '56 could choose a Dodge D-500 two-door hardtop, with 230-horsepower V-8 engine. Few Dodges of this caliber remain in existence today. Since its introduction three years earlier, the Red Ram V-8 engine had helped Dodge compile a string of endurance-run victories, illustrated by the sedan at rear.

In an ill-fated attempt to capture more female buyers, Dodge launched the "La Femme" hardtop in 1955 and continued into '56, complete with a matching umbrella, compact cases, and a handbag fitted into the front seatbacks.

In addition to a group of regular model*
Chrysler had the high-performance 300B coup*
(at rear), introduced at the Chicago Auto Sho*
This was the second season for the 300-serie*
which contained a 354-cubic-inch V-8 engin*
that developed as much as 355 horsepowe*
Chrysler promoted the 300B by advertising *
string of 37 victories in 1955 competition.

Make a date with the star of the show!

The fabulous Golden Hawk with sensational 275-hp skypower Engine

Studebaker THE BIG NEW CHOICE IN THE LOW PRICE FIELD!

Mercury launched a new model at the Chicago show: the Montclair "Phaeto*
hardtop sedan. The phaeton designation had been used in the Thirties *
denote convertible sedans.

Left: Studebaker gave its sedans and wagons a more conventional look *
1956, but retained the stylish European-influenced shape for a new line *
sporty Hawks. Topping the group: the Golden Hawk (shown), equipped with *
huge Packard V-8 engine. Studebaker and Packard had joined forces mid-ye*
in 1954.

Not many foreign cars stood on the auto show floor in
1956, but Volkswagen fielded a broad range of
models, from the growing-familiar "Beetle" sedan and
convertible to Microbuses and pickup trucks. Every
year, more and more Americans were falling for the
quirky-but-fun rear-engined VWs.

1957
49th annual Chicago Automobile Show
(January 5–13, 1957)

- "Motorevue of 1957" stage show adds to excitement at International Amphitheatre
- Twice-daily stage revue includes "motor opera" as well as automobile presentations by community "beauty queens"
- 3-dimensional stage has gold lace curtain, white satin backdrop ... revue said to have "pace and staging of a Broadway hit"
- Show again uses exposition hall, south of Amphitheatre
- Attendance sets record: 494,411 visitors
- Formal opening by Mayor Daley climaxes televised tour through WGN-TV facilities
- Imported makes at show include Austin, Singer, Humber, Hillman, Sunbeam, Jaguar, Volkswagen, Citroën, Morris Minor, Renault, and Volvo
- Ford has jet engine exhibit
- Mercury Turnpike Cruiser, evolved from show car, is loaded with gadgetry

Chicago's Mayor Richard J. Daley attends an auto-show banquet with wife Eleanor and three sons. The elder Daley had become mayor in 1955.

Chrysler's Imperial Crown Southampton four-door hardtop was all-new for 1957, featuring "Forward Look" styling from design chief Virgil Exner. Immense fins held what looked like gunsights, and curved side glass was an industry "first."

Mercury's Turnpike Cruiser two-door hardtop followed styling cues introduced on the previous year's concept vehicle, called the XM-Turnpike Cruiser. Special features included a reverse-slanted back window and dual-curve windshield. In its slogan, the company promised "dream-car design."

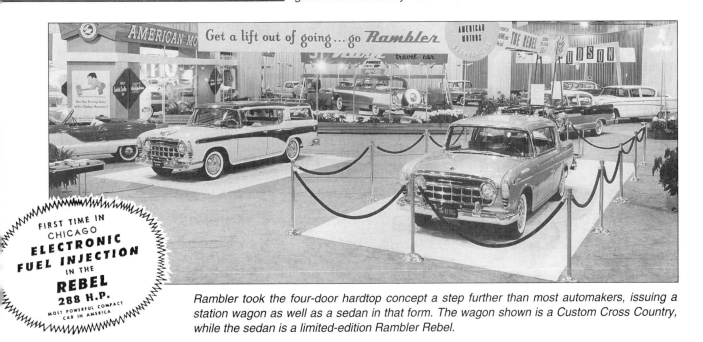

Rambler took the four-door hardtop concept a step further than most automakers, issuing a station wagon as well as a sedan in that form. The wagon shown is a Custom Cross Country, while the sedan is a limited-edition Rambler Rebel.

A two-seat Thunderbird is partia[lly] hidden in this view at the Ford displa[y], but the "boulevard" sports c[ar] continued to draw plenty of attentio[n]

Fords were restyled for 1957, with smaller tailfins tha[n] most makes. This Fairlane 500 hardtop sedan could ha[ve] a six-cylinder engine, or a choice of three V-8 sizes.

Chevrolet's display included a stylish Nomad station wagon, budget-priced One-Fifty sedan, and top-of-the-line Bel Air four-door hardtop.

Chevrolet might have had hopes for its hardtop sedans (first issued in '56), but the 1957 Bel Air two-door hardtops and convertibles eventually became sought-after cars on the collector market.

Plymouth had a big selection of station wagons, growing popular in suburbia—thus the designation, Sport Suburban, of this model. Showgoers could study Chrysler Corporation's new Torsion-Aire Ride on a bare chassis (right).

Above: Convertible fans had just one choice at Plymouth: the Belvedere V-8, priced at $2,638.

Left: Chevrolet introduced a flush-body Cameo pickup truck in mid-1955, with rear fender skins made of plastic and plenty of luxury extras. This model eventually became a popular collectible.

Studebaker stuck tall tailfins onto its sporty Hawk coupes. The Golden Hawk got a supercharged V-8 engine. Station wagon at right is a Packard Clipper; at left, a Studebaker Broadmoor. Packards were essentially rebadged Studebakers this year.

S.H. ARNOLT INC.

S.H. Arnolt was Chicago's foremost importer in the 1950s. In addition to importing a tantalizing array of European cars, from the Renault 4CV and Morris Minor to the MG sports cars, Arnolt developed the British-built Arnolt-Bristol roadster (foreground).

Sports cars and economy models weren't the only European machines imported by S.H. Arnolt. This is an Arnolt-Bristol 40: two-liter sports saloon (sedan), hand-built in limited quantities

Sleek is the word for Jaguar's XK140 MC roadster, with a 3.5-liter engine, wire wheels, and $4,160 price.

Ordinary shoppers probably didn't care much, but those in the market for ruggedness had a selection of tough trucks to study on the show floor. This is a Mack dump truck.

1958

50th annual Chicago Automobile Show

(January 4–12, 1958)

- Chicago Auto Show celebrates Golden Jubilee: fiftieth show to be presented
- International Amphitheatre again serves as auto-show site, with 500,000 square feet of exhibit space
- Record-setting 518,521 visitors attend the show during its 9-day run—first time over half a million
- "Motorevue of 1958" stage show traces cars from 1901 to 1925 to present day ... 21 community "beauty queens" participate in presentations
- Amphitheatre decorated with thousands of yards of gold lame, moonbeam satin
- Admission is 90 cents ... visitors can see more than 470 vehicles on display
- Imports include Austin, Austin-Healey, Bentley, Berkeley, Bianchi, Bristol, DKW, Citroën, Ferrari, Goggomobil, Hillman, Isetta, Jaguar, Mercedes-Benz, Morris Minor, MG, Opel, Panhard, Peugeot, Renault, Rolls-Royce, Simca, Skoda, Sunbeam, Triumph, Vauxhall, Volvo
- "Motor Memories" area features antique and classic cars
- Ford launches the Edsel as '58 model
- WGN-TV features two-hour telecast of auto show, on first Saturday

Yes, this was the fiftieth Chicago Automobile Show (by official count) to take place.

Once again this year, a bevy of community "beauty queens" added glamour to the presentation of new car models during the stage revue.

When it appeared onstage during the "Motorevue of 1958," the new Edsel looked just about as glamorous as the young woman helping with the presentation. Ford Motor Company had spent huge sums creating the Edsel, named for the son of Henry Ford. Sales fell far below expectations for a variety of reasons, but the Edsel name eventually became almost synonymous with failure in the public mind.

DeSoto launched the top-of-the line Adventurer hardtop in 1956. Only 350 Adventurer hardtop coupes were produced in 1958, along with 82 convertibles.

Below: Along with a totally reshaped body—wholly devoid of fins—Chevrolet had a brand new model in 1958: the top-of-the-line Impala, offered as a hardtop or convertible.

Youngsters were becoming more and more influential in purchasing decisions. Plymouth had been transformed from a dowdy family sedan of the 1940s and early '50s to a stylish attraction in '58.

Ford had introduced a Skyliner retractable hardtop for 1957, and continued the idea for '58. A complicated electrically-operated mechanism lowered the steel hardtop into position in the trunk area of the car—eating into luggage space.

American Motors continued to import the cute little Metropolitan from England, powered by an Austin engine. Seating three in a single seat, the Metropolitan came as either a hardtop coupe or a convertible, billed as the "world's smartest smaller car."

Star Chief was the designation for the poshest Pontiacs. Engine choices included a 300-horsepower Tri-Power (triple-carburetor) V-8 and a 310-horsepower V-8 with fuel injection. To the rear is a Bonneville convertible.

Resembling a scaled-down 1948 Ford Tudor sedan, the Swedish-built Volvo PV444 developed a reputation for sturdy construction. Volvo brought along a tractor for its exhibit at the Chicago Auto Show. Note the card table and chair—quite a basic display layout.

Exotic sports cars turned up at the Chicago Auto Show in the late Fifties, including Italian-built Ferraris: (left) a 250 Gran Turismo; (right) a 4.9 SuperAmerica.

Mercedes-Benz exported a variety of models from Germany, including the SL (super light) series. Featured here is a 300SL roadster. Note the big Mercedes sedan to its rear.

Studebaker always had a selection of commercial models at the Chicago show, including pickup trucks and utilitarian taxicabs. Two-toning gave the Transtar pickups a dose of glamour.

Ford abandoned its two-seat Thunderbird, turning out a four-seater instead for '58.

Pontiac dealers handled Vauxhalls, imported from Britain. Not too many of these Bedford minibuses went to American customers. Note the sliding driver's door.

Dodge trucks were known for ruggedness. Power Wagons (center) had been around since the late Forties. Note the engine display—a Super Power Giant 354.

1959
51st annual Chicago Automobile Show
(January 17–25, 1959)

- "Motorevue of 1959" stage show is seen twice daily, directed by Betty Gour ... features dancers, singers, and 18 "community beauty queens"
- Auto-show draws 481,358 visitors, to see more than 450 cars and trucks
- 25,000 attend Friday-night preview
- WGN-TV telecast precedes show opening
- Exhibit areas decorated with fabrics of silver lame, cream rayon, yellow percale
- Import popularity growing fast: new ones include Borgward, Goliath, Lloyd, NSU Prinz, Riley, Saab, and Taunus
- Toyotas now appear at auto show
- Rambler American debuts at Chicago
- Studebaker launches compact Lark
- Special exhibits feature historic cars, and military rockets and missiles
- Pontiac launches Wide-Track Bonneville
- Renault unveils Caravelle for first time

Lincoln's big Continental Mark IV came in six different body styles, including a convertible and seldom-seen, formal-roofed Town Car and limousine.

Studebaker launched the compact Lark for 1959, setting the pace for a series of small cars from other American manufacturers. Larks came in a variety of body styles, including a hardtop coupe and a convertible, with either a six-cylinder engine or a V-8.

Despite the aftereffects of the recession that had hit in 1958, more than 481,000 people turned out to see the '59 models at the Amphitheatre.

Renault introduced the French-built Caravelle at the Chicago Auto Show. Here, multi-talented entertainer Sammy Davis Jr. waves from a Caravelle convertible. Note the removable hardtop, suspended above.

Tailfins had grown taller and bolder through the late Fifties, but no manufacturer approached the soaring fins of the '59 Cadillac.

Cadillacs reached their zenith of gaudiness and chrome dazzle in 1959.

After disappointing first-year sales, Edsels emerged for '59 in onl one size—essentially reskinned Fords. Shown is the Village station wagon, available for either six or nine passengers.

Facelifted substantially fc 1959, Imperials abandone the "Hemi" V-8 engine in favc of a wedge-head design. Th simulated spare-tire cover o the decklid, available sinc '58, drew a few snickerin comments at the time.

Chevrolets were all full-size cars in 1959, so why shouldn't the trunk hold a full load of luggage? Chevrolet fins were horizontal this year, in contrast to the vertical units on the back fenders of most makes.

Pontiac followed the lead of many other automakers over the years, displaying one of its models up in the air at the 1959 show.

Dodges were available with the old flathead six-cylinder engine for the last time. Far more buyers drove home a V-8, packing as much as 5 horsepower.

Ford's truck line ranged from over-the-road haulers and tough pickups, down to the shapely Ranchero (left), which blended the appearance of a passenger car with some of the utility of a pickup truck.

BMW *Isetta*

SEE THEM AT THE SHOW—

-Amphitheatre, North Wing

Mages, the well-known Chicago sporting-goods emporiums, dealt in imported cars for time. Produced by BMW in Germany, the Isetta 600 (above) seated five. A smaller Isetta 300, with fewer doors, sold for as little as $1,048.

Left: Toyota made its first Chicago appearance in 1959. Wearing traditional attire, this woman points out the merits of the Toyopet, first imported in 1958. Japanese-built cars would not really catch hold in the U.S. market for another decade or so.

Sports cars attracted the interest of growing numbers of Americans in the late Fifties. Built in Britain, this Austin-Healey Sprite soon became known as the "bugeye" model as a result of its headlight design.

Triumph was another British sports car maker. Note the cut-down doors—a Triumph hallmark—on this TR3A roadster.

1960
52nd annual Chicago Automobile Show
(January 16–24, 1960)

- International Amphitheatre still serves as auto-show site
- 512,156 visitors attend the automobile show during its 9-day run
- "Motorevue of 1960" stage show is choreographed by Bob Frellson
- Community "beauty queens" participate in auto show for last time ... 21 in all
- $20 million production features more than 450 vehicles
- Amphitheatre color scheme is off-white this year ... stage area features gold pleated drapery for first time
- Close to three dozen import makes appear at show, including Deutsch-Bonnet and Fiat
- Scarab and Bocar race cars seen in import area
- High school students again participate in traffic-safety slogan contest
- Auto industry aims at economy: Chevrolet introduces rear-engine Corvair ... Ford has new compact Falcon ... Chrysler launches Valiant

Rambler called itself "America's most imitated car," having been launched as a compact long before the Big Three issued shrunken-size models. Shown is an Ambassador hardtop sedan.

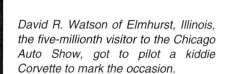

David R. Watson of Elmhurst, Illinois, the five-millionth visitor to the Chicago Auto Show, got to pilot a kiddie Corvette to mark the occasion.

Few spectators could have known, but this would be the DeSoto's last appearance at the Chicago Auto Show. A few '61 models were built, but production halted before the 1961 show.

All Mercury models were still full-sized in 1960. Convertibles came in Monterey or upscale Park Lane trim.

Among the imported makes that failed to last long in the U.S. market was the Dyna Panhard. The small coupe at the rear is a Deutsch-Bonnet, imported briefly into the United States from France.

Rolls-Royce didn't expect to sell large numbers of motorcars the Midwestern United States, but turned up at the Chicago sh regardless.

An old song referred to the "surrey with the fringe on top." Well, Willys put out a Surrey in 1960, as part of its four-cylinder Dispatcher series.

Saab had been sending its Swedish-built cars to the Chicago Show since 1959. Front-wheel drive at a time when virtuall cars were rear-drive, Saabs still used two-cycle engines instea the conventional four-cycle configuration. Oil had to be mixed the fuel. Saabs gained quite a reputation for ice-racing, courte: that front-drive design.

1961

53rd annual Chicago Automobile Show
(February 18–26, 1961)

- Auto show moves to McCormick Place, along the lakefront at 23rd Street
- Main exposition area of new $35 million facility is more than 300,000 square feet—bigger than six football fields
- For first time, all American and imported cars and trucks are in one vast arena
- Auto-show attendance sets record, with a whopping 789,734 visitors
- "Motorevue of 1961" introduces cars in series of musical, dramatized vignettes ... takes place in what will be called the Arie Crown Theatre, with seating for 5,000
- Import Car Salon is in main lobby—28 makes, from Austin to Riley to Triumph, comprise the display
- Amphicar (car/boat) is on display
- More than 400 cars and trucks on view
- Open 11 a.m. to 11 p.m. ... admission: one dollar
- New models at show include compact Buick Special, Oldsmobile F-85, Dodge Lancer, Pontiac Tempest
- Mayor Daley awards savings bonds to slogan-contest winners
- Manufacturers use farm, campground, Hawaiian garden, and Hong Kong waterfront as background for displays
- Fire-department snorkel lifts adventurous guests 45 feet, in bucket
- Show preparation takes 850 man-hours

DON C. MULLERY

"The automobile still is just about the most exciting of all commercial products," said Don C. Mullery, chairman of the executive show committee, in the 1961 program. "There's a thrill to owning a new automobile that, in the words of those who have had a succession of cars in their lifetime, is repeated over and over again." Chicago's auto show grew from a handful of makes at the first event to more than 400 this year, "in an immense, record-breaking single exhibit area of over 300,000 square feet."

Billboards throughout the city helped draw more than 789,000 people to the 1961 auto show—far beyond the previous attendance record.

Exhibitors had a lot more space to flaunt their products at McCormick Place than at the old Amphitheatre. The new facility even had a built-in theater, suitable for major stage performances.

Despite the increased crowds for the 1961 Chicago Auto Show, spectators had more elbow room inside than at prior events. City buses brought visitors right to the entrance.

Ford's Thunderbird moved into its third generation in 1961, wearing modest fins and huge round taillights. Note the Country Squire station wagon to its rear, with fake-wood paneling.

Imperials got a fresh look for 1961, which failed to win universal acclaim. Tailfins were more flamboyant than ever, and free-standing headlights were supposed to evoke memories of classic cars from the Thirties.

Chevrolet brought the XP-700 Corvette concept car (rear, left), created two years earlier, to the 1961 auto show. The production Corvette in front is fuel-injected.

"Albert—You're on my foot!"

real life at the auto show, attractive young women
ndeniably made a difference in getting male
ectators to listen to the presentation about each car.
ome young men were known to visit the show mainly
gaze at "pretty girls."

Rambler had introduced the little American in 1958, adding a convertible for '61.

Checker offered two series to the general public in 1961: a Superba, introduced a year earlier, and a new Marathon. Like the taxis, sedans could seat eight with optional jump seats. Note the early taxicab at the rear.

As its name suggests, the Amphicar could travel on water as well as highways. As one sign suggests, the company was seeking dealers as well as customers.

For a short time, Fiat marketed an Italian-built surrey vehicl[e] the United States.

Pontiac joined the compact-car parade i[n] 1961 with the Tempest. Technical quirk[s] included a curved driveshaft to feed th[e] rear-mounted transaxle.

American Motors designed and built the M-422 Mighty Mite, a 1/4-ton 4x4 with an aluminum V-4 engine, on a 65-inch wheelbase. It measured only 107 inches long.

Among the products of the British Rootes Group was the sty[le] Sunbeam Alpine sports car. It came either as a roadster or [as] a hardtop.

1962

54th annual Chicago Automobile Show

(February 17–25, 1962)

- McCormick Place hosts auto show for second season ... exposition hall is completely finished now
- Show includes three "prestige" dining rooms on President's Walk, 1,000-seat cafeteria, and many smaller dining rooms
- 723,639 visitors attend the show
- 5,000-seat Arie Crown Theater is used for free "Motorevue of 1962" stage show
- Revue uses popular TV shows as theme for entertainers and presentation of cars
- $1 admission; open 11 a.m. to 11 p.m.
- Auto show is a $25 million production
- European cars are exhibited in setting that features fountain effects ... biggest fountain projects 15-foot conical spray
- This year's imports include Alfa-Romeo, Austin, Commer, Daimler, Fiat-Abarth, Osca, Porsche, Opel, Simca
- WGN-TV again telecasts preview, on first Saturday of show
- Chrysler Corporation shows two gas turbine cars: Plymouth and Dodge
- New models of '62 include Chevy II, Ford Fairlane, and Mercury Meteor

Visitors to McCormick Place had cars and trucks to see on two levels.

With bucket seats inside and a standard 361-cid V-8, Polara 500 was the top model of the Dodge Dart line, downsized for 1962.

usual, Jaguar exhibited an impressive variety of vehicles at the auto show, including an XK-E coupe and roadster, and selected aloons" (sedans).

Oldsmobile had something new and special on sale in 1962: a Jetfire hardtop coupe with a turbocharged V-8 engine that demanded a unique water-injection system.

By 1962, most car-buyers knew that a Volkswagen Beetle was different in construction from other makes. Note the spare tire, mounted at the front of the trunk.

Studebaker took its basic coupe, as styled by the Raymond Loewy team nearly a decade earlier, and transformed it into the rakish Gran Turismo Hawk for 1962. This woman could be speaking about the car's Thunderbird-style roofline or its 289-cid V-8 engine.

After launching the compact Falcon two years earlier, Ford trotted a mid-size Fairlane for '62, promoted here by a gingham-c presenter.

ng before anyone coined the term "sport-utility vehicle," ernational had this Scout, which easily meets the modern finition.

Each day during the auto show, crowds grew thick by evening; but weekends attracted the most visitors.

their second season, compact Valiants got Plymouth badging, ding a hardtop coupe body style.

Ford of Britain produced the Consul Capri hardtop, new for 1962. Note the sculptured bodysides, tiny fins, and kinship to American-built Fords. Price: $2,331, with a 56-horsepower four-cylinder engine.

For mid-1962, Chevrolet decided to turn the rear-engined Corvair into a sporty machine, courtesy of a turbocharged engine, tachometer, four-speed gearbox, tauter suspension, and Monza Spyder designation.

The Excitement Continues (1963-73)

Taking different paths might be considered the automotive theme of the 1960s. By 1962, a crop of compact cars had been on the market for a couple of years, and some not-quite-so-compact models were about ready for sale. "Muscle" was beginning to rear its head, in the form of ever-greater horsepower ratings and emergence of the first floor-shifted four-speed gearboxes. Dad might still prefer a column-mounted gearshift, but chances were that Junior was drawn to "four on the floor."

More than 817,000 people flooded McCormick Place in February of 1963, setting an auto-show record. That year's "Motorevue" in the Arie Crown Theatre, featuring the Lou Breese orchestra, took the form of a "sightseeing tour" of the city to showcase all the American-built automobiles. Imports had appeared at the show since the early 1950s, of course, but never were they part of the stage revue. The 1963 foreign-car crop, on the lower level of McCormick Place, included everything from Alfa-Romeo, Arnolt-Bristol and Citroën, to DKW, Fiat, Peugeot, Simca, and the Israeli-built Sabra.

If that wasn't enough "foreign" influence, a visitor could stop by the exhibit from the Sports Car Club of America. An auto-show guest might also learn something about air pollution, at an educational exhibit sponsored by the Automobile Manufacturers Association. Americans were just beginning to hear about primitive efforts to control engine emissions, starting in California.

Compacts might offer frugality, but style wasn't forgotten, either—not with such cars as the brand-new Buick Riviera and the futuristic Studebaker Avanti to please one's eyes.

The Chicago Automobile Trade Association celebrated its 60th birthday in 1964. Another attendance record was broken, as that year's "Motorevue" featured a presentation of automobile advertising. In addition to that twice-daily stage revue, visitors could enjoy continuous movies at the "Little Theater." Imports could be seen in two places: on the main floor, and in a salon on the lower level.

Ford wasn't quite ready to launch its Mustang, but Chicago showgoers got to see a concept version, called Mustang II. Buick and Oldsmobile introduced new station wagons with raised roofs that contained glass panels. Performance continued to attract attention, especially from the younger set. Pontiac, for one, was ready to respon issuing the GTO—considered by many to be the first tr "muscle car." Naturally, Chicagoans got a good look at it.

Toyota-built Toyopets had been seen in small numbe since 1958, but Datsun sold its first car to a Chicago buyer the auto show. The Japanese onslaught of econoca wouldn't take place for another decade, but early exampl were trickling onto the market.

Not long after the '64 auto show, Studebaker was gor moving temporarily from Indiana to Canada before expiri completely. That left only the Big Three in Detroit, alo with American Motors in Kenosha, Wisconsin.

Performance, sport, luxury—those were the hallmarks the 1965 auto show. Even the compact models we becoming a bit bigger and more plush, responding Americans' desire for convenience features.

Overall attendance dipped a bit in 1965, but the fir weekend set a record—and Midwesterners reportedly we ready to buy new cars. Astro Guys and Astro Girls herald automotive progress at the Arie Crown's "Motorevue while the Little Theater—right off the main lobby McCormick Place—showed manufacturer-produced movi

Among the cars seen for the first time at the Chica show were AMC's Marlin and the Chevrolet Caprice.

Just weeks before opening of the 1967 a show, McCormick Pla burned virtually to ground. Above is a r dering of the new M Cormick Place, oper in 1971.

128

dition to production models, the show floor included an
triguing batch of 20 "dream cars," from the Dodge
Charger II to a Mercury Comet Cyclone Sportster. More
compelling to younger visitors were the Monza Juniors, built
n go-kart chassis, given away each day at the Chevrolet
and. Go-karting had become popular in the Chicago area,
as well as elsewhere in the nation.

After starting up on the West Coast, "go-go dancers"
ad made their way into clubs and bars in the heartland. So,
hat better theme for the 1966 "Motorevue" than "History
n the Go-Go," billed as a lighthearted view of history—
utomotive and otherwise. To bring the stage production
oser to the audience, the Arie Crown's stage now reached
ver the orchestra pit, so the Lou Breese musicians sat right
o on stage.

Several vehicles were seen for the first time at Chicago's
ow, including the Dodge Charger and the Kaiser Jeep
uper Wagoneer, as well as a couple of Chevrolet concept
rs and Ford's Magic Cruiser. American Motors exhibited an
xperimental AMX, destined to lead to a production version
few years later.

A new "Winners' Row" exhibit featured great cars from
e past. Auto-show attendance broke a record, topping the
48,000 mark.

A few weeks before the 1967 auto show opened,
hicagoans were digging out from the worst blizzard of the
entury. For days, the city was virtually shut down: cars
ldom seen on any streets, public buses not running, many
usinesses and stores closed for the duration.

Disaster in another form struck, to threaten the very
xistence of this year's auto show. Just four weeks before the
7 show was scheduled to open, a dreadful fire destroyed
cCormick Place. Planners at the Chicago Automobile Trade
ssociation rushed into action, and managed to get the
ow moved back to the International Amphitheatre, its site
ntil 1961.

Even though time did not permit setting up an elaborate
age performance at the Amphitheatre's Arena, a
Motorevue" did take place in 1967. Opening-day
tendance set a record, though the final tally dropped
arply from previous figures.

Sport and muscle again ruled. Chevrolet introduced the
amaro in 1967, to go head-to-head against Ford's
ustang. Pontiac's Firebird debuted for similar duty.

Various city and state agencies participated in the auto
ow over the years, including the Illinois Secretary of State's
ffice. This year, the Chicago Police Department displayed a
ripped, stolen car, calling attention to the growing problem
f auto thefts.

No one could have realized what a tumultuous year lay
head for 1968. By summer, Robert Kennedy and Martin
uther King, Jr. would have been assassinated. In August,
ational Guard troops would be called out to quell
nprecedented disturbances during the Democratic National
onvention.

When the auto show opened in February, however,
ore peaceful pastimes were in order. Chicagoans simply

Driving home an auto-show Corvette

In February 1967, 18-year-old Hugh T. Edfors and his
dad attended the auto show. "While we walked around the
International Amphitheatre," Hugh recalls, "I spotted a car
that stopped me in my tracks." It was a 1967 Corvette
coupe, painted bright Sunfire yellow with a black accent
stripe. The car had a 427-cid, 435-horsepower engine with
three two-barrel carburetors, four-speed transmission, side
exhaust pipes, and leather interior.

Hugh stood transfixed for several minutes, dreaming
about this car. "I didn't give much thought to the car after
the show, until August of '67 when I saw a small ad for a
Corvette in the auto section of the Chicago Sun-Times, from
City Auto Sales on South Michigan Avenue."

Ed and his father went to look at the car, which was
stored in the rear of the third floor of the building. The dealer
pulled the cover off and it was the car that appeared at the
auto show. Paperwork confirmed that fact, as did the fluorescent light fixture still attached to the inside roof, installed
for the show.

With an all-new Corvette to debut soon, no one seemed
interested in this '67. "The dealer was happy to unload the
$5,700 car to me for about $4,300. I couldn't believe I even
got a deal on the car of my dreams." Hugh still owns that
Corvette, stored in the mid-Eighties with 28,000 miles on it.

paid their $1.50 admission to see more than 450 vehicles,
again exhibited at the International Amphitheatre.

For the last time, a "Motorevue" was part of the
festivities. After 1968, stage performances at the auto show
would fade into history.

As usual, manufacturer exhibits at the auto show had a
variety of extra attractions, including a ventriloquist and
magician as well as sports celebrities and "fever girls,"
representing the heavily advertised "Dodge Fever."
Oldsmobile liked to have the current Miss America at its
exhibit area, and this year's winner, Debra Barnes, was no
exception. AMC brought Craig Breedlove, holder of the
world land-speed record, to its exhibit. E.M. "Pete" Estes,
general manager of Chevrolet, named Chicago's show "the
outstanding one in the country."

The 1969 auto show opened a little later than usual: on
March 8th. AMC used Chicago as its launch pad for the
performance-oriented SC/Rambler, while Pontiac flaunted
its coming-soon Trans Am. "Freddy Ford," an 8-1/2-foot
robot, fielded questions at Ford's stand. For the twentieth
time, students participated in a safety-slogan contest.

Whereas compacts had been the trend a decade earlier, at the time of the 1970 auto show a handful of smaller-yet subcompacts were being prepared for introduction. Import brands of comparable size had been marketed for years, of course, but finally the American automakers were recognizing growing interest in economical driving.

Not that performance was forgotten. Not yet. Buick, for one, exhibited its hot GSX sports coupe. Chevrolet and Pontiac used Chicago for the debut of their second-generation Mustang-fighters, the Camaro and Firebird, respectively. Ford mixed economy and sport, announcing a new Mustang Grabber as well as a subcompact Maverick Grabber.

Vans had been another growing trend through the Sixties, and compact Dodge vans for 1970 were seen for the first time, at the Chicago show.

Losing McCormick Place to that tragic fire in 1967 didn't mean a lakefront exposition center was ignored. Far from it. Chicago had immediately begun plans for a *second* McCormick Place.

Finally, the brand-new structure was ready, in time for the 63rd annual auto show, in February 1971. Midwesterners responded eagerly, giving organizers a new attendance record—topping the previous figure by nearly 94,000.

Chicago still had four major daily newspapers, though that total soon would begin to shrink. Auto editors from all four wrote essays for the 1971 auto-show program, including Dan Jedlicka of the *Sun-Times* and Jim Mateja of the *Tribune*—both of whom continue to provide automotive reports Chicagoans.

The emphasis on automotive performance was beginni to ebb in the early Seventies, due in part to increasing stringent emissions regulations, but also to growing insuran costs for "specialty" vehicles. Soon, the "muscle car" e would be over, though other trends sprung up to take place. Recreational Vehicles (RVs), for one, drew plenty attention at the 1972 auto show.

Some 550 vehicles in all were available for inspection. A more than 935,000 folks flocked to McCormick Place in 19 to exercise that privilege. Several sports cars could be seen the first time, including a Lotus Europa Twin Cam and t Jensen Interceptor, as well as examples from the British Squi and TVR companies.

Attendance in 1973 set another record, coming just sho of 950,000. Safety was becoming a major issue, prompti several car divisions to create and display experimental safe vehicles.

Americans faced an uncertain future late in 1973, wh the OPEC nations initiated an oil embargo that resulted in fuel crisis. Like all Americans, Chicagoans soon had to de with gasoline shortages, gas-station lines, and the threat rationing.

Suddenly, those big guzzlers didn't look so tempting aft all. Econocars, no longer the brunt of jokes, looked like t wave of the future.

Dan Jedlicka—on the auto-journalist job since 1968

Dan Jedlicka joined the Chicago Sun-Times *in 1968, as assistant financial editor. A lifelong auto enthusiast, he soon began to write about cars as well as finance. By 1973, he had his own auto column. Mr. Jedlicka was interviewed at a restaurant near his Chicago office.*

Dan Jedlicka grew up in the Little Village area of Chicago, near 24th and Lawndale. His journalism career began early, working summer vacations in the early Sixties, covering the police beat in his Volvo PV544. After a period in Harrisburg, Pennsylvania, Dan returned to Chicago in '68, joining the *Sun-Times*. Late that year, he began to write bylined stories about cars. He also covered "muscle cars" for *Esquire* magazine. Since 1973, Dan has had his own auto column at the *Sun-Times*. The "Auto Times" section started in the Nineties.

"The crowds then were so reverent toward these cars," Dan recalls. "People would line up three deep" to look them over.

"I remember as a kid," age 12 or so, "I was most enthralled at the auto show by the dream cars: the Pontiac Bonneville [and] Buick dream cars. These dream cars were so incredible ... incredible shapes." There were "fairly wild" dream cars as late as 1969, but "not like the Fifties." In contrast, "you don't see a lot of far-out stuff" nowadays.

"They did a good job of making it a family show," Jedlicka contends. Even in the Seventies, which he calls a "dreary time" in the industry, "there was always something that they managed to come up with."

All told, "I think the Chicago show does what it's suppose to. It's a good selling show." Still, "the Amphitheatre always struck me as more personal" than McCormick Place.

Of the many auto-industry leaders he's met over the years Jedlicka had special praise for John DeLorean, when he heade Chevrolet in the early Seventies. He describes DeLorean as "ver candid, very outspoken [with] a good sense of humor. I had a lot of respect for the guy, professionally."

Auto-show events that stand out include the "human hood ornament," an attractive woman who decorated a vehicle one year in the Seventies. "We thought nothing of it at the time,' Jedlicka recalls. He describes the female presenters as "very professional," adding that "you got to see the models as they really were. They'd be human beings."

Jedlicka believes "Chicago is very much a car town—more than Los Angeles." In Chicago, people drive even if they don't have to. "I think there's a real love of cars in this city."

An ardent enthusiast with a particular interest in sports cars Jedlicka has owned many collectible vehicles, including a Studebaker Golden Hawk and this Maserati Mistral.

1963
55th annual Chicago Automobile Show
(February 16–24, 1963)

- 817,482 visitors flock to McCormick Place—attendance sets auto-show record
- "Motorevue of 1963" uses "sightseeing tour of Chicago" to present the 16 American makes of cars in Arie Crown Theatre ... twice-daily revue billed as "The Car is the Star"
- Five-channel stereophonic sound enhances impact of stage revue ... orchestra is headed by Lou Breese
- 450 cars and trucks are on display
- Admission again $1; open 11 a.m. to 11 p.m.
- McCormick Place heating/air conditioning system works automatically as crowd size increases or decreases
- Imports at salon on lower level include Alfa-Romeo, Arnolt-Bristol, Citroën, DKW, Daimler, English Ford, Ferrari, Fiat, Jaguar, Mercedes-Benz, Peugeot, Simca, Porsche, Renault, Saab, Sabra, Triumph, Volkswagen, and Volvo—plus models from British BMC and Rootes groups
- Sports Car Club of America has exhibit at auto show
- Educational display in main exhibit area, sponsored by Automobile Manufacturers Association, illustrates air pollution
- Chevrolet launches "Sting Ray" Corvette, penned in part by Larry Shinoda
- Studebaker puts dramatically styled Avanti on sale ... Buick launches Riviera
- Hillman Super Minx said to be first economy import with American automatic transmission—seen for first time at show
- All cars adopt amber front turn signals

Buick introduced the sophisticated and shapely Riviera personal-luxury coupe for 1963, borrowing a name first used in '49 for the company's first pillarless hardtop coupe.

Introduced two years earlier, in 1961, the Continental convertible was the first soft-top four-door American car sold since Frazer issued a small number in the early Fifties. Note the "suicide" (rear-hinged) back doors on this '63 model. Continentals also came in the four-door hardtop body style.

Left: Concealed headlights helped identify the latest Corvette model: the '63 Sting Ray. Evolved from a GM show car of that name, as conceived by design chief William Mitchell, the production Sting Ray soon became one of the most collectible Corvettes. Both a coupe and a convertible were offered.

Right: Some folks in this scene look awed by the powertrain for a Corvette Sting Ray, others look curious—and some appear unsure of what they're seeing. Three of the Corvette's V-8 engine choices were carbureted, but one used fuel injection.

Once again, Miss America (this time, Jacquely
Jeanne Mayer, of Ohio) helped promote Oldsmo
biles. Notice how tiny she looks next to an Old
98 hardtop sedan in 1963.

Left: Chrysler had another "letter-series" car at the 1963 show: the 300J, presented at the stage revue. The Prudential Building, pictured in the mural, was then the highest structure in Chicago. Today, it looks almost tiny next to the huge skyscrapers that have been constructed since.

Above: Almost psychedelic i
style, this sign looks like
might have been created late
in the decade; but it was see
all over McCormick Place
during the nine-day run of the
1963 Chicago Auto Show.

Left: Studebaker had launched the futuristic, fiberglass-bodied Avanti "boulevard" sports car in 1962. Lacking a conventional grille, the Avanti held a 289-cid V-8, supercharged or not. Seen here at the 1963 "Motorevue," Avantis would still be produced by a separate company, after the demise of Studebaker in 1966.

Introduced a year earlier, the 1963 Studebaker Gran Turismo (GT) Hawk could be equipped with an Avanti V-8 engine—
with or without supercharging. Note the Avanti at rear, on a pedestal.

Cadillacs still had tailfins in 1963, but toned down from the flamboyance of 1959-61. Sedan de Ville was the name for the company's four-door hardtop.

Right: What gave the Ford Galaxie a "Ten Million Dollar Ride?" Evidently, that was the amount Ford Motor Company spent developing this full-size model.

Below: Not many showgoers would have guessed that the Sabra sports car was produced in Haifa, Israel. Fiberglass-bodied with modern disc brakes, it carried a twin-carburetor engine that made 110 horsepower. Styling was unlike any other sports car on the market, but few Sabras found customers during the make's brief life span.

1964

56th annual Chicago Automobile Show

(February 8–16, 1964)

- McCormick Place sees record 821,208 visitors to auto show during its 9-day run
- "Motorevue of 1964" stage show brings familiar auto ads alive, with cast of fifty ... curtain used in Arie Crown Theatre is largest of its kind in the world
- Imports are on main exposition level, and also in special salon on lower level
- Little Theater shows continuous sound-and-color motion pictures
- Performance is reported to be auto show's dominant theme
- Buick and Oldsmobile station wagons, with raised roofs, are seen for first time
- Ford displays concept Mustang II ... will evolve into production Mustang, launched later in spring of 1964
- Chrysler engineers answer questions about company's turbine cars
- Pontiac exhibits new Tempest GTO
- Mercury display looks like mountain, to recall Pike's Peak Hill Climb victory
- American Motors has Tarpon show car
- Chicago Automobile Trade Association celebrates its 60th anniversary
- Studebaker leaves South Bend, Indiana, this year; begins production of cars in Hamilton, Ontario, Canada

Billed as the "world's most luxurious automobile," the Grand Mercedes ranke as best of the best.

Young gentlemen gaze intently at a cutaway of the 196 Pontiac Grand Prix, its hardtop coupe body tilted up to mak viewing easy.

Above: *After trying out its turbine engine in a nearly-stock Dodge and Plymouth, Chrysler created 50 specially-bodied Turbine cars. Though experimental in nature, they were driven for about three months each by 203 "consumer representatives."*

Right: *Designed in America and reminiscent of Ford's Thunderbird—but sporting a projectile-shaped rear end—these turbine cars were built by Ghia, in Italy. Turbine power failed to catch on.*

Oldsmobile called its new station wagon the Vista Cruiser. Equipped with a glass dome overhead, it was billed as "the newest thing in view."

This woman might have been pointing out the anodized metal on the bodysides and rear of the Cheyenne wagon, created by Rambler (American Motors).

Dodge had a sporty version of its compact Dart on sale in 1964, dubbed the GT.

A transparent hood permitted eager spectators to get a close look at the "Super Stock" 426-cubic-inch engine, which was available in 1964 Plymouths. Developed mainly for drag racing, the 426-cid V-8 found its way into quite a few cars from Chrysler Corporation.

For its fourth generation, in 1964, Ford's Thunderbird got all-new sheet metal with a sculptured look.

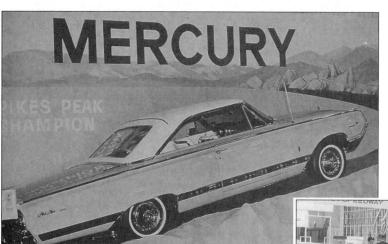

Above: As always, auto-show visitors waited patiently in long lines to enter McCormick Place. The auto show was open 12 hours a day.

Left: Mercury exhibited this Park Lane Marauder on an incline, capitalizing on the make's success in the Pikes Peak Hill Climb, powered by the 427-cid V-8 engine. Parnelli Jones won that event in 1963 and '64, driving a Mercury built by Bill Stroppe.

Right: Race driver Rodger Ward met fans at the Mercury stand, alongside a Comet Caliente hardtop that made an arduous Safari run.

Left: Jeep wagons had been marketed for years, but the fully-updated Wagoneer carryall debuted in 1963 and continued unchanged into '64. All Wagoneers had six-cylinder engines.

Ferrari's display included the Pininfarina-bodied 400 Superamerica coupe with removable hardtop. Note the tail of the "Spirit of America" (at rear), the vehicle in which Craig Breedlove set the world's land speed record.

1965

57th annual Chicago Automobile Show

(February 20–28, 1965)

- Progress is theme of "Motorevue of 1965" stage show, again seen in Arie Crown Theatre at McCormick Place
- Revue features the Astro Guys and the Astro Girls
- Main lobby contains giant sculpture—16 feet wide, 32 feet long, 30 feet high—with multi-colored panels (many of which rotate) bearing names of automobiles
- Auto show attracts 786,871 visitors— reported to be "in a buying mood" ... final weekend attendance sets record
- Datsun sells its first car in Chicago, right at the auto show
- Little Theater off main lobby shows films produced by manufacturers: races, rallies, equipment testing, and "great events"
- Sport and luxury said to highlight Chicago show
- AMC Marlin and Chevrolet Caprice debut at Chicago show, as does limited-edition Ford Thunderbird Special Landau coupe
- More than 450 vehicles exhibited at show, including 20 "dream cars"
- Ford has experimental LTD limousine and Mercury Comet Cyclone Sportster
- Plymouth displays VIP concept car
- Dodge shows Charger II "idea car"
- Chevrolet gives away Monza Junior each day—built on go-kart chassis

When the Ford Mustang debuted as a 1964-1/2 model, no fastback body style was included. That omission was rectified in the 1965 season, complete with louvers in the space normally occupied by a quarter-window. Looks like the auto-show crowd was pleased by the sight.

Chrysler offered three convertibles in 1965: Newport, New Yorker, and 300L.

Buick introduced a Gran Sport option for its 1965 Skylark (right), with a Wildcat 401 V-8 engine, Super-Turbine 300 automatic transmission, and oversize tires. Buick's LeSabre (left) fell between the modest-size Skylark and the big Electra 225, in both price and size.

Left: Rambler entered the personal-car competition with its fastback Marlin, which evolved from the Tarpon show car of '64. Sales never took off, and the model lasted only three seasons.

Below: After departing from Chrysler Corporation legendary designer Virgil Exner created the Mercer Cobra for the Copper Development Association. Purpose: to demonstrate uses of copper, brass, and bronze. Exner borrowed the Mercer name and some styling cues from the classic era, but set it up for a 271 horsepower V-8.

Most men bending over car hoods seemed to get an intense expression on their faces. This closely-cropped fellow is studying a 1964 Dodge stock car engine.

Ford's exhibit at the 1965 auto show ranged from the family-focused, full-size Galaxie 500 (left) to a GT40 racing machine (right).

In store windows throughout the Chicago area, signs reminded passersby that the 1965 auto show was coming.

Plaid-patterned paint was not a standard choice for a TVR Griffith. Bodies were built in Britain, but Ford V-8 engines were installed in the United States, prior to sale.

The French-built Simca 1000 promised an ample set of standard equipment, but in 1965 that list did not include a radio. Sedans were squarish and ordinary, but shapely Simca 1000 coupes wore bodies from Bertone. Simca came with a 5-year/50,000-mile warranty.

In 1965, not that many Americans were familiar with BMW's reputation for excellence in engineering. Displays of imports at the auto show tended to be basic, often mixed in with aftermarket products.

Launched in 1963 as a successor to the old 356 series, the Porsche 911 attracted aficionados because of its rear-engine handling skills. Actually, it wasn't much swifter than some big American cars of the mid-Sixties.

HORSEPOWER 150
COMPRESSION RATIO 9:1
NO. CYLINDERS 6
5 SPEED TRANSMISSION

THE ALL NEW

PORSCHE 911

MAX. SPEED 130 +
ACCELERATION 0-60 8.5 SEC
¼ MILE 16.7 SEC
SPEED END of ¼ MILE 87 MPH

1966

58th annual Chicago Automobile Show

(February 19–27, 1966)

- Theme of "Motorevue of 1966" stage show at Arie Crown Theatre is "History on the Go-Go," a lighthearted view of historical events with an automotive touch
- Revue has cast of more than 60—variety acts, singers, dancers—plus orchestra directed by Lou Breese
- Stage extends over orchestra pit, to bring production closer to audience
- Pageant is presented in salon setting
- Kaiser Jeep Super Wagoneer debuts at Chicago show ... production Dodge Charger seen for first time at any auto show
- Chevrolet shows Caribe and Concours "idea cars" for first time—also Mako Shark
- American Motors has experimental AMX
- Mercury has two-seat Comet Escapade ... Ford shows Magic Cruiser for first time
- Chrysler shows 300-X research car
- Safety influence noted at auto show
- Attendance breaks record: 848,031
- Import Salon consists of three areas, each 40 feet in diameter
- New "Winners' Row" exhibit features a dozen great cars of the past
- Mercedes-Benz 250-S makes U.S. debut
- Studebakers seen for last time; production in Canada ceases in '66

Above: Following the trend toward bucket-seat versions of mid-size cars, Plymouth's Satellite came with a standard 273-cid V-8. In 1966, however, Satellites could be equipped with the brawny Hemi V-8 engine instead.

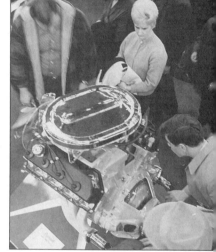

Right: Looks like one or two of these chaps might like to try his hand at a Plymouth with this 426-cubic-inch Hemi V-8 engine. Rated at 425 horsepower, the Hemi actually delivered closer to 500 horses.

In mid-1964, Pontiac had launched the GTO, a Tempest offshoot considered by many to be the first "muscle car." GTO bodies were lengthened and smoothed for '66.

Left: The "Geo-Sphere" served as a centerpiece for the 1966 auto show at McCormick Place.

Above: Ramblers didn't always lure youthful male car fans in the mid-Sixties, but what youngster could fail to fall for a convertible, regardless of make? Rambler had two convertibles in '66: the 770 (shown) and a smaller American.

Left: Chevelles ranked high on the "wish lists" of rabid "muscle car" fans—especially in Super Sport (SS) trim with the big 396-cid V-8 tucked beneath the hood, packing 325 horsepower.

Right: Even Chevrolet's El Camino car/pickup could have a 396-cubic-inch V-8 engine installed.

Below: Oldsmobile became the first American automaker in modern times to issue a front-drive vehicle: the Toronado, which debuted for 1966.

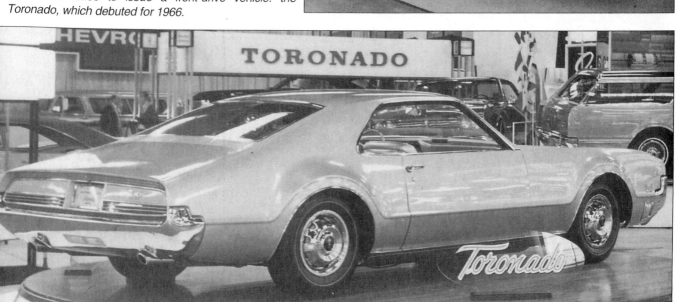

What? A Ford Thunderbird with four doors? It's true, the Landau sedan (with "suicide" doors) went on sale for 1967 and lasted into '71. All Thunderbirds were restyled this year, losing what little was left of their original sporty nature.

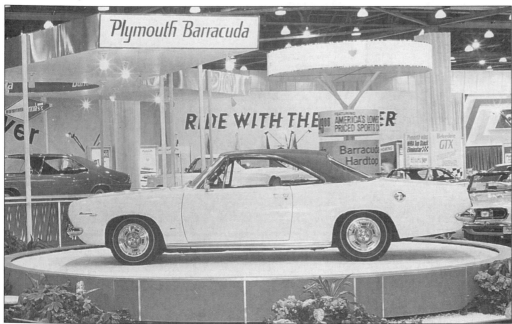

Plymouth tried to capture the youth market with a Barracuda fastback, issued for 1965. Barracudas earned an ample facelift and length increase for '67, adding a convertible and hardtop to join a shapelier fastback. Note the competition-type gas cap.

Full-size Chevrolets, like this Impala convertible, sold in impressive numbers during the Sixties, despite competition from intermediates and compacts. This convertible has a 327-cid V-8, but a six-cylinder engine was standard, and bigger V-8s could be ordered.

A year after Oldsmobile introduced the front-drive Toronado, Cadillac switched its Eldorado personal-luxury coupe to front-wheel drive. Note the sprinkling fountains around the pedestal display.

Ford displayed the GT edition of its Fairlane 500XL hardtop coupe at the 1967 auto show. To the rear, on a pedestal, is a Mach II concept car.

Left: Styled by Pietro Frua and produced from 1963-70, Maserati's two-passenger Mistral came in coupe and convertible form. Dual-overhead-cam six-cylinder engines came in two sizes.

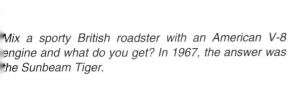

Mix a sporty British roadster with an American V-8 engine and what do you get? In 1967, the answer was the Sunbeam Tiger.

1968

60th annual Chicago Automobile Show

(February 24–March 3, 1968)

- Chicago Auto Show again takes place at International Amphitheatre
- 653,120 visitors attend auto show
- Admission this year is $1.50, to see more than 450 vehicles plus 50 displays of accessories and allied equipment
- WGN-TV has 90-minute color telecast from auto show on first Sunday
- Preview session for auto executives and media draws 31,000 ... opening-day crowd sets record at 76,573
- "Motorevue" performance returns after year's absence and is seen twice daily; will be last year for stage revues
- Two models seen for first time at Chicago show: luxury Continental Mark III and AMX two-seat sports car (from AMC)
- Miss America, Debra Barnes, appears at Oldsmobile exhibit
- Dodge display includes ventriloquist, magician, stock-car drivers, "fever girls"
- Craig Breedlove, holder of world land-speed record, is at AMC exhibit
- Lincoln-Mercury display has sports stars to sign autographs
- Chevrolet dealers again offer free shuttle buses from downtown
- Officials say three-hour visit is needed to see the show properly
- Chevrolet General Manager E.M. (Pete) Estes calls Chicago show "the outstanding one in the country"

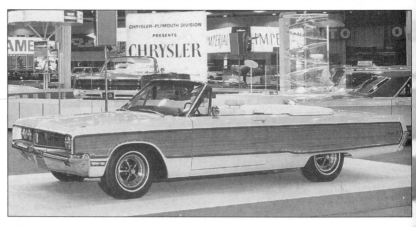

Simulated woodgrain panels decorated the bodysides of a Chrysler Newport convertible or hardtop with the "Sportsgrain" option, a mid-season special that cost $126 extra.

As the sign suggests, Oldsmobile assaulted the youth market in the late Sixties with its 4-4-2 model. When it debuted in 1964, 4-4-2 stood for a four-barrel carburetor, four-speed manual transmission, and dual exhaust. Those details soon changed, but the designation stuck.

AMC (American Motors) brought out the two-passenger AMX coupe (right) for its mid-1968 debut, following up on an earlier AMX show car. The sporty and shapely Javelin (left), shown in SST trim, was AMC's answer to the Ford Mustang.

A woman in fringed headdress and miniskirt helped present the merits of the Dodge Charger R/T, a performance-focused mid-size hardtop.

Signs induced car fans to visit the 1968 Chicago Auto Show—held again at the Amphitheatre, because McCormick Place stood in ruins.

Introduced for 1968, Lincoln's Continental Mark III personal-luxury coupe was considered a direct descendant of the graceful Continental Mark II of 1956-57. Corporate chairman Henry Ford II chose the ultimate design, from a batch of proposals.

Note the vastly long triangular quarter windows on this Buick Wildcat hardtop coupe. Wildcat was the sporty member of the big-Buick family, packing a standard 430-cid V-8 engine.

Buick dealers continued to market the mini-sized, German-built Opel Kadett, dubbed the "Mini-Brute." Kadetts got a modest restyling for '68, with more rounded edges.

Ford had plenty of "better ideas" for performance-car fans, even in its full-size Galaxie 500 line, which included a 500XL hardtop coupe and convertible.

Above: Plymouth's Road Runner was the first low-budget muscle car, shown on stage as part of the 1968 "Motorevue." Named after the Warner Brothers cartoon character, the Road Runner even had a horn that mimicked the character's "beep-beep" sound.

Above: Homely "Beetles" had established Volkswagen in America, but the stylish Karmann Ghia captured the hearts of thousands of enthusiasts. Karmann Ghias came in convertible and hardtop body styles, with the same powertrain as the Beetle.

Right: Imported sports cars were relegated to the fringes of the exhibit area, alongside aftermarket displays. Shown here is a Lotus Elan.

1969
61st annual Chicago Automobile Show
(March 8–16, 1969)

- 655,716 visitors attend the show during its 9-day run
- AMC launches SC/Rambler Hurst at show ... Pontiac exhibits Firebird Trans Am, to go on sale in April
- New Ford Maverick held back for public debut at New York's show
- Show cars include Mercury Super Spoiler, Chrysler Concept 70X, Plymouth Duster I
- Drag racer "Dyno Don" Nicholson appears at show ... so does "Dodge Fever Girl" Joan Parker
- Chevrolet exhibits dramatic Astro III
- Lincoln-Mercury exhibit includes slot-car race
- Sports stars at display include Bart Starr and Jesse Owens (Lincoln-Mercury), Jean-Claude Killy and O.J. Simpson (Chevrolet)
- WGN-TV telecasts auto-show preview for 18th time
- "Freddy Ford" robot, 8-1/2 feet tall, answers questions at Ford exhibit ... he's actually second-generation robot
- Safety-slogan contest held for 20th time—more than 20,000 entries received

Pontiac launched the Trans Am as a mid-1969 model—most assertive member of the Firebird clan. This one was hard to miss, with its big twin blue racing stripes stretching from front to rear of the white body. Only 697 were built in '69, nearly all with a 335-horsepower Ram Air III V-8 engine.

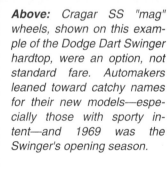

Above: *Cragar SS "mag" wheels, shown on this example of the Dodge Dart Swinger hardtop, were an option, not standard fare. Automakers leaned toward catchy names for their new models—especially those with sporty intent—and 1969 was the Swinger's opening season.*

Left: *Three muscular machines highlighted Chevrolet's exhibit at the 1969 auto show: a T-top Corvette in foreground, compact Nova (left), and Camaro (right), which was ready for a redesign during the following season.*

Auto-show crowds continued to enjoy the stage revues at the Amphitheatre, where cars were presented one after another. At this moment, the "star" is an AMC Javelin.

Skits were part of the fun of presenting facts on new models during the "Motorevue." This group is calling attention to the Mercury Cougar convertible.

Above: Not many Saab Sonett coupes went to customers in America, but the Swedish-built sports car helped draw attention to conventional Saab sedans. A German Ford V-4 engine was installed, and the body was made of fiberglass.

Left: Before creating its Z-series sports cars of the 1970s and '80s, Datsun issued a distinctively-styled 1600 roadster and then a 2000 (shown) roadster.

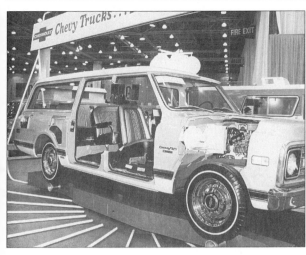

Chevrolet cut away a section of its Custom 10 Suburban to give showgoers a better view. Suburban wagons have a history dating all the way back to 1936.

Above: *Auto-show exhibits often presented a vehicle in a simulation of its "natural" environment. For a Jeep, that might be a patch of rocky and hilly terrain.*

Left: *No, Civic wasn't the first Honda to hit American shores. In the late Sixties, Honda had the little 600 sedan, with a two-cylinder engine.*

Left: *With its Land Cruiser, Toyota was one of the pioneers of the sport-utility vehicle—long before SUVs became a trend. The first Land Cruisers had been imported in 1960.*

Below: *Rotary engines, as used in the innovative but short-lived NSU Ro-80, looked promising in the late Sixties. Only Mazda, however, would stick with rotary power for a long period.*

1970

62nd annual Chicago Automobile Show

(February 21–March 1, 1970)

- Small cars predominant trend at Chicago Auto Show
- Auto-show attendance totals 662,743 visitors
- "Geo-Sphere" hangs in main lobby of exhibition hall
- Buick exhibits GSX sports coupe
- Compact Dodge vans seen for first time, at Chicago show
- Chevrolet spotlights second-generation Camaro and latest Corvette, both appearing for first time at Chicago show
- Pontiac launches redesigned Firebird at Chicago show
- Chevrolet exhibit includes cheerleaders from Michigan State University
- Ford announces two new sport-economy models at show: Mustang Grabber and Maverick Grabber
- Oldsmobile Rallye 350 debuts at Chicago Auto Show
- Chrysler exhibits Cordoba de Oro styling exercise
- Experimental Opel Aero GT is seen for first time in U.S.
- Experimental rotary-engined Mercedes-Benz C-111 debuts at Chicago show
- John DeLorean announces that new small Chevrolet will debut in August

Although this Oldsmobile Cutlass Supreme coupe appears to be stock, it has a few special items installed, including wire wheels and a padded top.

Introduced this year, the Monte Carlo was a full-size "personal" coupe, with the longest hood ever installed on a modern Chevrolet model. Monte Carlos were available with a choice of potent powertrains—topped by a new 454 cubic-inch V-8 engine that delivered 360 horsepower.

Motor Trend magazine selected Ford's Torino as its "Car of the Year." Torino debuted for 1968, lengthened and reshaped for '70. To the left is an LTD hardtop sedan.

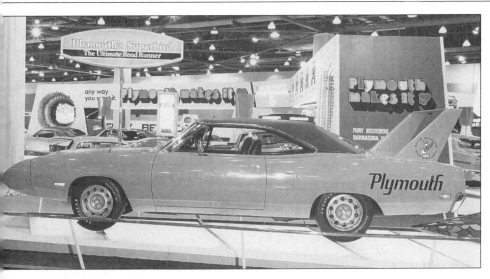

Superbird topped Plymouth's muscle-car lineup for just one season. Only 1,920 were built, easily spotted by their monstrous rear wing. Naturally, one of the hottest Plymouth V-8 engines might be installed.

Below: Entrepreneur Malcolm Bricklin helped launch Subaru in America, serving as the Japanese company's U.S. distributor. The tiny Model 360 used an air-cooled two-cylinder engine.

Above: A 289-cid Ford V-8 went into the sleek and low DeTomaso Mangusta, which featured gullwing doors. A Ford V-8 engine was installed in the Italian-built two-seater.

Below: A special, sporty "Grabber" edition of the new compact Ford Maverick was dubbed "Thrifty Swifty." When the Grabber went on sale for '71, a 302-cid V-8 was available.

Above: After releasing a series of practical Kadetts in the Sixties, Opel turned out a stylish little sport coupe, dubbed the Opel GT. Styling mimicked that of the Chevrolet Corvette, if on a smaller scale. To the rear, on the pedestal, is a GT concept car.

1971

63rd annual Chicago Automobile Show

(February 20–28, 1971)

- Auto show moves into new McCormick Place exhibition center
- Record-setting 942,029 visitors attend the show during its 9-day run—beats previous record by almost 94,000
- Auto editors from Chicago's four major daily papers contribute essays to auto-show program: Jim Mateja (*Tribune*), Dan Jedlicka (*Sun-Times*), Cliff Bielby (*Chicago Today*), Dan Miller (*Daily News*)
- Ford unveils Pinto hatchback Runabout at Chicago Auto Show
- Pontiac introduces Ventura II compact at Chicago show
- Chevrolet has Astro II concept at show, and introduces "Heavy Chevy" Chevelle and Rally Nova option packages
- Opel 1900 seen for first time in U.S.
- Dodge displays Diamante roadster—blend of Charger Daytona and Challenger
- Dodge tests Hot Apricot color scheme on Charger SE
- Ford displays experimental Mustang Milano two-seater, plus Wildflower rendition of 4WD Bronco in psychedelic hues
- Lincoln-Mercury has Montego Sports-Hauler that holds small vehicle inside

RICHARD V. LYNCH

The Chicago Auto Show had returned "to the scene of its greatest triumphs," said Richard V. Lynch, chairman of the executive show committee, in the 1971 program. During its return to the Amphitheatre, "the quality of the event never suffered. The cooperation of the Chicago new car dealers and the manufacturers was beyond expectations and the label the 'World's Greatest' persevered." Nevertheless, planners were "extremely proud" of the new McCormick Place, "which is both beautiful and exciting to see, and which imparts an inviting environment suggesting a leisurely browse through a fantastic mechanical montage."

At last, a new McCormick Place was ready—in time for the 1971 Chicago Auto Show. Attendance leaped to a new record.

Chevrolet exhibited a pair of performance machines: the "Heavy Chevy" (left) and Rally Nova. The "Heavy Chevy" was a special Chevelle with a black grille, side stripes, and rally wheels.

Left: Note the semi-padded roof on this Plymouth Satellite Sebring Plus hardtop, equipped with a 383-cid V-8. Distinctive roof treatments grew popular in the Seventies.

Below: Porsche unleashed the 914 in 1970, with a Volkswagen four-cylinder engine or a Porsche six-cylinder. Both engines were mid-mounted, a departure from Porsche's traditional rear-engine layout. The 914 arose out of a joint venture between Porsche and Volkswagen.

bove: Not many Lamborghini Espada upes found customers in the United ates, but exotic machines always drew ns at the auto show. This one used a 12 engine.

'ght: Built in Britain, the Jensen terceptor II sports car ran a Chrysler 8 engine, rated at 330 horsepower. nly 742 were produced during 1971.

1972

64th annual Chicago Automobile Show

(February 26–March 5, 1972)

- Chicago Auto Show flaunts about 550 vehicles for visitors to peruse
- Auto show attracts 935,341 visitors
- Four daily-paper auto editors again contribute essays to auto-show program
- Lincoln Continental Town Car makes its debut at Chicago Auto Show
- Ford announces Pinto station wagon as mid-season model
- Buick exhibits experimental Silver Arrow III Riviera at auto show
- Lotus introduces new Europa Twin Cam model at Chicago show ... Renault 17 sports coupe also displayed
- Jensen Interceptor III debuts in Chicago ... Squire and TVR make their first U.S. appearances at Chicago show
- Ford "idea cars" include Berline III, a modification of LTD
- Pontiac has three customized show cars, including Casa Blanca Grand Ville
- Large recreational-vehicle exhibit includes International Harvester prototype motorhome
- CATA sponsors contest to rank salesmen's performance on show floor—idea had proven successful before

Plymouth Barracudas came only in hardtop coupe form for 1972—basic or 'Cuda guise. Convertible Barracudas and big-block engines were gone.

Fashion designer Pierre Cardin lent his name to a "Cardin" edition of the spo AMC Javelin, equipped with a special interior and emblems.

A Galaxie 500 hardtop was the five-millionth Chicago-built Ford. Note the Model T Ford to its rear, with a 1914 Illinois license plate.

Topping the Chrysler line was the New Yorker, shown in hardtop coupe form. Regular and Brougham editions were available in '72.

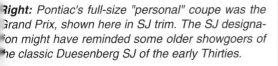

Above: A GT hardtop led the mid-size Mercury Montego lineup. Montego was one of five Mercury models displayed at the auto show.

Right: Pontiac's full-size "personal" coupe was the Grand Prix, shown here in SJ trim. The SJ designation might have reminded some older showgoers of the classic Duesenberg SJ of the early Thirties.

Above: The final edition of the Lotus Elan +2 coupe remained on sale as late as 1974. Like other imported sports cars, Lotus models were consigned to a separate area of the auto show, apart from domestic cars.

Right: Ever since the Fifties, Volkswagen Camper buses had been popular, seen all over the nation's highways in summertime. Tilting up the roof gave quite a bit of headroom inside. Campers could hold a whole family, equipped for sleeping and cooking.

1973

65th annual Chicago Automobile Show

(February 24–March 4, 1973)

- Some 550 vehicles seen at auto show
- 949,829 visitors attend the show during its 9-day run—total tops previous record
- Subcompact Chevrolet Vega wagon available with new Custom-Estate option
- Chevrolet unveils XP-898 "idea car" at Chicago show, with plastic-sandwich body and Vega running gear
- Mazda exhibit includes cutaway exhibit of company's Wankel rotary engine
- "Now Car" electric sport coupe is exhibited
- Several car divisions display an experimental safety vehicle
- "Muscle car" era is waning, as impact of governmental regulation is felt
- OPEC oil embargo begins in fall of 1973; Chicagoans, like all Americans, face gasoline shortages and gas-station lines

As horsepower ratings declined during the Seventies, automakers took to installing flamboyant decorations to convey an image of raucous behavior. Pontiac's "chicken" on the Trans Am hood was one of the best-known emblems for a while.

Right: Assertive is the word for this Mustang Mach I with a "tu-tone" hood and tie-downs. The "muscle-car era" was ending, but Ford gave it one more try in '73, before shrinking to a Mustang II.

Below: Sunroofs weren't quite as common in 1973 as they are today, but this Continental Mark IV had one. Sales doubled when the prior Mark III turned into a Mark IV for 1972—longer, heavier, and gobbling up more fuel. As the fuel crisis emerged later in 1973, and long queues at gas stations became everyday occurrences, owners of these big boats may have wondered whether a smaller car would have been wiser.

"boattail" rear end helped give the 1971-73 Buick Riviera a far *ifferent* personality than its predecessors. Not everyone cared *r* that back-end look, and it disappeared after '73.

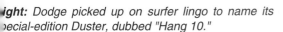

bove: Plymouth's Gold Duster was a "spring special," *tended* to attract customers to dealerships after the *ard* Chicago winter. A free canopy vinyl roof was in- *uded.*

ight: Dodge picked up on surfer lingo to name its *pecial-edition* Duster, dubbed "Hang 10."

Above: *Two breeds of AMC Gremlin made the auto show in 1973: plain (in foreground) and equipped with a new "Levi's" interior (rear). The "Levi's" edition featured seats and door panels in blue spun nylon, with copper rivets to resemble the familiar blue jeans.*

Nothing else at the auto show looked anything like the Citroën SM-Maserati, blending the French company's air-oil suspension with a Maserati V-6 engine. Front-wheel drive assured better winter traction—thus, the skis mounted on the roof of this model at the auto show.

6

Dream Cars—the Early Years
(1950-73)

Dreams. They're what the auto industry is made of, when all is said and done. That's been the case since the beginning. If people didn't dream of driving home another car, a better car, there would be little need for auto shows—or for the auto industry as we know it. Whether it's a Broadway show, a movie show, or an auto show, most of those who attend are there to dream a little.

Dreams vary widely in dimension, of course. Some are modest; others grandiose. Given the opportunity, automobile stylists tend to gravitate toward the latter end of the spectrum. Most stylists express a preference for working on designs that reach well beyond the conventional limits, stretching their creativity and exercising their imaginations to the greatest extent possible. Contributing to the development of a "dream car" can be seen as a virtual reward for working on more mundane tasks, on regular production vehicles.

Whether they're called "dream cars" or "show cars," "concept cars" or "experimental cars," the basic idea began in 1938 with the debut of General Motors' "Y-Job." Seen at countless events, then and for years afterward, that stylish one-of-a-kind convertible demonstrated what GM's designers of that era could do, if left unshackled by thoughts of real-world production.

A couple of years later, Chrysler followed suit with some concept vehicles of its own: the Thunderbolt and the Newport. Evolved from regular production models, these lavishly-shaped machines let Chrysler demonstrate a few ideas that revealed the company's potential creativity, even if they never turned up on real-world automobiles.

Chrysler led the way in the Fifties, issuing a long string of dream cars, from the K-310 to the D'Elegance, the DeSoto Adventurer to the Dodge Firearrow. Most of them were built with the assistance of the Ghia company, a renowned styling firm in Italy.

General Motors took its own path early in the decade, developing a succession of fantastic automobiles to exhibit at the GM Motoramas, which toured the country through the Fifties. These GM specialty vehicles also began to trickle into the auto show each year. The GM "dream" list started off in 1951 with the streamlined and supercharged Buick XP-300, which could run on methanol. GM then moved into such fanciful vehicles as the Pontiac Parisienne and the Cadillac LeMans. Several smaller-scale "dreams," such as the

LaSalle II and the Buick Wildcat, were created in part to te fiberglass body construction—as used on the new-in-19? Chevrolet Corvette. GM even created a concept truck, call L'Universelle, which flaunted features that would not appe in production until the minivans of the 1980s.

Some of the "dream cars" of the Fifties we unabashedly futuristic—especially the "bubble-toppe models, such as the Pontiac Bonneville Special and Cadill Cyclone, as well as the Ford Mystere. Some served as te beds for far-out technology. Ford's Gyron of 1962, a rath extreme example, represented the possibility of using gyroscope for stability, riding on just two wheels instead the customary four-wheeled layout. Needless to say, th one never led to any marketable vehicle.

In the case of some cars seen at the Chicago Auto Sho you might have to look closely to determine that they we meant to fulfill many "dreams." Quite a few were basica stock, with the exception of special paint treatments and, many cases, exotic interiors. The Oldsmobile Palm Beach 1951, for instance, was notable mainly for its iridescent su green paint job, topped by a sand-colored roof. Lincol Mercury brought a long list of "specials" to the auto show the Fifties, not too far removed from their regular-producti counterparts. Some of those weren't meant to be sold, b others were intended to give local people something unique the dealerships—in effect, a "Chicago" model, though it mig actually have any number of names, or no specific name at a

Buick displayed its Century Cruiser at the 1969 Chicago Au Show, equipped with "all the comforts of home," from refrigerator to a TV set.

Even when a concept vehicle was never planned for production, certain features soon found their way onto regular-production cars. The built-in exhaust tips of the 1953 Cadillac LeMans, for example, went into '54 Cadillacs. So did a variant of that car's wraparound windshield. Mercury's production Turnpike Cruiser of 1957 borrowed several features from the recently-seen XM-Turnpike Cruiser concept, including its compound curved windshield and back-slanted rear glass.

Although most "dream cars" in the Fifties came out of the Big Three's design studios, independent automakers also got into the act now and then. Shortly before it turned into a Studebaker offshoot, and then quietly disappeared, Packard created a flamboyant Predictor, built by Ghia with such features as a swivel-out passenger seat. Hudson, just prior to its absorption into American Motors in 1955, exhibited a stylish Italia, wholly unlike any Hudson that had ever left a dealership. In fact, a couple of dozen Italias were built and sold, so a few people had an opportunity to own and drive a "dream."

That result was not typical, however. Most show cars were destroyed soon after their auto-show appearances. Some were kept by the company, at least for a while, before disposal. A handful managed to escape the crusher, winding up in the collections of a couple of specialist collectors of early-day "dream" machines.

European automakers brought few concepts to the Chicago show, but Simca displayed a bizarre Fulgur in 1962, looking like it belonged on "Star Trek" rather than on any highway.

Some concept cars, such as the Ford Cougar 406 of '62 and the Plymouth VIP of '66, appeared for the first time in Chicago. Not all of the "dream" vehicles seen at the Chicago Auto Show made their official debuts at the Amphitheatre or McCormick Place, however. Many had first appeared elsewhere: at another auto show, perhaps, or at a special company event.

Hosting a debut of a show car came to be perceived as quite a coup. Chicago organizers managed to obtain a sizable lot of official debuts over the years. They continue to do so today, acting even more zealously to make the Chicago show the official launch pad for as many special cars as possible.

Dream cars, then, have come in three basic levels:

1. Exercises in imagination, on the part of stylists, engineers, or more often, both. Here, designers are given license to let their minds run free, coming up with concepts that couldn't possibly be produced in the foreseeable future, in the form shown. Many of these have been "test beds" for future technology, from the potential of atomic power in the Fifties to turbine engines in the Sixties and hybrid-electric powertrains today.

2. Close-to-stock specials. More of a marketing tool than a design exercise, these are offshoots of production vehicles, given special interiors or exterior trim, and a catchy name. At the auto shows over the years, visitors were likely to encounter several automobiles that served as "spring specials," intended to give the Chicagoland audience a unique vehicle and to attract them into dealerships after the show ended. Because the Chicago Auto Show took place in the depths of the Midwestern winter each year, something extra was needed to spark attention, and send consumers into the dealership as the snow and ice ebbed.

3. Customer-reaction exercises. Here, marketers have the stylists and engineers come up with a new idea, displaying it at the auto show to see how consumers react. Auto-show patrons might be asked to fill out comment cards. Or, observers might simply watch and listen to what people say, or study their gestures.

Even if comments are overwhelmingly favorable, there's only a slim chance that a vehicle like it will be found at dealerships a few years hence. More likely, certain elements will be borrowed from the concept vehicle and installed on a production model. A body curve here, a new gadget there—pieces from concept cars are far more likely to come to life than is the vehicle as a whole.

Of course, if a concept car gets an unmitigated "thumbs-down" from the auto-show audience, most likely it will be relegated to the scrap heap.

For the most part, concept vehicles of the Sixties and early Seventies toned down a bit. Not so many exhibited quite the level of flair and flamboyance that marked the breathtaking Fifties versions. But then, production cars, too, weren't so dramatic as they'd been in the tailfinned Fifties.

Still, a few stunners did make the auto-show rounds periodically. So did a number of high-performance machines, demonstrating that the potent engines that powered production vehicles during the "muscle-car" era could be stretched further yet in concept form. Social trends managed to find their way into the auto show, too. As surfing grew popular on the West Coast, for instance, you could count on a few concept cars that would feature a surfboard motif—even if no one in Chicago was likely to climb upon a 'board and ride the waves.

As electronic technology gathered steam, too, concept cars began to display the latest advances in gadgetry—some of it useful, some not. From the beginning, "dream cars" were designed to incorporate all that had been achieved in automotive design and engineering up to that point, and then reach well beyond the previous limits.

Chicagoans had always liked a good show, and eagerly sought to get a look at the latest ideas. Even if they drove back home in a style-free, low-tech sedan—and their next purchase wouldn't be much more *avant garde*, either—it was nice to know what was possible, and what might be rolling down the road in the next few years. Every winter, Midwesterners had an unfailing opportunity to spend a day finding out what was new on the automotive scene.

Why so many concepts? That's no mystery. Postwar automakers believed that the person who was enthralled by a "dream car" just might be similarly entranced by a more prosaic coupe or sedan, down at the dealership. They quickly learned the lessons of motivation researchers in the Fifties, who discovered that red convertibles drew American men into showrooms—even if they wound up driving away in a brown station wagon. Shouldn't a far-out concept produce even greater sales results?

161

Green alligator-skin and lacquered yellow wicker door-panel trim highlighted the Oldsmobile Palm Beach Holiday coupe, seen at the 1951 auto show.

Oldsmobile's special 98 Palm Beach Holiday coupe was painted in iridescent s green. The steel top was cabana sand color with a crackle finish.

Marjorie Needham, 21 (Miss Berwyn-Cicero in 1951), poses with Buick's streamlined XP-300 concept car, wearing a tapered chrome fin down the center of its trunk. A 335-horsepower, supercharged V-8 engine lurked beneath the hood. The two-piece trunk lid opened from either side.

Based on the Capri sedan, Lincoln's "Maharajah" was one of four special Lincoln models that appeared at the 1953 Chicago Auto Sho Also on hand: the "Anniversary" Capri convertible, "Cadet" Capri sedan, and "Midshipman" Capri coupe.

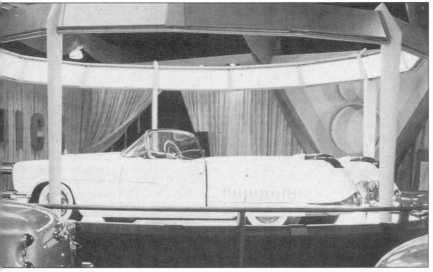

Built to test fiberglass body construction, Buick's Wildcat featured a sharply-sloped wraparound windshield—unseen on production cars in 1953. The convertible top folded into a body recess, needing no separate boot.

Not all "dream cars" looked futuristic. Based on the Monterey coupe, the Mercury Bahamian was one of several Mercury concepts released for the auto show in 1953.

Pontiac's Parisienne, seen at the 1953 show, was a cut-down Chieftain Catalina hardtop with a landau half-roof and wraparound windshield. Several details were borrowed for the production '55 Pontiacs.

Starfire was Oldsmobile's fiberglass-bod[ied]
sporty personal car, with seating for six. Billed [as]
the "X-P Rocket" and serving as a lab on whee[ls,]
it featured what Olds called a "daring new l[ow,]
poised, waist-high silhouette." Innovatio[ns]
included a panoramic windshield that exten[ded]
around door openings. An Orlon convertible [top]
lowered into a recess with a metal cover.

Cadillac's 1953 LeMans wore a wraparou[nd]
windshield and integral exhaust tips similar [to]
those that would appear on regular producti[on]
Cadillacs a year later. Beneath the hood: [a]
250-horsepower V-8 engine. Cadillac als[o]
displayed an ensign blue Series 60 Spec[ial]
sedan with Naugahyde roof to demonstrate [its]
new air conditioner.

This was no ordinary 19[53]
Hudson. Designed by Spring a[nd]
built by Carrozzeria Touring [of]
Italy, on a Jet chassis, the Ita[lia]
stood nearly 10 inches lower th[an]
a regular "Step-down" Hudson[. A]
114-horsepower Hudson [Jet]
engine was installed. Dubbed [a]
practical car with producti[on]
possibilities," the Italia actua[lly]
went on sale at $4,800, but o[nly]
25 were built in 1954-55.

See the Plymouth Belmont at the Chicago Automobile Show March 13 thru March 21

Though huge by modern standards, the two-passenger Plymouth Belmont—displayed at the 1954 show—was called a sports car in the promotional literature.

Riding a standard Dodge chassis with a 114-inch wheelbase, Plymouth's Belmont had a reinforced fiberglass body, aviation-type seats in white leather, a tachometer, and luggage compartments behind each seat. The Belmont stood less than 33 inches tall, to the top of the door.

Close-coupled in profile, the four-passenger DeSoto Adventurer used many stock DeSoto chassis parts. Note the full wheel openings and exposed exhaust system, as well as the long, flat hood. A racing-style fuel filler sat on the rear deck. Under the hood: a 170-horsepower FireDome V-8.

Dodge promised "a glimpse into the future" beyond 1954 with the Firearrow, designed by Chrysler and Ghia (the Italian styling firm). Standing just 46-1/4 inches tall to the top of the curved, sharply-raked windshield, it blended European sports-car thinking with contemporary American conveniences.

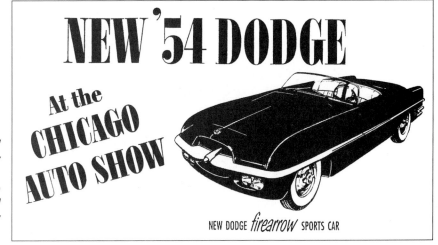

NEW '54 DODGE

At the CHICAGO AUTO SHOW

NEW DODGE *firearrow* SPORTS CAR

A plastic "bubble" canopy on the 1954 Pontiac Bonneville Special was hinged a counterbalanced to allow occupants to enter: Pontiac called it "the pattern for tomorro General Motors created a long series of "dream cars" in the early Fifties, many seen f at the GM Motorama.

Cadillac called its fiberglass-bodied, two-passenger 1954 La Espada convertible a "completely functional dream car." A companion hardtop, named El Camino, also was developed under the leadership of Ed Glowacke, head of Cadillac styling. These two paved the way for the 1957 Cadillac Eldorado Brougham.

Devoid of windows that opened, the 1956 Ford Mystere had to rely on air conditioning to comfort its occupants. Front glass curved all the way to the pillar at the rear of the door, raising for access. A roof vent sat at the windshield top. A gas turbine engine went into the rear.

Mercury promised that the XM-Turnpike Cruiser of 1956 "anticipates future motoring needs." *re enough, Mercury soon issued a production Turnpike Cruiser that borrowed a number of *tures, including the compound curved windshield and back-slanted rear glass.

Relatively small by 1956 standards, the Buick Wildcat III seated four and wore a fiberglass body and fine screen-type grille. A 280-horsepower V-8 with four carburetors provided the power.

*rysler Corporation promoted its "Forward Look" with the assistance of the concept DeSoto Flight Sweep I, a *r-seat sport convertible with "clamshell" front fenders.

Above: Although most "dream cars" are strictly for show, some turn into reality. Before readying a costly Brougham for production in 1957, Cadillac created a show car of that name, brandishing distinctive side trim and fins when it appeared at the 1956 Chicago Auto Show.

DeSoto displayed its Indianapolis pace car at the 1956 auto show. To the rear is a conc Chrysler Plainsman station wagon, with its spare tire inside the back fender—an idea soon to put into production on Dodge and Plymouth wagons. The Plainsman also had an "observati car" rear-facing third seat and a roll-down rear window.

What's behind the scenes in the truck-world?

SEE THE GMC EXHIB

Like many General Motors show cars, L'Universelle appeared first at G Motorama in 1955; and then at the Chicago Auto Show.

Auto-show visitors had to marvel at the features of this GMC L'Universelle concept panel truck, many of which would appear on minivans three decades later. In addition to front-wheel drive and car-like styling, the truck featured dual fold-up side doors, a mid-mounted Pontiac V-8, a roof vent for cooling, and torsion-bar front suspension.

ilt by Ghia on a Clipper chassis, the Packard Predictor heralded "an
xciting promise of all the great things to come" from the company. Note the
ll fins with antennas, and the concealed headlamps. Production Packards
ere flamboyant in '56, too, but the make would not be around much longer.

A swivel-out passenger seat was one of many
convenience features in the Packard Predictor,
seen at the 1956 Chicago Auto Show.

You'll see a special showing of the Impala—Chevrolet's fascinating experimental five-passenger sedan. It sparkles with delightful new ideas throughout!

Left: Chevrolet's five-passenger Impala had a
fiberglass body, V-8 engine, and rode a 116.5-inch
wheelbase. Painted in two shades of blue, it had an
integral bumper and grille, plus chromed wire wheels
with knock-off hubs.

ront and rear styling of the 1957
hevrolet Impala leaned more to-
ard Corvette, with little kinship to
onventional coupes or sedans.

Dale Robertson's TV sh[ow]
"Wells Fargo," inspired [a]
custom Buick convertible, b[uilt]
on a Limited chassis. Except [for]
trim, it doesn't look far fr[om]
stock.

Like its competitors, Ford looked ahead to a
"World of Tomorrow" when giving its stylists
license to create concept cars.

Above: One successful concept car often led
another. Ford's "La Galaxie" show car w[as]
inspired by an earlier dream vehicle: the 19[--]
Lincoln Diplomat.

Special models were developed with region[al]
themes, such as this 1959 Buick Texas statio[n]
wagon, complete with a sunroof.

A one-piece plastic canopy on the 1960 Cadillac Cyclone was coated to
protect against sun rays, and gave a full 360-degree view. Hinged at the
rear, the canopy raised for entry and the door slid back. Radar in huge
nose cones could warn the driver of obstacles ahead.

Something out of "The Jetsons" TV series? No, it's the Simca Fulgur, seen at the 1961 auto show. French companies did not often bring concept vehicles over to the United States.

ot every show car was a amatic, futuristic creation. This hevrolet Impala convertible s simply billed as "a special r from the world of fashion."

Evolved from a privately-run race car of the late Fifties, the Corvette Stingray Special became an official Chevrolet show vehicle. Visitors to the Chicago Auto Show got to see it in 1961.

Electrically-operated gullwing doors and a low profile (only 49.5 inches tall) added to the futuristic appearance of the Ford Cougar 406, seen for the first time by the public at the 1962 Chicago Auto Show. Ford promoted it as a luxury personal two-seater, not a performance car. A 406-cid V-8 engine went into production Fords in mid-1962, but the Cougar name would not be used until '67, on Mercury's cousin to the Mustang.

THE GYRON

Ford used the Gyron, a 1962 show car, to speculate on possible use of a gyroscope for stabilization. The delta-shaped car had only two running wheels and no steering wheel—a steering dial instead. Engineers were seeking innovative ways to sever, at long last, the link between the automobile and the horse-drawn carriage.

When Chrysler Corporation tucked its new CR2A turbine engine into a pair of 1962 vehicles, they looked virtually stock. This is a Plymouth, but a Turbine Dodge Dart made a coast-to-coast run and both cars toured extensively. Chrysler had been experimenting with turbines since 1954, when a turbine-powered Plymouth Belvedere ran successfully.

This 1962 Lincoln-Mercury Palomar wagon probably wouldn't pass muster today in terms of safety—not with a passenger sitting up on the "flying bridge," on an elevated rear seat.

Built on a shortened version of the mild-mannered Tempest's chassis, Pontiac's experimental Monte Carlo convertible featured a rakishly chopped wraparound windshield and supercharged four-cylinder engine. Intended to gauge interest in a Pontiac sports car, the two-passenger Monte Carlo sat in the middle of the company's 1962 display.

rysler used this monster-finned Turbo Flite with lift-off top as one of the showcases for its turbine engine. The Turbo Flite appeared he 1962 Chicago Auto Show, along with a near-stock but turbine-powered Dodge and Plymouth. The car's top rose automatically doors opened.

Called the Turbo Power Giant, this Do[...] truck held one of Chrysler Corporati[...] turbine engines, appearing at the 1[...] auto show. A stake-body truck had b[...] turbine-powered a year earlier.

Above: Note the opened rear wheel w[...] on this mildly modified Cadillac converti[...] seen at the 1962 Chicago Auto Show.

Cadillac used virtually the same displa[...] 1963 as it did in '62, to show off yet ano[...] close-to-stock dream convertible.

Oldsmobile's 1963 "el Torero" show car was a custom-fitted 98 convertible, colored in Firefrost gold.

A distinctive Spanish-motif interior in "el Torero," highlighted by gold brocade fabric on door panels, matched this woman's cape. Four naturally-contoured bucket seats were upholstered in white leather with red satin striping.

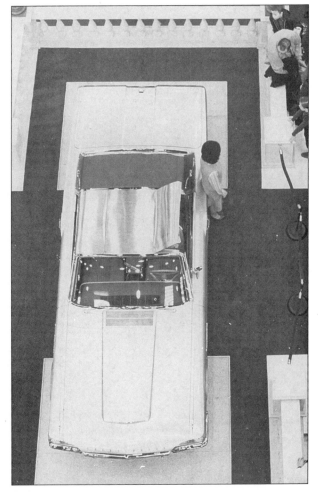

How much did this special Ford Thunderbird differ from production models in 1964? Hard to say from an overhead view, but a lot could be accomplished when starting with an appealing basic automobile, then tinkering with trim and details.

...erformance was the theme for Buick's Wildcat Sprint in 1964. Note the ...ctangular headlights—a shape illegal in the United States at the time, ...d not used on production cars until years later.

Just the thing to attract young buyers' attention was the Pontiac LeMans Flamme of 1964, a special Firecracker Red convertible.

Rambler's Tarpon "dream car" aimed the youth market. A fastback styli study, the sporty compact hinted at t production Marlin that would come so to Rambler dealers.

Dodge's first Charger concept, in 1964, was a convertible. Note the strange, tall headrests. The Charger II, seen later, was a long fastback that evolved into a production Dodge model.

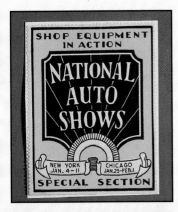

Throughout the early years of the auto show, and into the 1950s, special stamps and stickers were produced to commemorate the occasion. Those pictured span 1910 to 1954.

Official cars of the auto show needed to have an "official" license plate. This one was used in 1954.

...sitors to the 41st annual auto show got a ...ket like the one shown at top. Special passes ...re issued each year to employees and others ...ofessionally involved with the show.

Industry executives, auto dealers, and specially-invited guests might have been given season passes to the auto show.

Members of the Chicago Automobile Dealers Association got this window decal in 1956.

Show programs were issued even in the early years. These two were produced for the 1916 and 1920 auto shows. Both used the figure of Mercury holding a steering wheel—a theme of the show.

In the teens and Twenties, exotic and expensive automobiles appeared at a separate Salon, in one of the downtown Chicago hotels. Salons had their own souvenir catalogues.

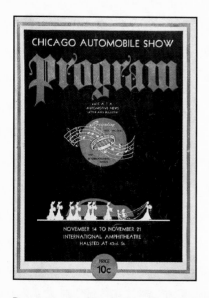

Program covers for auto shows from the late 1930s to mid-1950s ranged from straightforward to highly colorful and imaginative, sometimes imparting the flavor of that year's stage revue. No auto shows were held between November 1940 and January 1950—World War II and the immediate postwar years—when cars were in short supply.

The auto show moved into McCormick Place in 1961. Like each annual program in its era, the 1961 edition contained a floor plan, comments from show officials, ads for current models, and details about the "Motorevue."

This was a typical sight at the auto show each year. Here, a vendor is pushing 50-cent programs at the 1955 event. Programs gave details on the new car models, maps of the show floor, and rundowns on the stage revues—plus a few words from leaders of the Chicago Automobile Trade Association.

For the 1971 auto show, an all-new McCormick Place was ready, as pictured on the program cover.

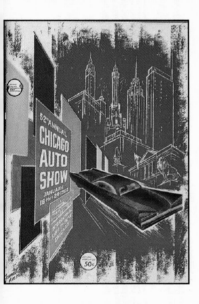

…rams pictured above and below span 1955 to 1998. Vendors enthusiastically sold programs at the entryways to each year's show.

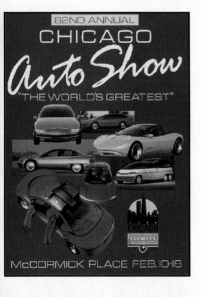

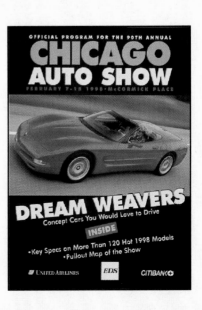

Exhibitors at the 19[10]
Chicago Automobi[le]
Show would have [worn]
this pin, featuring t[he]
mythical Mercury
symbol.

Exhibitors, dealers, journalists, and others were issued pins to wear during
the auto show. Pictured are pins used each year from 1950 through 1973.

A similar pin was
issued for the 1912
show, using the sam[e]
figure of Mercury.

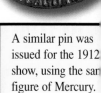

Not too many peop[le]
got to wear a
"Lifetime" pin for [the]
auto show.

Pins shown were issued for executives and other special visitors to the Chicago Auto Show from 1974 through 1998. Some were issued to political figures, including the Mayor of Chicago and Governor of Illinois.

Looks like this young fellow has been busy, picking up product literature at the various display areas of the 1960 show. His crown came from the Sirloin Room, a restaurant adjoining the Amphitheatre. Patrons typically snapped up hefty quantities of product brochures and giveaway items while wandering the show floor.

Product brochures, mixing hard facts and specifications with inducements to buy, wound up in the hands of hundreds of thousands of auto show visitors each year. Many manufacturers offered shopping bags to hold all that loot. Dealers, of course, hoped the giveaway items would help encourage prospects to stop in at a dealership later—and drive home a new car.

This plain-covered brochure was issued by Ford, exclusively for the 1956 Chicago Auto Show.

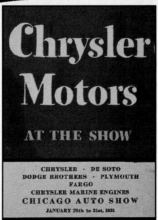

Chrysler Motors offered this brochure at the 1931 auto show.

In the teens and Twenties, some organizations issued their own directories of the autos. This 1925 edition was published by the *Free Press* newspaper.

...ing gowns were part of the "dress code" for young women participating in the 1959 auto show as "community and suburban queens." They appeared ...ge at the revue, along with professional performers.

Typical showgoers look over a 1960 Ford station wagon—a popular item in suburbia at the time. Not only did entire families visit the auto show, but until recent times it was common to wear Sunday clothes for the occasion.

...DeSoto name soon would disappear, but few of the folks who took in this 1960 display ...have guessed the car's fate. Most automobiles still had tailfins at this time.

Even automobile enthusiasts a lot older than this enthralled young gentleman, seen at the 1961 auto show, didn't know much about the components that went into the air-cooled, rear-engined Chevrolet Corvair.

To allay any fears that a compact car might lack sufficient storage space, Mercury displayed its 1961 Comet with a row of luggage that could supposedly fit into the trunk.

Seen at the Chicago Auto Show as a concept car, in 1961, the Corvette Stingray had a racing history and evolved into the production Sting Ray Corvettes of 1963.

Studebaker's exhibit area in 196? featured a Gran Turismo Hawk (foreground), compact Lark (left) and futuristic Avan? sport coupe (in enclosure). A year later, Studebaker moved from South Bend, Indiana, to Canada; and the marque expired in 1966.

Oldsmobile exhibited this J-TR F-85 roadster at the 1963 Chicago Auto Show. Note the stylishly simple white dress and matching shoes on the narrator. Neat attire was typical of the times—but women's fashions soon would undergo drastic change.

American Motors exhibited this AMX concept car in 1966, and it soon evolved into a production model.

This young woman in an evening gown, in the driver's seat of a Corvair, exemplifies what might be called the "prom look" in the early Sixties.

Formal gowns were the rule among presenters in the early Sixties. Shown is a Ford Sunliner convertible. Note the wide white-wall tires, still popular at the time.

This curiously helmeted woman didn't look quite human in 1966, at the Dodge truck exhibit area. Styles of women's clothing were changing fast by the mid-Sixties, with miniskirts coming on strong.

e Seventies, the auto show had adopted a more cosmopolitan look as nters of various racial and ethnic backgrounds took to the stage at manufac-e exhibits.
si

By the late Sixties and early Seventies, miniskirts and flamboyant colors were "in." This young woman's outfit closely matches the appearance of the special Dodge Yellowjacket.

Live animals—suggesting the company's Cougar and Bobcat models—were the main attractions at Lincoln-Mercury exhibits in the Seventies. Note the sign, which identifies sports celebrities scheduled to appear in 1978.

Chicago Mayor Jane Byrne was hard to miss when she toured the 1982 auto show, husband McMullen at her side. The man stepping ahead the mayoral group is Ross Kelsey, general manager of the show. To their rear is Joseph Bidro, CATA president and Ford dealer.

Mercedes-Benz models appeared on a banked section of track at the 1983 auto show, suggesting their competition heritage.

Entertainers took many forms at the auto show. This fellow twirled hoops with his feet for Nissan, in 1987.

...eryone passing by might have realized that a "prancing horse" was the ...of Ferrari, but they couldn't miss this golden-hued large-scale model ...1987 auto show.

Familiar Disney characters met with Robert Burger, former general manager of Chevrolet division, at the Chevrolet stand in 1989, to help promote the new Lumina APV minivan.

Every year at the show, visitors face a cornucopia of possibilities: cars, trucks, entertainment, and souvenirs.

Through the decade of the Eighties, a Vector supercar was promised but never went into production. Finally, prototypes appeared at the 1991 Chicago Auto Show. A handful were built for sale.

John Weinberger of Continental Motors was responsible for giving Chicagoans a chance to gaze upon the dramatic Bugatti EB112 at the 1995 show, just as he had a year earlier with the EB110. Production was supposed to begin, but the Bugatti company went into receivership.

Manufacturers would do just about anything to get attention, it seemed. This Ford Explorer "aquarium" was filled with water and fish in 1995.

For many years, the Sports Car Club of America exhibited special vehicles in the lobby outside the auto show floor. So did the Volo Auto Museum, wh truck is seen here at the 1996 auto show.

nd-new McCormick Place (South) was ready e for the 1997 Chicago Auto Show.

Vice-President Al Gore and the Russian Prime Minister toured the auto show floor on opening day in 1997, before the general public could enter. Seen on that occasion are (l-to-r): Prime Minister Viktor Chernomyrdin (with his interpreter), Gore, Mayor Richard M. Daley, Illinois Secretary of State George Ryan, and CATA leaders/dealers Patrick Fitzgibbon, Ray Scarpelli, and Lee Weinman.

hibits could go on one floor at the new McCormick Place building, opened in 1997.

used a dramatic light show to highlight its riced NSX sports car in 1997.

Chrysler President Robert Lutz donned a cook's uniform to introduce a Ram pickup with a third door—as well as a batch of concept cars—to the media prior to the opening of the 1997 auto show. The display looked like a genuine diner.

Welcome To CHICAGO AUTO SHOW

Everyone is welcome to attend the auto show, each and every year.

During the charity event for the 1998 auto show, Grand Prize winner J[?] Pollard won a new Corvette. Sharing in her excitement were auto show Chairman Ray Scarpelli (left) and Chevrolet General Manager John Middlebrook.

Motorcars weren't the only attractions at the Jaguar stand in 1998. This Jaguar Special Edition Beech King Air C90B airplane was said to be the first in a line of special planes to be marketed jointly by Jaguar Cars and Raytheon Aircraft.

The limited-edition Plymouth Prowler, bringing back memories of hot rods from the Fifties, was seen in a new color at the 1998 auto show: bright yellow—a true crowd-pleaser. Early Prowlers had all been painted purple.

A rock-climber edged up the wall to reach this Toyota at the 1998 auto show. Automakers always try to take advantage of the latest trends to attract audiences to a display.

Nothing quite like the Plymouth Satellite II, with its open front roof, ever went on sale. Narrators at the 1964 auto show told how Dodges and Plymouths were "taking all comers at the stock car racetracks."

Buick's Riviera concept of 1964 didn't look dramatically different from the stock Riviera, introduced a year earlier, apart from its lower stance. GM's renowned styling chief, Bill Mitchell, hung onto Riviera concepts for his own use.

e innovative sliding roof on a Studebaker Daytona agonaire made it possible to attach a camper top—an creasingly popular pickup-truck accessory in 1965. udebaker already had moved from Indiana to Ontario, nada, and would be out of the car business a year later.

Seen for the first time at the 1965 Chica[go] Auto Show, the Plymouth VIP was nea[rly] all glass from the beltline up, bisected [by] a longitudinal roll bar. Each glass sect[ion] retracted fully into the trunk. N[ew] photochromic glass darkened in brig[ht] sunlight. The console served as [a] traveling office and entertainment cent[er.] Officially dubbed XP-VIP, this car was o[ne] of the first concepts credited to Elwo[od] Engel, the recently-appointed head [of] Chrysler styling.

Visitors to the 1965 auto show had an opportunity to see a pre-production Ford Thunderbird Town Landau, months before the car went on sale. Opportunities to check out "coming soon" models, well ahead of their official debut date, helped draw large crowds to each year's show.

Oldsmobile didn't have to change [the] Cutlass 4-4-2 convertible much [to] turn it into a 1965 "dream ca[r."] Heavy-duty performance comp[o]nents were installed, the grille w[as] revised (front bumper deleted), a[nd] body-contoured "astronaut" se[ats] went inside.

An imitation tiger-skin interior highlighted this 1965 Pontiac GTO convertible, part of the GTO's "Tiger" theme. Tiger stripes decorated the seats, belts, and door trim, with fur-like carpeting below.

Introduced at the 1965 Chicago Auto Show, Chevrolet's "Surfer I" concept was displayed towing a race boat. The roadster-pickup was essentially a stock El Camino car-pickup, with its roof snipped off and various custom extras added. Mahogany paneling went on lower bodysides and the tailgate. No provision was made for a roof of any kind, but cleats could hold ropes or a cargo top.

re wheels and a half-padded roof e among the improvements to 1965 Ford Galaxie 500 LTD dtop sedan, to transform it into a d dream car.

195

Called a "design experiment...to te
public response," the 1966 AM
prototype had three-way seating and
cantilever roof—no front pillars. Unusu
fastback styling would evolve into
production AMX.

A vinyl-covered roof with blind
quarters decorated the 1966
Continental Coronation coupe.
Note the wide woodgrain band
along the lower bodyside,
framed in metal.

Ford called its 1966 toples
cut-down, one-of-a-kind sp
cial edition of the 4x4 Bron
the "Dune-Duster."

Ford's Fairlane GT A Go-Go helped call attention to its all-new intermediate model of 1966. Designed by the Corporate Projects Studio and constructed in California by customizer Gene Winfield, the "A Go-Go" featured such special accents as canted hood air intakes, a straight-bar grille, side trim ending in exhaust outlets, and a Sport Shift transmission.

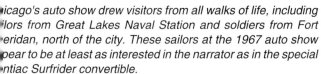

Chicago's auto show drew visitors from all walks of life, including sailors from Great Lakes Naval Station and soldiers from Fort Sheridan, north of the city. These sailors at the 1967 auto show appear to be at least as interested in the narrator as in the special Pontiac Surfrider convertible.

Above: Full-sized Fords still got custom treatment for display at the 1967 Chicago Auto Show, as this Interceptor two-door hardtop demonstrated. Based on the XL, it featured special grillework, covered headlights, air vents behind front wheels, built-in exhaust outlets—and no door handles.

Left: Dodge used a series of clever names in the Sixties to promote its performance image, from "Dodge Fever" to the "Scat Pack." This specially-built D-100 Scat Packer pickup truck drew notice at the 1968 Chicago Auto Show.

Built by the Alexander Brothers from a design by Harry Bradley, the 1968 Dodge Deora was essentially a reskin of the A-100 van. Features included a center-hinged front door and upward-lifting windshield.

Below: Oldsmobile named this modified 4-4-2 convertible Apollo, billed as "straight out of the space age." A 455-cid V-8 provided the power.

Metallic candy red leather upholstery with black suede accents went into the 1969 Olds Apollo. Four contoured bucket seats were patterned after space-capsule "couches."

Mercury displayed this Cyclone-based Super Spoiler, with a rakish cutdown windshield and not-so-functional spoiler, at the 1969 Chicago Auto Show. At the height of the "muscle car" era, concept cars tended—logically enough—to focus on performance. Mercury also wanted to promote its recent NASCAR victories.

ne of two production-based concept Fords attracting throngs at the 1969 auto show was the Super Cobra (left), based on the Fairlane ortsRoof hardtop. The car's top was lowered two inches, windshield swept back five degrees, and nose extended eight inches. A haker" hood scoop fed air to the Cobra Jet Ram Air V-8. A flatter, extended nose and lengthened roof pillars marked the Thunderbird turn II (right), which contained computerized trip control, travel monitors, a CB radio, and a portable tape recorder.

yone entering the 1969 Pontiac Cirrus concept car had to proach from the rear, aircraft-style. Taillights shined blue while ising and red while braking, an idea that some thought might come standard.

Duster I, exhibited at the 1969 Chicago Auto Show, was a high-performance concept based on Plymouth's Road Runner, featuring a Hemi engine, low curved windshield, and a shortened wheelbase. Big wheel openings accommodated giant H60x15 tires, and the built-in rollbar had adjustable-airflow spoilers. Production Dusters soon would go on sale. Note the short dress, strange hat, and go-go boots on the young woman.

Folding down the front seatback allowed access to the rear of Chrysler's massive Concept 70X, seen in 1969. Developed by Chrysler Research Styling, the stylized four-door featured parallelogram-hinged side doors and see-through mesh headrests. The center armrest doubled as a rear-facing child seat. An ultrasonic proximity warning device could show the presence of nearby vehicles, perhaps in the "blind spot."

A low center of gravity helped keep GM's Astro III stable. Exhibited at the 1969 auto show, it was considered a potential high-performance vehicle for restricted access highways. Astro III had a tricycle-type wheel layout, a rear-mounted Allison gas turbine engine, and rear-vision closed-circuit TV.

Above: Initially designed as the Firebird IV in 1964-65, Buick Century Cruiser of '69 seated fc and might be used for cruising on automated highways. An e trance canopy slid forward a up. Hand grips were used to ste manually. Inside were swivel co tour, semi-reclining seats.

Lincoln's topless Mark III dual-cowl phaeton of 1970 featured twin windscreens mounted atop front seatbacks. Front fenders were extended four inches from the standard model.

Chrysler first used the Cordoba name for a 1970 limited-edition model. The concept variant, named Cordoba de Oro (shown), was a design exercise by Chrysler's styling chief, Elwood Engel. Note the strong wedge profile. The cantilever roof had no A-pillars and the rear spoiler raised automatically.

...ght: A little vehicle could slip into ... rear of the Mercury Montego ...orts Hauler, exhibited at the 1971 ...o show.

...low: Buick's Riviera Silver Arrow III, ...played in 1972, featured a low roof-...e, plus high-level taillights above the ...ck glass. Triple beam, high-intensity ...adlamps had a special freeway ...am. A sensor in the mirror could de-...t bright light and switch to night non-...re position. Note the pillar inside the ...r quarter window.

Two decades before Ford issued its *Explorer* sport-utility vehicle, that name was used on a concept truck. Unveiled at the 1973 Chicago Auto Show, the low-profile *Explorer* was Ford's idea of a futuristic pickup that could be used for camping. A mid-mounted 429-cid V-8 provided the power, and a foldable tent was included.

7

Show Time—Extravaganzas and Promotions

Not until the Chicago Automobile Trade Association (CATA) took over the Chicago Auto Show in 1935 did the idea of an all-out annual extravaganza come into fruition. Entertainment had reared its head at previous shows, and the Coliseum had always been decorated lavishly, as for a festive occasion. On the whole, though, those earlier auto shows were down-to-business affairs, dedicated mainly to getting the publicity job done.

Unlike Europeans, who tended to prefer serious-minded auto shows, Americans—including Chicagoans—liked to be entertained. They loved a spectacle, having flocked to the Columbian Exposition back in 1893. They swarmed to the Century of Progress in 1933, and again in that fabulous exposition's second season.

Because the CATA had been involved in that 1933–34 world's fair, their executives doubtless took careful note of the teeming crowds—especially at the automotive displays. It seemed only natural, then, that auto-show organizers decided that their annual event needed to "go all the way" into showmanship. Looking over the latest crop of cars is serious business when you're contemplating a purchase, of course. But who ever said a person couldn't be entertained and informed at the same time?

Under the leadership of A.C. Faeh, successor to Samuel Miles as show manager, the Chicago Auto Show turned into a true extravaganza after the mid-1930s. Cars would continue to be the "stars," but each year's new models were presented to the public with a fanfare unheard of at past automotive events, in Chicago or elsewhere.

In the spirit of the times, attractive young women became an integral part of the show. First came the twice-daily parade of fur-bedecked women, helping to call attention to the '36 vehicles at the November 1935 auto show. Decorated with a "Hall of Stars" motif in rich blue and silver, the International Amphitheatre featured a huge central arena (238 x 150 feet), allowing plenty of space for stage revues. Promoters promised "brilliant and spectacular feats of showmanship...destined to make this pageant take its place as the supreme automobile show of them all." Adding to the emphasis on glamour, 40 attractive "usherettes" were selected and trained by Andy Frain.

Organizers immodestly advised that the 1936 show was "generally regarded by the public and the industry as by far

the most brilliant and successful ever held in Chicago [or] elsewhere throughout the United States." Show manag[er] A.C. Faeh noted that this "marked the first time that t[he] various makes of cars enjoyed the spotlight individually[,] presenting them one by one in an ensemble of beauti[ful] women and gorgeous fur styles."

A year later, the arena featured a "Brides of the Nation[s]" revue, focusing on Chicago as a "melting pot," with the '3[?] cars to be "glorified, as they well deserve, in an even mo[re] novel and daring manner."

Another revue theme came each year. "Fashions of t[he] World" for 1938 was followed by "An Age of Wheel Print[s]" (complete with a promenade of "nationality queens") an[d] "Dame Fashion" with a cast of 100. *Automobile Top[ics]* magazine described how the 1940 "automobiles monop[o]-lize the spotlight as they appear, one by one, by contra[st] with past shows which presented them with pretty girls ste[p]-ping out of the car. The beauties are to be seen in profusio[n] but they have other parts in the show." The Amphitheatre stage was the largest ever built in Chicago, equipped with [a] pair of electrically-controlled turntables to show off the veh[i]-cles. Offstage, visitors could get a look at something new—television.

Another stage spectacle, "Non-Stop America," dre[w] audiences twice daily in November 1940. Instead of ethn[ic]

Miss America of 1969, Judith Anne Ford, encouraged people [to] visit the auto show in this publicity photo for Oldsmobile.

ing women, this revue featured neighborhood and
urban "queens."

Stage revues continued with the revival of the auto show
1950. That year's "Wheels of Freedom" featured huge
ntings of Washington and Lincoln, as well as what one
gazine called "gorgeously gowned glamor girls" chosen
community queens. Through the Fifties and into the
ties, each year's show spotlighted a revue—even after the
ve to McCormick Place. Neighborhood "queens"
appeared after 1960, but attractive young women
nained part of the auto-show scene.

"They would play dramatic music as the cars came out,"
alls CATA President Jerry Cizek, "to keep the audience
erested.... But in between, there'd be acts. There'd be
ncers, there'd be jugglers." Cars sat in a staging area.
hey'd get so many cars in, then they'd have a little break.
en those cars left, the next batch of cars came in."

Even after the stage revues disappeared, a theatrical
nosphere continued to prevail. The entertainment simply
ved off the stage, and into the show-floor exhibits
mselves. Magicians, singers, dancers, gymnasts, skaters,
d sporting feats. If it was entertaining and drew crowds, it
bably appeared at the auto show.

Many of the same performers would appear year after
ar, Cizek recalls, such as "the guy who did tricks with the
per bags." Cizek even remembers hearing of a "truck
ed with a plastic liner, and somebody diving in it."

Chevrolet had its singers and dancers. Lincoln-Mercury
ariably trotted out a sports panel. Celebrities signed
tographs and chatted with the audience. Naturally, the
imate goal was to lure folks into the exhibit, to look over
cars—and perhaps buy one later on.

Jim Mateja of the *Chicago Tribune* notes that Dante the
agician, at Oldsmobile, issued a challenge that he could
:ape from anything: "If I don't get out, you win a car."
ery time, "Old Dante would get out."

This autographed photo of Walter Payton was obtained at the auto show. The Chicago Bears football great signed autographs and met fans year after year, in the Seventies and Eighties.

Mark Sweet gave a special performance of his magic act for blind youngsters, Mateja recalls. "He put on a great show," working free, early in the morning. At the booth of Harry "soft-touch" Ryba, "every kid got a box of fudge."

Sports celebrities gained a strong presence at the auto show during the Seventies and Eighties, comparable to their growing position as role models for young people. Some were already well known; others were on their way up. Mateja remembers Michael Jordan as "a quiet guy" during his first appearance as a Chevrolet spokesman, adding that visitors "basically bypassed this kid."

Each year's auto show echoed the flavor of its predecessors, but they changed with the times. Voluptuous models in low-cut gowns gave way to conventionally-dressed presenters who knew the facts about the cars. Attractive women still played a role; but for the most part, the scanty outfits faded away in the Eighties and Nineties.

Video replaced film strips. High-tech electronics emerged in manufacturer displays. Yet, the main purpose of the show never changed: to show off the cars in the most appealing and exciting way possible.

Paul Brian: broadcasting from the auto show

Known today as communications director of the CATA, Paul Brian has a long tie to the auto show. Growing up in Chicago, Paul visited each show with his father.

"Going to the auto show was a real big deal in our family," he explains, "not just a casual affair. They'd always yank us out of school for the day—my brother Bruce and me." The family would stop at the Pump Room downtown for a "memorable meal." Or possibly Fritzel's, or Old Heidelberg. "I remember seeing the Studebaker Super Hawk coming on stage and thinking it was the coolest thing on wheels."

In the Army in 1974, Paul was stationed at nearby Fort Sheridan, working in public relations and recruiting. He suggested getting something automotive, to draw attention. "How about a tank?" he asked. And that's what they

brought to the auto show. How did people react? "Oh, they loved it."

In the mid-Eighties, Paul was recruited by WGN and co-hosted the TV presentation from the auto show. He also broadcasted from the show floor, from the Chevrolet stand. Among his many on-the-air interviewees were Craig Breedlove, Jean Lindamood, and Brock Yates. "Most memorable" were Bob Sinclair (Saab) and Peter Schutz (Porsche). "They were genuine personalities ... genuine rogues."

In 1993, Paul got a call from Jerry Cizek. Soon, he was occupying an office at CATA headquarters.

"This is a fabulous palette to paint on," Paul says of his CATA job. He also hosts "Drive Time" on AM radio.

"Nationality Queens"

From the 1936 show to the 1940 show (in November 1939), each ethnic group in the Chicago area selected a representative to participate in the auto show as a "Nationality Queen." Contests were held in various city neighborhoods, where large numbers of people of a particular ethnic extraction had taken up residence. Chicago had long been known as one of the foremost "melting pot" cities, but new immigrants typically chose to live among people of similar background, speaking the same language. Chicagoans took pride in their heritage, and pageants using native costumes were not uncommon. So, it seemed only natural that a pageant might be initiated for the annual auto show.

Miss Ireland, Jill Riley, poses with a Cadillac at the auto show in November 1939.

Each young woman wore a costume reflecting her own heritage while participating in auto-show festivities. Though not considered strictly a "beauty contest," women were selected at least in part for the sort of "pulchritude" that was thought to be representative of their backgrounds.

Miss Poland, Genevieve Lawnicki, got drive a kiddie car in this publicity shot f the 40th annual Chicago Auto Show.

"Nationality Queen" at the 38th auto show (November 1937)

Miss Lithuania: Julia Kazlauskis Bartosch

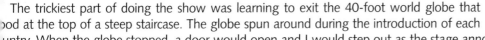

At the Chicago Auto Show to introduce the 1938 car models, Julia Kazlauskis was one of 19 young women chosen to represent specific ethnic groups. Now Mrs. Kazlauskis Bartosch, she was interviewed in her home in Chicago's western suburbs.

I'm of Lithuanian extraction. My parents read about the city-wide nationality contest in the Lithuanian newspaper. They entered my photo (left). I was 17 years old at the time, a petite 5'3". I graduated from Kelly High School in February 1936, at age 16. This was not a typical beauty contest, but went further in search for girls who best personified different ethnic heritages.

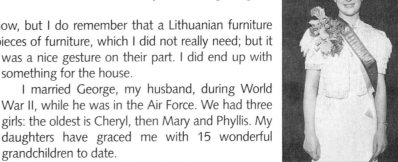

Mrs. Bartosch in 1998

When I was chosen as Miss Lithuania, the contest people presented me with a traditional Lithuanian outfit to wear during the show. I had to return it after the last performance, which was on November 13th—my eighteenth birthday.

The trickiest part of doing the show was learning to exit the 40-foot world globe that stood at the top of a steep staircase. The globe spun around during the introduction of each country. When the globe stopped, a door would open and I would step out as the stage announcer introduced me. Music would begin to play from the live orchestra as I gracefully descended the stairs in high heels. We were taught never to look down at our feet while we walked, and to always smile pleasantly toward the audience.

As I reached stage level, a car drove up onto the stage. Mine was a Ford convertible during the run of the show. After entering the vehicle, I was chauffeured around the arena so everyone could get a good look at the latest Ford, while I waved to the crowd.

We were not paid any money for doing the show, but I do remember that a Lithuanian furniture company, which sponsored me, offered some nice pieces of furniture, which I did not really need; but it was a nice gesture on their part. I did end up with something for the house.

I married George, my husband, during World War II, while he was in the Air Force. We had three girls: the oldest is Cheryl, then Mary and Phyllis. My daughters have graced me with 15 wonderful grandchildren to date.

The show seems like a hundred years ago. When I look at these photos I can't remember being that young, but I can honestly say that I have only fond memories of being a "queen" during the Chicago Auto Show.

Above: Julia Kazlauskis (middle) is wearing a crown of Rue—a parsley-like plant. "Lithuanian custom," she says, is "that when you wore Rue in your hair it signified you were a maiden." The girl at right is a professional model who appeared onstage, and whose gown was "created to represent a modern adaptation of the historic outfit that I wore" in the "Fashions of the World" pageant. The third girl was part of a fur show that ran in conjunction with the auto show.

For the first several years of the stag[e] revues, Philip Cavallo Senior (show[n]) served as musical director, along wi[th] Philip Cavallo Junior.

Performers wore big hoop skirts on stage in the "Dame Fashion" revue at the auto show in November 1939.

Lucille O'Connor (left) and Donna Laron served as "page girls" at the "Dame Fashion" revue in November 1939.

A patriotic theme was suggested by this group of costumed performers—logic[ally] enough, since World War II was looming.

Left: Each year, stage-revue developers needed to come up with new ideas, themes—and costumes. These outfits for the 1954 show appear to have originated with Flash Gordon or Buck Rogers.

Below Right: Clowns and other individual entertainers appeared on stage between automobile introductions. This fellow with his little car—a popular act at circuses and carnivals—is seen at the 1953 show.

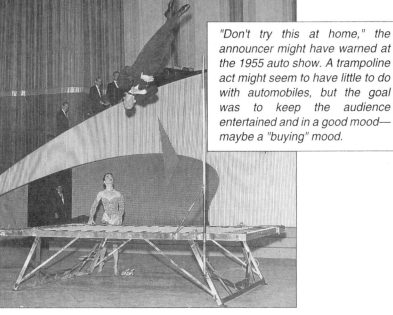

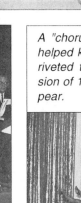

A "chorus line" of high-kicking dancers helped keep the attention of showgoers riveted to the stage—where a succession of 1960 car models soon would appear.

the 1964 auto show, orchestra leader ou Breese entertains with a banjo solo.

"Don't try this at home," the announcer might have warned at the 1955 auto show. A trampoline act might seem to have little to do with automobiles, but the goal was to keep the audience entertained and in a good mood—maybe a "buying" mood.

crobats were among the separate acts mployed for the "Motorevue" each year. This oup performed at the 1952 auto show.

Neighborhood and Community "Beauty Queens"

Left: Finalists in the Garfield Park group for the 1951 "community queen" contest pose with an auto-show poster.

Right: Each young woman had to endure a session before the judges, before selection as a "community queen." This woman is shown running that gauntlet prior to the 1952 auto show, judged by a select committee that included choreographer Dorothy Hild as well as show executives.

"Community queens" wore evening gowns during the stage revue. Note the turntable, which would rotate to reveal all the contours of each car, including this 1956 Rambler station wagon.

Community "Beauty Queens"

June Marie (O'Connell) Platenka
Miss Berwyn-Cicero (1954)

At the 1954 Chicago Auto Show, June Marie O'Connell was one of twenty "community queens" who appeared on stage to help introduce the new car models. We interviewed Mrs. Platenka in her suburban Chicago home.

My parents wanted me to enter the pageant. They sent in the pictures and filled out forms. I was 19 years old at the time, and had graduated from Jay Morton East High School, Cicero, Illinois, in 1952.

The first step after entering was to attend an event at the Palmer House Hotel, where the twenty queens were chosen from the entries. I was picked as Miss Berwyn-Cicero (top center, photo at left).

At the time I was entered into the contest, I was attending Morton College. Even though I was an A and B student, I had a hard time convincing the school Dean to let me take a week off.

Next stop, we were sent to Carson Pirie Scott department store. A wardrobe mistress took each queen and found an appropriate gown that best complimented her, and then had shoes dyed to match. I ended up with a pastel pink strapless gown. We were able to keep the outfit when the show ended.

About a week before the show, we began dress rehearsal at the International Amphitheatre. We had to dress in a long, narrow dressing room located high up in the building.

The routine was to enter our assigned cars waiting in a narrow passageway, and be driven onto the show stage by a chauffeur. I was in a butterscotch and white Pontiac Catalina two-door hardtop. While live music played, the stage announcer introduced me and the car as it came on stage. The car stopped halfway and a tall, handsome usher (right—Jack Gallagher: see page 9) opened the door and I would exit gracefully.

I remember that we would then stand alongside the car for several minutes. The car would then be driven off-stage, and I would walk up a tiered grandstand stairway to join the other queens who came before me. We all stood and smiled while the next car and queen came onstage. When all twenty queens and vehicles were presented, we then left the stage together, amid more music and applause.

On the last night of the show, as we exited the car, the usher handed us a large bouquet of roses. That day, March 21, was my 20th birthday.

We appeared at both afternoon and evening shows, and would stroll around the Amphitheatre between shows. During one afternoon, I met Ronald Reagan (left), who was the show marshal. I asked Mr. Reagan if I could have my dad take our picture together, with my trusty Argus C3 camera. He said okay, and while my dad was adjusting the camera, four or five other queens jumped into the picture.

I introduced one of my brothers, Jack, to Miss Uptown—Maria Schank (top left, in top photo)—and they dated for about two years. We were provided dinner each night at the Stock Yard Inn restaurant, and we received $10 a day to appear. I was so excited about doing the auto show that I almost forgot to go pick up my check.

Appearing as Miss Berwyn-Cicero was an exciting time for me. It was so profitable, not in money or gowns, but in the richness of the experience, the friendships and camaraderie between the various queens, and the wonderful memories of those days.

Mrs. (O'Connell) Platenka today, with husband Melvin.

Max and Cherie, seen here onstage at the 1961 auto show, called their imaginative dance act "Head On Collision."

A highly-publicized attraction at the 1973 auto show was a "live hood ornamer kneeling on a Dodge Charger.

Gymnasts performed at the Nissan exhibit area in 1987.

If clowns were popular, clowns tossing souvenirs into the audience were better yet. This tall fellow prepared a supply of twisted balloons for eager onlookers in 1963.

Dancers entertained at many exhibits over the years. This "Street He group performed at the Chevrolet stand in 1985.

210

Each year at the auto show, drivers could renew their licenses the Illinois Secretary of State's booth. Seen here is the 1991 exhibit. The City of Chicago and Chicago Police Department also set up booths at the show, often promoting safety issues.

Looking at this kid-size Chevy Jr. might be fun, but a lucky youngster got to take the gasoline-powered car home in 1967.

Oldsmobile put a sculptor/designer to work right at the show in 1976, creating a futuristic automobile in clay.

Auto-show visitors who were too young to drive—yet—could be tempted by driving simulators in 1969.

Freddie Ford, a likable robot, appeared at the Ford exhibit for several years—this time in 1970. Made of Ford parts, Freddie could see, hear, and answer questions, giving a spiel to promote a Ford vehicle.

Above: *Auto-show exhibitors tried to capitalize on trends. Slot-car races were popular among youngsters in 1962.*

FAMOUS SPOKESPERSONS

Spokespersons for Oldsmobile in the early Fifties were "Lucille and Johnny" (actually, Jean Ruth and William Lechner), seen in this publicity photo with a Classic 98 Holiday coupe.

TV star Jack Webb appeared at the 1955 auto show. Note the number on the license plate, which was the badge number of Detective Joe Friday, the character played by Webb on "Dragnet."

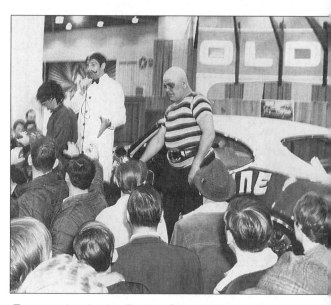

Zany mad scientist Doctor Oldsmobile and his henchma Elephant Engine Ernie, brought their humorous skit to the flo of the Chicago Auto Show in 1969.

Joan Parker was "Miss Dodge Fever" in 1968, at the height of Dodge's high-performance era. Looks like she had quite an enthusiastic group of fans.

NASCAR driver Cale Yarborough appeared at the Mercu stand during the 1968 auto show.

Chicago Bulls superstar Michael Jordan, seen at the 1991 auto show, served as a spokesperson for Chevrolet products.

Miss America of 1960, Lynda Lee Mead, greets visitors at the Oldsmobile booth.

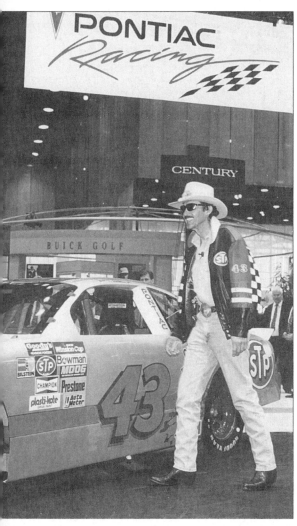

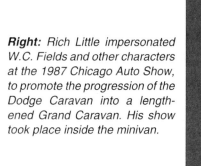

Right: Rich Little impersonated W.C. Fields and other characters at the 1987 Chicago Auto Show, to promote the progression of the Dodge Caravan into a lengthened Grand Caravan. His show took place inside the minivan.

NASCAR legend Richard Petty turned up at the 1996 auto show to help unveil the redesigned Pontiac Grand Prix. Sports, auto-racing, and Hollywood celebrities visited the auto show.

Actor Jack Palance (left) helped launch the Ford PowerForce concept truck at the media preview for the 1997 Chicago Auto Show, assisted by Ford Division General Manager Ross Roberts. Some celebrities have appeared only at media events, while others remained available during public days at the show.

8
Toned Down for the Duration
(1974-83)

Many Americans thought nothing would ever interfere with their enjoyment of the automobile. They were mistaken. By 1974, considerable change already had occurred, and more was imminent.

Governmental regulations played a major role in the changes taking place. Pollution laws led to stringent tightening of exhaust emissions and other noxious offshoots of the motorcar. Safety regulations also came into play.

Even though engines shrunk and lost their vigor, Detroit (and the still-growing import brands) managed to create plenty of distinctive automobiles each season, to tempt auto-show visitors.

At show time in 1974, the OPEC oil embargo remained in force. Gasoline lines were the rule. Rationing had not occurred, but tempers grew short when gas stations limited sales to a few gallons—and more so when less-patient motorists tried to get to the pump without waiting their turns.

Fuel shortages notwithstanding, more than 928,000 visitors passed through the gates at McCormick Place to see the 1974 Chicago Auto Show. Quite an impressive turnout, under the circumstances.

Airbags were something new to study. About to go into several thousand General Motors models, airbags were displayed at the Oldsmobile stand—but it's safe to assume that interest was less than brisk. Safety features were not yet integrated into the public mind.

Installation of seatbelt interlocks, for instance—which prevented engines from starting until occupants were belted—brought grumbles of protest from motorists across the nation. Seatbelt buzzers, which sounded an annoying warning until the belt was buckled, drew no applause, either. Even those who were ardent advocates of driving while belted failed to appreciate being forced into buckling up by an aggravating device.

Despite the growing trend toward lackluster vehicles, several imported brands took a back seat to no one with their dash and dazzle. The Citroën SM and Maserati Bora, for instance, as well as Ford's Capri and Pantera, rose far above the pack. Judged by striking vehicles of this caliber, one could easily believe that nothing of a negative nature was happening in the industry.

On the other hand, 1974 was the year when Ford abandoned the traditional Mustang and launched a tame Mustang II, shrunken in size and devoid of V-8 power. Chicago did not yet require emissions testing, but free pollution tests were given not far from McCormick Place, for drivers who wondered if their cars could pass muster.

Attendance rose in 1975, as a collection of stylish compact cars made their debuts. Ford launched the Granada, with its Mercedes-like grille; Mercury, the closely related Monarch. Chrysler introduced the Cordoba, hiring Ricardo Montalban—he of the smooth Latin voice—to promote the car. Before long, just about everyone seemed to pronouncing that name—Cor-DOH-Bah—in varying-quality imitations of Mr. Montalban's passionately rhythmic utterances.

American Motors had a brand-new vehicle on the market, too: the Pacer. Consumers failed to respond in droves to its curious shape and uninspiring performance.

Honda, on the other hand, was demonstrating its leadership in responding directly to governmental challenges. Instead of complaining that it would be difficult, if not impossible, to meet ever-tightening emissions standards, Honda developed the CVCC stratified-charged engine as one potential answer to the pollution problem. Most likely, though, the number of auto-show patrons who spent time with the live cougars and sports figures at the Mercury Cougar display area overshadowed those who studied the workings of the CVCC engine.

American-built convertibles made their final appearance in 1976, in the form of the Cadillac Eldorado. Ragtops would return again, but not until 1982. Many consumers though

Fuel economy suddenly became crucial in the Seventies, prompting consumers to take a new interest in minicars. Not many frugal models were in the Big Three picture, so they turned to imports, such as this 1977 Plymouth Arrow (built by Mitsubishi in Japan).

fety regulations were about to outlaw convertibles, but that dn't happen. Instead, soft-tops were simply victims of unging sales.

Attendance set a record in 1976—again. More than 51,000 folks got a look at some 650 vehicles, as well as a election of entertainment. Dodge, for example, brought in a i team to perform, as well as Nancy del Corral, billed as a motorized" mannequin. Seen at the Dodge display more an once, Ms. del Corral performed with mechanized ovements and an expressionless face, after challenging nlookers to make her "lose it" and start laughing or grinning. e didn't. Dante the magician, meanwhile, went through his pertoire at the Ford stand.

Pontiac chose the 1976 Chicago show to make the official ebut of its limited-edition Trans Am, painted in black and old. Technology exhibits ranged from Ford's stratified-charge ngine to Chrysler's turbine car and GM's Electric Pedestrian lover. Vans were big in the Chicago area, and Ford had a itaway version for people to study.

How did Chicago's show stack up in America's centennial year? Clint Mahlke, manager of Ford's display, ld the *Chicago Tribune* that the Chicago show not only was e biggest, but the "most comfortable, where people stay nger." A typical show tour took nearly four hours.

What? Another record? Sure enough, attendance neared 70,000 at the 1977 show, which featured a big display of ckup trucks and campers. General Motors downsized its big rs this year, setting the stage for a shrunken automotive orld. Sporty cars weren't extinct, though, as Chevrolet unched its revived Camaro Z28 at the Chicago show and ntiac revealed a Can Am sport coupe.

Most of the 600 vehicles at the 1978 show were smaller d lighter than before, led by downsized mid-size models m GM. Choices this year stretched all the way from the tle new Ford Fiesta to neo-classic Stutz and Clenet replicars, ith massive price tags.

Oldsmobile's familiar V-8 engine was transformed into a esel—an unwise move for GM, as it turned out, because the esel developed serious reliability problems. Americans turned vay from diesels after that fiasco, even though other types d not suffer such troubles.

Chevrolet had issued a rear-drive subcompact Chevette in 976, but Chrysler went the next step in '78, turning out a ir of front-wheel-drive subcompacts: the Dodge Omni and ymouth Horizon.

In the past, presenters at the manufacturers' displays had een expected to look nice, but not necessarily have a orking knowledge of the vehicle they were promoting. That as beginning to change. Subaru, for one, insisted that its esenters be dressed in regular street wear and be fully aware the cars' merits. Scantily-dressed young women did not sappear, but little by little over the next decade their imbers would dwindle, edged aside by women in business serious casual attire.

Ford abandoned the Mustang II after 1978, creating a ew—and bigger—Mustang for the following season. In fact, 979 was quite a good year for new and redesigned models, cluding the Buick Riviera, Cadillac Eldorado, and Oldsmobile ronado; a downsized Ford LTD sedan; and sporty little

Dodge Omni 024/Plymouth Horizon TC3 coupe offshoots of Chrysler Corporation's subcompact sedans. One of this year's concept cars, the Mercury XM, even had a rumble seat—a feature not seen on production models for decades.

Another fuel crisis erupted during 1979—not as severe as the 1973-74 shortage, but serious enough to send consumers' tempers flaring. Faced with possible bankruptcy, Chrysler Chairman Lee Iacocca petitioned the federal government for a massive loan to keep the company afloat. He got it, too.

Close to 700 vehicles showed up for the 1980 Chicago Auto Show, including several electrics. General Motors had launched a fresh crop of compacts as early '80 models, but those highly-touted X-cars soon suffered a rash of recalls and complaints from consumers, never quite recovering from that tarnished reputation.

Disco dance clubs remained active around the nation, but the Chevrolet exhibit featured disco *skaters*. Ford and Oldsmobile relied on robots to entertain the customers.

Manufacturers assembled another group of entertainers for the 1981 auto show, helping to set another attendance record. More than 700 vehicles vied for attention, drawing onlookers with the assistance of sports celebrities, dancers, magicians, and ventriloquists.

As for the cars themselves, Ford had its new front-drive subcompact Escort ready. Chrysler Corporation issued a pair of front-drive compacts: the Dodge Aries and Plymouth Reliant. Before long, that platform would serve as the basis for a whole string of Chrysler-built passenger cars.

Not only could visitors to the Chevrolet stand at the 1982 auto show have a chance to win a Celebrity sedan—new that year—but they could watch a magician, juggler, and dancers while scrutinizing the new models. Chrysler Corporation had a Dodge 400 available, not to give away but to be used for a year. Robots were nothing new at the auto show, but Peugeot's exhibit featured mechanical creatures who actually "drove" cars, at the French company's test facility.

For many, the most exciting event of the 1982 automotive year was the return of the convertible, after a six-season absence. Chrysler led the way with its LeBaron and related Dodge 400, along with the lavish but short-lived Buick Riviera. Chrysler's ragtops initially were converted from coupes by an outside company; but a few years later, the company would begin producing its own convertibles. Ford came next with a convertible Mustang, issued in 1983. Chevrolet and Pontiac issued convertibles of their own that year, in subcompact size.

After years of hesitation, consumers were taking a greater interest in cars again. Auto-show attendance set yet another record in 1983, topping 979,000. Presenters at the Ford stand now wore business suits, instead of more revealing garb— certainly more serious in nature, if disappointing to some gentlemen in the crowd. Patrons at the show got to see Ford's new compacts, the Tempo and Topaz, well ahead of their on-sale date as '84 models.

Gymnasts performed at the Nissan stand, while celebrities—from stock-car legend Richard Petty to TV star David Hasselhoff—signed autographs elsewhere on the show floor. Excitement was returning to the American auto scene; and as usual, Chicagoland folks got to see much of the revived action first.

1974
66th annual Chicago Automobile Show
(February 23–March 3, 1974)

- 928,112 guests visit auto show
- Showgoers can see Ford's Capri and Pantera, Citroën SM, Maserati Bora, Lotus Europa Special, Ferrari Dino, Jensen-Healey, and rotary-engined Mazda
- In auto-show program, Jim Mateja notes importance of big cars, Dan Jedlicka writes of the politics of safety and ecology, and Cliff Bielby talks of RVs
- Visitors learn how airbag works—and sounds—at Oldsmobile exhibit
- Chevrolet exhibits two experimental rotary/mid-engined Corvettes ... 1974-1/2 models are in "Spirit of America" colors
- Datsun shows 260Z 2+2 for first time in U.S. ... also 1937 Datsun roadster
- Peugeot debuts two diesel cars
- British Leyland has tiny commuter car
- Buick displays Opel Diplomat show car
- Pontiac exhibits Banshee dream car
- Antique car exhibit and daredevil team help entertain auto-show guests
- Ford Mustang II debuts ... display also has Mustang-based Sportiva roadster, talking robot, Ghia-designed Mustella
- Toyota has Experimental Safety Vehicle and futuristic F101 sedan
- New interlocks prevent engines from starting until seatbelts are fastened
- "Muscle car" era makes its last gasp
- City of Chicago gives free pollution tests near McCormick Place
- OPEC oil embargo is lifted in March

Pontiac introduced an "All American" edition of its Grand Am for 1974. Note the vertical louvers over rear quarter windows.

Chevrolet displayed a trio of specially-decorated "Spirit of America" cars at the 1974 auto show: a Nova (shown), Vega, and Impala. Each was painted in red, white, and blue.

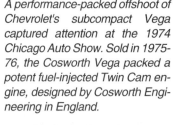

A performance-packed offshoot of Chevrolet's subcompact Vega captured attention at the 1974 Chicago Auto Show. Sold in 1975-76, the Cosworth Vega packed a potent fuel-injected Twin Cam engine, designed by Cosworth Engineering in England.

After issuing a decade's worth of potent and popular Mustangs, Ford turned to a smaller, lighter Mustang II for 1974. No more V-8 engines were available, but the Mustang II could at least get a V-6 instead of the standard four-cylinder.

216

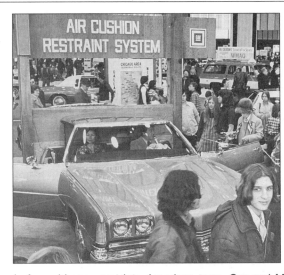

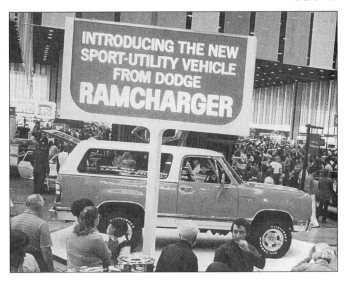

Long before airbags went into American cars, General Motors experimented with the idea. Several thousand primitive airbags, dubbed the Air Cushion Restraint System, went into mid-1970s Oldsmobiles, starting with the Toronado.

Was Dodge the first to use the term "sport-utility vehicle?" Could be, since that phrase went on a sign promoting the Dodge Ramcharger at the 1974 auto show.

Through the Seventies, Maserati sent a modest number of Merak coupes into the U.S. market, powered by a mid-mounted V-6 engine with a five-speed gearbox. Powertrains and other details were similar to the Citroën SM.

In addition to open roadsters, Fiat now offered the tiny two-passenger Targa-roofed X1/9, with a mid-mounted engine. Were these gentlemen in the front row more interested in the Fiat, or the short-skirted presenter?

Ford is credited with improving the 1973-74 version of the DeTomaso Pantera (left), powered by a 351-cid V-8 and styled largely by Tom Tjaarda at the Ghia studio in Italy. Lincoln-Mercury dealers marketed the European-built Capri coupe (right).

1975

67th annual Chicago Automobile Show

(February 22–March 2, 1975)

- McCormick Place sees 943,924 visitors to auto show during its 9-day run
- More than 550 vehicles are exhibited
- Auto show has full lineup of compacts
- Lincoln-Mercury introduces pair of small cars at Chicago show: Bobcat and '76 Capri II—seen for first time in U.S.
- Ford launches Granada and Mercury Monarch ... Granada display lets visitors participate in videotaping of "ads"
- New vehicles at Chicago show include AMC Pacer, Triumph TR7, and Mercedes-Benz 450 SE
- Visitors can see cutaways of Chevrolet Nova and AMC Pacer
- Honda exhibits Civic CVCC with stratified-charge engine
- Dodge Silver Duster is displayed—follow-up to Gold Duster
- Two live Cougars—and sports celebs—are seen at Mercury Cougar XR-7 area
- Mercedes-Benz ESV-24 Experimental Safety Vehicle makes its U.S. debut
- Antique and competition vehicles exhibited by Sports Car Club of America
- Chrysler introduces Cordoba—far smaller than prior models ... actor Ricardo Montalban will serve as spokesman

A Buick Century Custom coupe paced the 1975 Indianapolis 500 race in May—but visitors to the auto show got to see it first. Limited-edition replicas went on sale, painted red, white, and blue.

Ford launched the luxury compact Granada for 1975, borrowing a few styling touches from Mercedes-Benz. Soon, it became Ford's top-selling model.

Above: *Mayor Richard J. Daley (left) and two associates visited the auto show in 1975. Here, they're studying the rear hatch of an AMC Pacer X. Late in 1975, the Mayor suffered a sudden heart attack and passed away.*

Below: *AMC (American Motors) launched the Pacer this year, with styling unlike anything else on the road. Billed as "the first wide small car," the Pacer was originally planned to use a Wankel rotary engine, but got a conventional six-cylinder engine instead.*

Offered as a hatchback (left) and a station wagon (right), Bobcat was Mercury's new version of the Ford Pinto, which had been around for several seasons.

By the mid-Seventies, the automotive world was changing fast. Big V-8 engines hung on a while, but in detuned form to meet tightening regulations. But that didn't deter car fans from visiting the auto show each winter.

Convertibles wouldn't be around much longer, from U.S. manufacturers. This Cadillac Eldorado stickered for $10,354, and was one of just five domestically-built ragtops on the market—all from General Motors. A year later, Cadillac would be the only one; and then it, too, would be gone.

Triumph introduced the wedge-profiled TR7 for 1975, the latest member of a long series of British-built "TR" sports cars. Instead of an open roadster, as before, the TR7 was a closed coupe.

A new engine was the big news from Honda in 1975: the CVCC (Compound Vortex Controlled Combustion) four-cylinder, with an extra spark plug and intake valve for each cylinder. Operating with a leaner mixture than usual, the CVCC engine promised greatly improved emissions.

1976
68th annual Chicago Automobile Show
(February 21–29, 1976)

- Record attendance: 961,677 visitors see auto show at McCormick Place
- Show features more than 650 vehicles
- Buick exhibit is a simulated TV newsroom ... AMC exhibits 15 "Great Americans" in life-size paintings
- Buick shows Century pace car ... Japanese-built Opel (Isuzu-built) debuts
- GM displays Electric Pedestrian Mover ... Ford, a stratified-charge engine ... Chrysler, a turbine car and engine
- Dodge exhibits XS-22 dream car
- Ski team performs at Dodge ... Nancy del Corral, "motorized" mannequin, challenges spectators to "break up her act"
- Simulated Italian villa promotes Plymouth Volare
- New Jaguar XJ-S seen for first time in Chicago ... 4 Datsuns make U.S. debuts
- International shows two new models
- Limited-edition Pontiac Trans Am, in black/gold, is unveiled at Chicago show
- Chevrolet has experimental Monza Super Spyder II ... Ford shows Ghia Flashback sports car
- Gina "kit car" debuts at Chicago show
- Dante, the magician, performs at Ford display
- Showgoers are surveyed about the future of the automobile
- America's last convertible (for a while), the Cadillac Eldorado, enters final season
- Subcompact Chevette goes on sale
- Mayor Daley dies on December 20, 1975

A simulated Italian villa was the setting for Plymouth's revived Road Runner, based on the Volare that was to debut in mid-1976. Volare was a near-twin of the Dodge Aspen, and this Road Runner was merely an option group.

Fans of "Starsky & Hutch" on TV could drive home a Ford Torino with this special paint job, based on the characters' vehicle.

Chevrolet tilted up the body of a compact Monza to reveal its engine and chassis.

Based on the Nova but unknown to most modern-day enthusiasts, a limited-edition Chevrolet Shark 1 went on sale this year.

A third generation of Datsun's Z-car debuted late in the 1975 model year; the 280Z, with a bigger, newly fuel-injected six-cylinder engine. Its predecessor, the 260Z, had lasted less than two seasons.

Below: The Italian-built Lancia returned to the U.S. market in 1976, in two forms: front-drive Beta and mid-engine, rear-drive Scorpion.

Oldsmobile introduced the GMO in mid-1976 as a regional special. "GMO" stood for "Gallant Men of Olds," the company's theme at the time.

No Capris were imported from Germany or Great Britain in 1975, but by '76 the sport coupe was back, with four-cylinder or V-6 power, as the Capri II.

Dodge set up a ski jump in its display area, which drew big crowds. Stage revues hadn't been seen for years, but manufacturers took up the slack, providing mini-extravaganzas of their own.

1977

69th annual Chicago Automobile Show

(February 26–March 6, 1977)

- Attendance sets another record: 969,837 visitors to auto show
- More than 600 vehicles are exhibited
- Japan leads in number of import makes displayed at show
- Show includes biggest-ever display of trucks and campers
- Datsun displays four new models at show, including 200SX sport coupe
- GM downsizes its full-size cars
- Volkswagen unveils diesel Rabbit
- Chevrolet exhibit includes new Caprice Landau, Monza Mirage, Nova Rally, and Camaro Z28—revived for mid-year debut
- Experimental Corvette Mulsanne on view
- Chrysler revives LeBaron nameplate
- Dodge Diplomat goes on sale this year
- Ford unveils Thunderbird Town Landau and shows off new Continental Mark V ... sporty mid-year versions of Pinto Runabout and LTD II are on display, too
- Spectators at Ford exhibit can make a TV commercial, see replicas of "Charlie's Angels" autos—and win $20 if they spot someone wearing a certain lapel patch
- Oldsmobile shows Delta 88 Royale that will pace the Indianapolis 500 race
- Pontiac unveils LeMans Can Am sport coupe and new Phoenix
- Three-wheeled Phantom coupe debuts
- Topless International Scout is displayed
- Five Volvo "safety cars" seen at show
- Walter Payton hands out autographed photos at Buick area ... other Chicago Bears players appear at GMC Truck
- Sports-car display moves to lobby—a result of show expansion
- Christopher cougar and Rick-O-Shay bobcat are at Lincoln-Mercury exhibit

Chevrolet exhibited its about-to-be-revived Camaro Z28 for the first time at the 1977 Chicago Auto Show. The high-performance "ponycar" was a mid-season addition to the Chevrolet lineup.

Manufacturers often used the Chicago Auto Show as a launch pad for mid-season models, and those coming in the following season. Chrysler revived the old LeBaron name on a mid-size coupe and sedan. Based on the Dodge Aspen/Plymouth Volare, the LeBaron sold well.

***Left:** McCormick Place had something for everyone each auto-show season, from colorful sport machines to plain station wagons to ever-so-practical trucks.*

An Oldsmobile Delta 88 Royale coupe with a unique removable roof was selected to pace the Indianapolis 500 race in late May. But first, it made an appearance at the Chicago Auto Show.

222

Introduced in 1976, Sunbird was Pontiac's version of the subcompact coupe and sedan, related to the Chevrolet Monza and available with a sporty Formula option package (shown).

For mid-1977, Ford introduced a "T-top convertible" version of the Mustang II.

Porsche exhibited the drivetrain of its front-engine 924 at the auto show. A 2.0-liter overhead-cam four-cylinder engine up front drove a rear-mounted transaxle. Until 1977, all production Porsches had rear-mounted, air-cooled engines.

Yes, that's a porthole mounted at the rear of the Ford Pinto Runabout, which also featured distinctive side glass and colorful striping.

The Milwaukee-based Excalibur company displayed its Series III SS Phaeton with the top down, and also with the soft roof in closed position.

1978

70th annual Chicago Automobile Show

(February 25–March 5, 1978)

- 966,349 visitors see auto show at McCormick Place
- In auto-show program, columnist Jim Mateja advises visitors to study the cars; Dan Jedlicka offers automotive dictionary
- Cars are smaller and lighter this year
- More than 600 vehicles are exhibited, including revived Stutz, Panther, Avanti II, Hurst, and little Ford Fiesta
- $40,000 neo-classic Clenet replicar seen
- 440-cid V-8 available for last time in Chryslers ... Oldsmobile offers diesel V-8 engine, as does Cadillac Seville
- Ford Futura sport coupe debuts, as part of new-for-1978 Fairmont line
- Ford exhibit features $10,000 Diamond Jubilee Thunderbird, plus four "idea cars" including Megastar and Corrida
- Chrysler introduces subcompact front-drive Dodge Omni/Plymouth Horizon, aided by space people from "planet Omni"
- Mid-size Dodge Magnum goes on sale
- Chevrolet has split Sportvan: street-van interior on one side, workshop on other
- Mid-size GM cars are downsized
- Oldsmobile introduces Starfire Firenza, Holiday 88 coupe, and sport-painted Cutlass Supreme as mid-season models
- Buick has 75th-anniversary Riviera, plus turbocharged V-6 engine display
- Toyota has all-new Cressida sedan
- Experimental Mercedes-Benz C-111 diesel sports car appears at Chicago show
- Pontiac unveils Trans Am Type K van/wagon prototype at Chicago show
- Auto-show displays feature electronic puppet, twin cougars, games for prizes
- Speakers for Subaru and some other makes no longer wear skimpy costumes, and are expected to know car facts
- Admission is $2 ($1 for children)
- Members of "Little People of America" get in free, courtesy of Chrysler Corp.
- Lee Iacocca is fired from Ford, moves to top post at Chrysler Corp.
- Volkswagen begins to produce Rabbits in the U.S.

Dodge used a pair of space-suited presenters from the planet "Omni" to extol the virtues of its all-new Omni—America's first front-drive subcompact. Plymouth's Horizon differed little.

Mercury exhibited a new Zephyr Z-7, close kin to the Ford Fairmont Futura. Note the distinctive side-window design.

Anyone might walk into a Chevrolet dealership in 1978 and order a "Black Sterling," billed as a "designer's version" of the new Malibu Classic.

Spotting a Dodge Magnum on the street wasn't difficult—not with that bold slat-style grille leading the way. A 400-cid V-8 was available in 1978, but a 318-cid engine was standard.

Ford introduced the LTD II in 1977, evolved from the prior Torino. Note the unusual two-tone paint treatment.

Painted in black and gold, the special Jeep Honcho featured a rollbar in the pickup bed. Honcho was an option group for the short-wheelbase version of the J-10 Jeep pickup truck.

Mercedes-Benz exhibited this futuristic, bright orange C-111 sport coupe at the 1978 Chicago Auto Show, equipped with a turbocharged five-cylinder diesel engine. The experimental car had averaged 156.5 mph for 10,000 miles, setting three world records.

Borrowing a legendary name (but nothing else) from the distant past, the limited-production Stutz Blackhawk featured big headlamps, a small classic-style grille, and an exposed exhaust pipe. Virgil Exner, Chrysler's former design chief, earns credit for the styling, which is not unlike the short-lived 1966 Duesenberg revival.

1979
71st annual Chicago Automobile Show
(February 24–March 4, 1979)

- McCormick Place sees 964,288 visitors to auto show during its 9-day run
- In auto-show program, Jim Mateja writes about diesels; Dan Jedlicka outlines cold-weather driving techniques
- Chrysler-Plymouth holds drawing for scaled-down Plymouth Volare wagon, used by Herve Villechaize, aka "Tattoo" on TV's "Fantasy Island" series
- Toyota unveils Celica Supra at show
- Police exhibit vandalized automobile
- WGN-TV again broadcasts from auto show, hosted by "Hee Haw Honeys"
- AMC introduces new Spirit model
- Ford Mustang is redesigned—will pace Indianapolis 500 race in May
- Pontiac displays four "idea cars," plus 10th-anniversary Trans Am
- Chevrolet exhibit features W.C. Fields impersonator ... Dodge has Don "Big Daddy" Garlits
- Concept cars include Mercury XM with rumble seat, Ford Fiesta Tuareg off-roader, and Ford Megastar II
- New-for-1979 cars include Buick Riviera, Oldsmobile Toronado, Cadillac Eldorado, Ford LTD, Mercury Marquis and Capri, Chrysler New Yorker and Newport, Dodge St. Regis, and Dodge Omni 024/Plymouth Horizon TC3
- California Custom Coach exhibits four-door Corvette ... Aston Martin has Volante convertible ... DOME-1 hails from Japan

Redesigned in 1977, the Continental Mark V came with a "Collector Series" option group this year, including a color-keyed umbrella and leather-bound owner's manual. Even with a hefty $13,067 sticker, close to 76,000 went to customers.

Buick introduced a wholly redesigned Riviera for 1979, downsized and switched to front-wheel drive. A turbocharged V-6 engine was available.

Oldsmobile often teamed with the Hurst company to create special performance vehicles. At the 1979 auto show, this Hurst/Olds W30 Cutlass Calais went on display, with a four-barrel 350-cid V-8, special black/gold or white/gold paint, and a sport console with a Hurst floor shifter.

Chrysler brought back the "300" designation on a 1979 model, related to the Dodge Magnum. Actually a Cordoba option group, it featured a cross-hair grille, bucket seats, and 360-cid V-8 engine. This 300 would last only a single season.

rd redesigned the Mustang for 1979—bigger and more powerful than the 1974-78 Mustang II. A Mustang was signed to ace the Indianapolis 500 race.

After Studebaker expired in 1966, Newman & Altman in South Bend, Indiana, had continued to produce an updated version of the Avanti—dubbed Avanti II. Through the Seventies, the Avanti II remained available (and appeared at the auto show), though selling little more than a hundred copies annually.

o one had an opportunity to buy a four-door Corvette, but hevrolet had one to gaze at in 1979. Not everyone cared for the oncept of adding a back seat to "America's sports car."

Created in Japan by an independent company, the Dome-1 attracted attention at the Chicago Auto Show, but the name never reappeared.

ubaru DL station wagons (left) came in front-drive or four-wheel rive. Subaru also offered the oddly-named BRAT pickup (right). RAT stood for Bi-drive Recreational All-Terrain Transporter.

Right: Visitors to the Chrysler-Plymouth display area could sign up for a chance to win "Tattoo's Fantasy Wagon." Manufacturers liked tie-ins to popular TV shows—in this case, "Fantasy Island," which featured a short-statured character named Tattoo (played by Herve Villechaize). Ricardo Montalban, Chrysler's spokesman for many years, also appeared in the series.

1980

72nd annual Chicago Automobile Show

(February 23–March 2, 1980)

- 946,215 visitors see auto show at McCormick Place
- Auto show adds floor space: 600,000 square feet, featuring about 700 vehicles
- Specialty cars this year include Berlina coupe, Guanci SJS-1, Arntz Cobra, Clenet, 1920s-style Creighton, Commuter Electric, Lectric Leopard, Cabriolet Cadillac, and Excalibur Series V Phaeton
- GM promotes front-drive compact X-cars, led by Chevrolet Citation
- AMC introduces four-wheel-drive Eagle
- "Bustleback" Cadillac Seville debuts
- Ford Thunderbird is downsized ... exhibit includes Mustang IMSA concept
- Chrysler shows Poly Car, in attempt to make plastics more acceptable
- Cadillac V-8 uses digital fuel injection ... new Fleetwood Brougham coupe seen
- Miniature Oldsmobile Omega with gasoline engine is given away each day
- Datsun shows three mid-year cars, including 10th-anniversary 280ZX
- Ford has Fiesta GTK, billed as station wagon of the future
- Disco skaters perform at Chevrolet
- Robots entertain audiences at Ford and Oldsmobile exhibits
- International puts turbo engine into 4WD Scout ... also offers 5-year/100,000-mile warranty
- Plymouth promotes Turismo Spyder two-seater, to gauge consumer reaction
- Volkswagen shows new Jetta—on sale in late spring
- Dodge exhibits Mirada Magnum show car
- Mercury displays Antser electric car
- Average new car gets 21 mpg, versus 13.9 mpg in 1974

A turbocharged V-6 engine went into Pontiac's Turbo Trans Am, which was selected to pace the 1980 Indianapolis 500 race.

AMC (American Motors) turned to something different for 1980: a four-wheel-drive passenger car, named the Eagle. Eagles came in sedan and station-wagon form.

Trucks were displayed on the lower level of McCormick Place, named for the late Colonel Robert McCormick, long-time publisher of the Chicago Tribune.

Quality and safety problems soon would surface, but when GM introduced its X-cars as early-1980 models, they drew praise from many quarters—and were even named Motor Trend "Car of the Year." Chevrolet's Citation (shown), was closely related to the Buick Skylark, Pontiac Phoenix, and Oldsmobile Omega. At left (partly hidden by a pillar) is the sporty Citation X-11.

me cars warranted presentation by a formally-attired narrator. *edesigned dramatically for 1980, Cadillac's Seville featured a "ustleback" rear end. Reminiscent of some old Rolls-Royce *dies, Seville drew high praise as well as criticism. Standard *gine was a diesel V-8, which proved troublesome.*

Dodge had a sporty new Omni 024 coupe (left) on the market. The DeTomaso edition (right) was actually a $1,575 option package including bright red or yellow paint, a black lower body, spoilers, sport suspension, and rear-quarter louvers.

*t everyone realized it, but for a while, the Italian Fiat company so controlled Ferrari. Seen on a single platform at the 1980 *to show were a targa-roofed Lancia Zagato coupe (front), *errari 308 GTS (center), and Fiat Spider 2000 roadster (rear).*

Quite a few battery-powered vehicles edged into the marketplace in the Seventies and early Eighties, including the Lectric Leopard.

Powered by a transverse mid-mounted V-8 engine, the seldom-seen Guanci wore a fiberglass body—and a $5,400 price. Planned production totaled only 50 cars per year.

1981
73rd annual Chicago Automobile Show
(February 21–March 1, 1981)

- McCormick Place draws record 974,129 visitors to auto show during its 9-day run
- More than 700 vehicles exhibited in two halls—675,000 square feet in all
- Manufacturer exhibits include dancers, magicians, ventriloquists, sports celebs—plus live animals
- 26 import makes are from five nations
- Plymouth exhibits Reliant-based prototype convertible—planned for 1982
- Specialty cars include Zimmer, Griffith, Excalibur, Clenet, Lotus, Maserati
- Krueger electric is seen ... so is Valiente fiberglass roadster
- Furor erupts as battery-powered car is denied permission to exhibit ... civil rights groups then picket McCormick Place
- In auto-show program, Jim Mateja notes that all cars are economy cars; Dan Jedlicka explains difficulty of car-making
- Dodge Aries and Plymouth Reliant debut near-twin front-drive compacts
- Ford promotes new subcompact Escort, unveils Ford EXP and Mercury LN7 two-seater offshoots
- Disgruntled motorists can punch gas pump at Chrysler exhibit
- Buick exhibits Regal that will pace the Indianapolis 500 race on Memorial Day
- Pontiac promotes mini-size T1000 ... Datsun introduces turbocharged 280ZX
- Concept Fords include two-seat Super Gnat, Mustang RSK, and subcompact Montana Lobo 4x4 with bubble doors
- Auto-show exhibits include replica of 1929 gas station

Chrysler Corporation launched its front-drive compact K-cars for 1981: the Dodge Aries and similar Plymouth Reliant (shown). Motor Trend named the K-car its "Car of the Year." Starting at $5,880, they were billed as the most frugal six-passenger U.S. cars on the market.

Illinois State Representative Josea Williams (right) confers with Edmund X. Ramire. Sr., president of Amectran—claimed to be the only minority-owned car manufactur ing plant in the United States in 1981. Ramirez's prototype battery-powered Ekar wa: banned from the auto show, due to alleged financial irregularities with the company—but reinstated later in the week, after the threat of civil rights protests.

Ford introduced the EXP, a two-passenger offshoot of the Escort, as a 1982 model. Visitors to the 1981 auto show got an early peek. Mercury's LN7 was similar.

Stage revues had disappeared years earlier, but manufacturer continued to provide plenty of entertainment at their own displa areas. Here, women in western garb perform at the Chevrole stand.

1982
74th annual Chicago Automobile Show
(February 27–March 7, 1982)

- 970,383 car fans visit the auto show at McCormick Place
- In auto-show program, Dan Jedlicka reports on driver attitudes; Jim Mateja notes the return of style in cars
- Auto-show exhibits include stainless-steel DeLorean—but company soon sinks into receivership
- Chevrolet Camaro and Pontiac Firebird adopt new downsized form ... Z28 Camaro will pace Indianapolis 500
- Showgoers with fat wallets can study Aston Martin Lagonda saloon (sedan) and Rolls-Royce Silver Spirit
- Chrysler's Stealth concept sports car evolved from Plymouth TC3 ... concept limousine rides on stretched K-car platform
- Spectators can compete to win use of a Dodge 400 for a year
- Lincoln-Mercury shows "Commcar," a Continental set up for communications, as well as aerodynamic Concept 90
- Oldsmobile debuts subcompact Firenza
- Chevrolet has magicians, dancers, and juggler—gives away Celebrity sedan, too
- Peugeot exhibits robots that "drive" cars
- GM previews experimental, unnamed economy car, said to achieve 60 mpg
- Convertibles are back: Chrysler unveils LeBaron and Dodge 400 for mid-year debut, and Buick displays open Riviera
- In his *Tribune* column, Jim Mateja notes abandonment of carnival mood at show
- GM promotes its new series of subcompacts, led by Chevrolet Cavalier, plus A-body sedans including Celebrity

John Z. DeLorean, one-time head of Chevrolet, launched his own company to produce the DeLorean sports car. Introduced in 1981, the DeLorean—produced in Northern Ireland—had a stainless steel body.

Chrysler Corporation took the lead in reviving convertibles, issuing an open Chrysler LeBaron at mid-season, followed by a similar Dodge 400 (shown). Auto-show visitors had an opportunity to look over both ragtops, though the Dodge was not yet in production. Both cars were converted from steel-roofed coupes by Cars and Concepts, a Michigan conversion firm.

Major car manufacturers inevitably occupied the upper level of McCormick Place.

Chevrolet redesigned the Camaro for 1982, while Pontiac undertook comparable action with its Firebird. The new Camaro was nearly 10 inches shorter and 500 pounds lighter, with an all-coil suspension—and for the first time, a standard four-cylinder engine. The compound-curved backlight served as a hatch.

Mercury offered a cousin to the Ford Mustang, named Capri. By 1982, the strongest engine available under Mustang/Capri hoods was a "high-output" 302-cid (5.0-liter) V-8, developing 157 horsepower. Note the T-bar roof on this example—plus the sign promising rebates. Incentives to sell cars had begun to appear in the Seventies.

Aston Martin, of Britain, marketed a handful of Lagonda saloons (sedans) in the United States, blending posh luxury with vigorous V-8 performance. A Lagonda stickered for $150,000 and buyers of limited-production machines couldn't expect much of a discount. Over a 15-year period, only 645 were built.

Volkswagen offered a selection of models, including the Quantum coupe (right, on pedestal) and a Rabbit-based pickup truck (left). Performance leader was the sporty Scirocco.

Few would guess that the underpinnings of a costly ($59,500) Zimmer Golden Spirit, sporting neo-classic bodywork, came from an ordinary Ford product. Zimmers were produced in Pompano Beach, Florida, starting in 1980.

Sportiest Toyota on the block continued to be the Celica coupe. This year's version, enjoying a major restyle, is shown in ST trim.

1983
75th annual Chicago Automobile Show
(February 26–March 6, 1983)

- Attendance sets yet another record: 979,346 visitors to auto show ... industry leaders see signs of sales recovery
- Showgoers get to see next-generation Corvette—but only its chassis
- 1984 Ford Tempo and Mercury Topaz are displayed to public for the first time
- "Showgirls" wear business suits, not scanty attire, at Ford exhibit
- Chrysler gives showgoers "sneak peek" at '84 sports car
- Ford issues Mustang convertible
- Chevrolet puts ragtop Cavalier on sale, and Pontiac launches open Sunbird
- New-for-1983 models include Ford Thunderbird, Mercury Cougar, Ford Bronco II, Ford LTD/Mercury Marquis, Chrysler New Yorker and LeBaron Town & Country convertible, Renault Alliance
- Prototype of Dodge convertible with rumble seat is seen—will not be built ... prototypes of Chrysler Laser and Dodge Daytona are destined for production
- Toyota exhibits Camry, replacing rear-drive Corona ... Mazda launches 626
- Special exhibits include antique cars (from 1927 fire engine to Kaiser Dragon to Pontiac GTO), dragsters, "funny cars," and SCCA's Can Am racing collection
- Celebrities on hand include Natalie Carroll ("the Firebird girl"), David Hasselhoff (with "Knight Rider" Pontiac), and NASCAR legend Richard Petty
- Gymnasts perform at Nissan display
- Concept vehicles include Buick Questor, Ford Probe IV, Continental Concept 100, and Nissan NRV II research vehicle

Visitors to McCormick Place needed only to glance at the show-floor carpeting to realize this was the auto show's 75th anniversary.

Mid-1983 brought the revival of the Monte Carlo SS, a "muscle car" from the past. Sporting a fresh nose, heavy-duty suspension, and bold body graphics, the SS carried a 180-horsepower, 305-cid V-8 engine.

Mercedes-Benz's 380 series, with 3.8-liter V-8 engines, consisted of (r-to-l): the 380SEC coupe, 380SL roadster, and 380SEL sedan.

hrysler Corporation gave auto-show guests a close look at two sporty models, due for 1984: the Dodge Daytona (left) and related hrysler Laser (right). Both models could get a turbocharged engine, but Dodges sold a lot better.

Beneath the surface, Cadillac's Cimarron was essentially the same as a modestly-priced Chevrolet Cavalier. Only a four-cylinder engine was available in 1982-84 models.

Chrysler stretched the wheelbase of its familiar K-cars (Dodge Aries/Plymouth Reliant) to create an Executive sedan and longer-yet Limo (pictured).

Ford described the next-generation '83 Thunderbird as a "dramatic new balance of form and function." Stunningly aero-shaped, the T-bird came with a V-6 or V-8 engine—and at mid-year, as a Turbo Coupe.

Through the years, Buick had turned out a number of high-performance models. In 1983, it was the Grand National, a bold variant of the Regal with a turbocharged V-6 engine.

Long after other automakers had abandoned any thought of using a rotary engine, Mazda continued to install one in its RX-7 sports car.

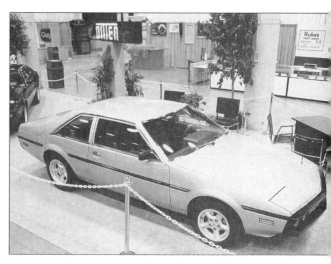

Built in Germany, a Bitter appeared at the 1983 Chicago Auto Show but did not go on sale until a later date. The make did not last long in the U.S. marketplace. The Bitter SC Coupe of the early Eighties used an Opel six-cylinder engine.

Jim Mateja: Covering the auto show for close to three decades

Working as the automotive writer for the Chicago Tribune *since 1970, James (Jim) Mateja has become one of the most respected auto journalists in the nation. We interviewed Mr. Mateja at the* Tribune *office in Vernon Hills, Illinois, northwest of Chicago.*

Jim Mateja joined the staff of the *Chicago Tribune* in September 1967, after college—but not to write about automobiles. Up to that point, in fact, Jim had never even *attended* an auto show. Instead, he handled financial news and served as a copy editor.

In 1970, he was assigned to the car beat, replacing John McDonnell. First assignment: the General Motors strike.

His initial opportunity to cover the Chicago Auto Show came in 1971—the first show at the new McCormick Place. That assignment was "kind of overwhelming," Mateja recalls, "because it was so damn big." The "first Sunday, that first weekend, it was just overrun with people." It was like "being thrown into the fire pretty fast." There was a "lot of competition at the time," and all four major Chicago daily papers sent someone to the show each day.

"Small cars dominated" that 1971 event, he notes. "Small was 'in.' You didn't see a lot of big cars....

"Back then, Chicago was *the* auto show," he explains. Detroit's annual show "wasn't really worth going to." Even Detroiters headed over to Chicago.

"Everybody that was going to show off a new car for spring" launched it at Chicago. "You'd get a lot of executives over here ... a lot of engineering types and designers," plus "contingents from Japan." They were "like bees swarming to honey" at the Chicago show, which was considered "neutral ground" for auto-industry people.

"Spring was right around the corner" when the auto show came to town, he adds. People looked at the "old beater" and began to wonder. "The timing of the show was just perfect."

In "those early days, there'd be a lot of families" at the auto show. "It was a picnic," an event that could "relieve your cabin fever."

Mateja first ran into the late Mayor Richard J. Daley at the 1971 auto show. The mayor's "bodyguards wouldn't let me get anywhere near the man [and] I had basically given up." But then, "he walked into me" while getting out of a convertible. "The mayor was always nice.... He was really a people person."

"Those were the years when a car buyer didn't buy a truck," Mateja explains. "People didn't even bother to go downstairs to look at trucks.

"The show has reflected what was going on at the time," Mateja believes. In the year of the oil embargo, for instance, a man brought in 10,000 locking gas caps, because it was "common for people to get siphoned." He sold them all in short order.

Curious events dot Mateja's recollections. At one time, Ford Chairman Donald Peterson didn't like the tires on the display cars. All of them were changed. At one Lincoln-Mercury exhibit, a man locked himself inside a car, refusing to get out. That incident prompted automakers to keep spare keys on hand.

During Friday preview night at one 1970s show, Fiat gave out magazines with a favorable story about their product. Soon, preview visitors realized it was a "girlie" magazine. "Mom was livid," Mateja recalls.

Also in the Seventies, Plymouth gave out "little metal clickers" on Preview night, to promote the Cricket. "All you'd hear were these crickets. It was mind-boggling. Clickers never made it to the actual show."

As chairman of Chrysler, Lee Iacocca came to Chicago once, to look at rival minivans. "When he walked in the door," Mateja recalls, "the show stopped."

Naturally, Jim met many celebrities, from Walter Payton and Michael Jordan to "Mean Mary Jean." The "guy that was really weird was the Lone Ranger," Mateja advises. Actor Clayton Moore "thought he *was* the Lone Ranger. He didn't like interviews [and] would not show himself out of costume."

Mateja believes "the show served as a great barometer." Observers could "pretty much tell what the mood was going to be that year. It never fails." To predict that 1998 would be a good year, all you had to do was watch the crowds around costly sport-utility vehicles. "The show is used to read the public mind."

Jim Mateja in the late Nineties, formally attired for the annual "First Look for Charity" event.

235

9

Revival of the Industry
(1984-95)

By the middle of the Eighties, a revival of excitement in automobiles already was evident. Convertibles were back, for one thing, led by Chrysler's LeBaron (and the related Dodge 400/600), along with the Ford Mustang, Chevrolet Cavalier, and Pontiac Sunbird. Even American Motors had a convertible: the Renault Alliance.

Engine outputs, too, were beginning to escalate again—slowly. Modern, efficient powerplants emitted far fewer pollutants than their ancestors of the Seventies, yet were able to deliver greater go-power. Engines of the Eighties yielded low emissions levels without resorting to the power-sapping add-on devices that had hampered prior models.

Revival of enthusiasm could be seen in auto-show attendance figures, too. Another record was set in 1984, as close to 989,000 visitors flooded through the gates at McCormick Place East. Among the patrons was Chrysler Chairman Lee Iacocca, in Chicago to survey the rear-drive minivan prototypes from competitive manufacturers—namely, the Ford Aerostar and Chevrolet Astro. Chrysler had its new front-wheel-drive minivans ready for sale this year: the Dodge Caravan and Plymouth Voyager, soon to set the pace in the growing minivan market.

If anyone had any doubt that sportiness was returning with a vengeance, a stroll through the '84 show floor would quickly dispel that notion. Chevrolet had its redesigned Corvette on display, having skipped the 1983 model year completely. Pontiac had a new mid-engined Fiero two-seater; Honda, a tiny two-passenger CRX. Nissan transformed its 280ZX sports car into a new 300ZX, while Ford showed a high-performance SVO offshoot of the Mustang.

Entertainment wasn't overlooked, of course. A pair of talking robots at the Dodge exhibit area were made to resemble Horace and John, the original Dodge Brothers from back in the teens. Plymouth employed a troupe of mimes to show off its Voyager "Magic Wagon."

Although most cars still looked rather boxy, Ford had another idea in the works. At the 1985 Chicago Auto Show, Ford unveiled the brand-new Taurus and its Mercury Sable sibling—aerodynamically-shaped sedans that would soon alter automotive styling practices almost across the board. A rousing performance by the multi-talented Ben Vereen at the Sable stand helped to draw interest.

Sports celebrities made their customary appearances, including the Chicago Bears' Walter Payton. Entertainers ranged from "Street Heat" Dancers at Chevrolet to a magician at Oldsmobile, to gymnasts promoting Nissans, to break-dancers somehow hinting at merits of GMC trucks.

Not much had been heard about airbags since the few thousand that were installed in GM cars in the mid-Seventies, but at the 1985 auto show, Mercedes-Benz demonstrated how they worked. Ford sold a handful of compact Tempo/Topaz sedans with airbags, mainly to fleet buyers, but they wouldn't go into general use for a few more seasons.

At the 1986 show, Pontiac displayed a concept Trans Sport minivan, remarkably similar to the slanted-snout GM minivans that would go on the market for 1990. Chevrolet meanwhile, flaunted a production convertible version of its Corvette—the first since 1975. Volkswagen installed a hotter 16-valve engine in its Scirocco coupe, in an attempt to capture a segment of the youth market.

Oprah Winfrey, not yet a TV super-superstar, appeared at the Dodge stand in 1986, while players from the Chicago Bears team showed up at Chevrolet. American Motors nearly on its last legs in the marketplace, dressed its presenters in western garb for the auto-show occasion.

Mid-year models had long been a fixture at the Chicago Auto Show—partly because it took place in late winter, and partly because it was inevitably considered the "selling" show. The mid-season crop of 1987 included a curvaceously restyled Chrysler LeBaron convertible, a sleek two-passenger Cadillac Allante (shipped from Italy, no less), and the Chevrolet Beretta coupe.

Chrysler had a new pair of subcompacts for 1987, named Dodge Shadow and Plymouth Sundance. Ford and Pontiac both brought out imported, Korean-built minicars.

Chrysler led the drive toward minivan popularity in the late Eighties and early Nineties. Pictured at the 1992 auto show is Plymouth Voyager, with its sliding door open.

he Festiva and LeMans, respectively. Showgoers could also lance at the tiny Yugo, built in Yugoslavia and issued during 86, promoted as the cheapest car in America.

Excitement was generated before the 1988 auto show ven opened. Former American Motors workers staged a rotest at the Drake Hotel, where media previews were nderway. The UAW workers were not pleased with hrysler's decision to close the Kenosha, Wisconsin, plant, fter taking over the fading AMC company during 1987.

Chrysler's new Jeep-Eagle division, evolved from that MC takeover, released a new subcompact Eagle Summit at he 1988 show, along with a larger Premier sedan. Sport-oupe fans got a look at the new Ford Probe.

Close, closer—but never all the way. Auto-show ttendance set a record again in 1989, but still fell short of he million mark: 990,858 visitors, to be precise. Star of the how might have been the Mazda Miata, a stunning two-eat sports car, loosely based on an old British Lotus model. On sale by spring of 1989, Miatas managed to induce avid hoppers to pay thousands of dollars above sticker price to e among the first to put one in the garage.

At the upper end of the sports-car spectrum, Acura used he Chicago show to unveil its aluminum-bodied NSX two-eater. Volkswagen had a sporty new Corrado on tap, ready o oust the Scirocco. Corvette fans got a gander at the ZR-1, acking a brand-new engine that made the regular orvette's V-8 seem almost a milquetoast.

Not too many concept cars wind up on showroom oors—at least not without drastic toning-down. That was efinitely not the fate of the burly Dodge Viper R/T 10, xhibited at the Chicago show in 1989. Overwhelmingly avorable public reaction helped induce Chrysler executives o put the muscular roadster, V-10 engine and all, into mited production a couple of years afterward.

Two brand-new makes could be seen at the 1989 show: exus and Infiniti, from the new luxury divisions of Toyota nd Nissan, respectively. Both were to go on sale as 1990 nodels. Subaru's new Legacy sedan was the first model of hat make to be built in the United States—a growing trend.

Safety got even more emphasis at the 1990 auto show. udi and Chrysler had airbag demonstrations, while Mercedes-Benz explained traction control. Cadillac showed n Aurora concept with a navigation system.

Buick's Bolero concept suggested the 1992 Skylark, ccompanied by a video that showed how the car was built. Iissan had a Gobi truck concept; Pontiac, a Sunfire with rear alf-doors; Chevrolet, a Geo California Concept Storm. leadlamps on the Ford Ghia Via used fiber-optic echnology. Chrysler's Voyager III showed how two vehicles night merge into one, some day in the future. Showgoers lso could see the new Chevrolet Caprice and Impala, the uick Park Avenue, and the Dodge Stealth.

In 1991, several names appeared on concept vehicles hat would later identify production cars. Mercury had a Mystique minivan; Ford, a Contour; Chrysler, a Neon with a wo-stroke engine. Several companies, in fact, showed two-trokes, believing they might fit into the near-future.

Pontiac's ProtoSport 4 "idea car" of 1991 suggested the ossibility of a four-door Firebird. Chevrolet's Monte Carlo redicted the next-generation Lumina. Showgoers got an early peek at the 1992 Ford Crown Victoria and Mercury Grand Marquis, as well as the Buick LeSabre, Pontiac Bonneville, and Oldsmobile Eighty-Eight. Judging by that list, big cars were making a serious comeback.

Sporty cars dominated the 1992 show, but electrics made an impact, too. BMW displayed an E2 Electric concept. Ford's Ghia Connecta also was electric-powered.

Acura had an FS-X aluminum concept car, Buick exhibited a Sceptre sedan, and Chevrolet had five different concepts of its Geo Tracker—plus a Corvette Sting Ray III show car. Lincoln's Marque X convertible predicted the coming-soon Mark VIII coupe. Chrysler displayed a Cirrus concept; Dodge, an electric EPIC minivan. Honda's EP-X blended sportiness with fuel-efficiency. Toyota offered an Avalon concept; Pontiac, a California-inspired Salsa in fluorescent orange. Oldsmobile's Anthem was supposed to suggest the Cutlass Supreme replacement for 1996.

Among production models, Dodge finally had a Viper on sale, while Ferrari showed a 512TR, successor to the Testarossa. Chicago debuts included a Toyota Camry station wagon and Mazda 626 sedan. Saturn showed off its station wagon, scheduled for release that fall. Ford unveiled its redesigned Probe. New this year was an Allstate Auto Safety Show, with crash-test dummies Vince and Larry offering advice on airbags and seatbelts.

Few would deny that the Plymouth Prowler, shaped like a Fifties street rod, was the big hit of the 1993 show. Fewer still believed it would ever see production. (Four years later, it did.) Hyundai's Scoupe convertible never went beyond the concept stage, but the HCD-II evolved into the Tiburon. Dodge displayed its 1994 Ram van, GMC its '94 Sonoma pickup truck, and Mazda a redesigned B-Series pickup. Showgoers could take home a toy model of the Volkswagen Eurovan. The Illinois Secretary of State's office set up a "Future Access" display, to show how high-tech methods might make license applications more efficient.

At the 1994 show, Buick used a product presentation theater to promote the new '95 Riviera. Ford teased auto-show audiences with its Profile concept—said to suggest the coming-soon Contour. Lincoln's Contempra concept foretold the '95 Continental. As their names suggest, the Dodge Venom and Chrysler Expresso concepts could hardly have been more different. Chevrolet's "TechnaVision" booth promised to take visitors on a "magic carpet ride" through a Monte Carlo.

Official debuts at Chicago included the Toyota Avalon, Mercury Mystique, Pontiac Firebird convertible, 1995 Chevrolet Blazer, and '95 Mitsubishi Eclipse/Eagle Talon.

Another grand batch of concepts turned up at the 1995 show, from the high-performance Ford GT90 to an Acura CL-X and potent Ford SHO-Star van. Oldsmobile showed the Antares, said to suggest a Cutlass Supreme successor. Ford's Triton predicted the next-generation F-150 pickup truck.

Once again, Chrysler had a lush bunch of dream cars. Just a glance at the Atlantic sedan revealed that modern Chrysler stylists had built on the legacy of the Exner years.

McCormick Place had seen a lot of change. Now, an all-new exposition center was in the works, and the "old" building had just one more season to host the auto show.

1984
76th annual Chicago Automobile Show
(February 11–19, 1984)

- Attendance sets another record, as 988,766 visitors see auto show at McCormick Place
- Chevrolet unveils Astro minivan prototype at auto show, and holds public clinic
- Ford exhibits Aerostar minivan prototype
- Chrysler Chairman Lee Iacocca visits auto show, studies rival automakers' rear-drive minivan prototypes as contrast to Chrysler's new front-drive minivans
- More than 700 vehicles are exhibited
- New sporty cars at show include Pontiac Fiero, Honda CRX, Nissan 300ZX, Ford Mustang SVO—plus the redesigned Corvette
- Chevrolet Cavalier Type 10 shown with special Chicago appearance package—an often-seen sales technique
- Ford displays Thunderbird that will pace PPG Indy Car World Series
- Concept vehicles include Mazda MX-02 with four-wheel steering, Nissan NX-21 (dubbed family car of the Nineties), Ford Ghia Barchetta convertible, mid-engined Toyota SV-3 prototype, Oldsmobile diesel Ciera ES, and Chevrolet's fiberglass Citation IV
- Plymouth Voyager "Magic Wagon" appears with performing mime troupe
- Talking robots featured at Dodge area—two look like the original Dodge brothers
- More cars come with turbo engines

Chicago Mayor Harold Washington (center) and Illinois Secretary of State Jim Edgar (left) cut the ribbon to open the 1984 auto show.

Right: *Pontiac's brand-new Fiero two-seater was selected to pace the Indianapolis 500 race in May 1984.*

Ford workers had their own exhibit at the auto show, featuring a cutaway LTD sedan.

Buick's stylish Riviera convertible served as Torch Relay Car for the 1984 Olympics. Produced from 1982-84, convertibles got a special heavy-duty suspension and power top, with quarter windows that lowered automatically.

The Alice Dysart Fantasy Players, a troupe of five mimes, performed on a stage within the Chrysler-Plymouth exhibit area. A magician helped demonstrate the ways to use the new Voyager's interior space.

Above: To help promote the all-new Plymouth Voyager, performers in a "Magic Wagon" demonstrated the minivan's potential for families.

Right: Honda introduced a two-passenger Civic CRX for 1984, borrowing mechanical components from the regular Civic sedan. Motor Trend magazine named CRX its "Import Car of the Year."

Left: Nissan introduced a 300ZX in 1984, to replace the 280ZX. Turbo power was available in the stylish sports car.

An all-new four-wheel-drive Jeep Cherokee and Wagoneer debuted for 1984, powered by four-cylinder or V-6 engines.

1985

77th annual Chicago Automobile Show

(February 9–17, 1985)

- McCormick Place gets 978,483 visitors
- Chevrolet's new subcompact Nova is unveiled at Chicago show—product of joint venture with Toyota Corolla
- Coming-soon Ford Taurus and Mercury Sable debut—destined to change shape of American cars ... singer/dancer/actor Ben Vereen appears at Mercury exhibit
- More than 700 vehicles are exhibited
- GM unveils N-body luxury compacts
- Special models include Bitter, Bertone, Maserati Biturbo, Ferrari Testarossa, Peugeot Quasar concept, and Concept Lotus with voice-activated controls
- Concept vehicles include Chevrolet Camaro GTZ, 4WD Ford Ghia Vignale, and Chevrolet Eurosport RS
- Toyota displays FX-1, a prototype for forthcoming Supra replacement
- Sports celebrities at show include Walter Payton (a perennial favorite) and Chicago Bears' Jim McMahon
- Break dancers entertain at GMC Truck
- Race driver Patty Moise demonstrates her Buick Regal
- Gymnasts perform at Nissan area
- Magician David Seebach entertains at Oldsmobile; 50,000 hats are given away
- Three models assemble new Pontiac Fiero GT body, every 90 minutes
- Mercedes-Benz deploys airbag at exhibit
- Chevrolet has magician Mark Sweet, Street Heat Dancers, and female drill team
- Ford sells first Tempo/Topaz models with driver-side airbags in 1985

Ford stunned the auto show with a pair of aerodynamic sedans, ready for introduction later in the year. Replacing the staid LTD, the Ford Taurus (top) helped send the company to the top of the sales charts. The Mercury Sable (above) was structurally identical, but offered more comfort/convenience features.

General Motors joined forces with Toyota to create a new subcompact Chevrolet Nova (shown) and a similar Toyota Corolla—both produced in California at a new plant. GM Chairman Roger Smith (third from left) posed with Toyota executives at the auto show.

Volkswagen tilted a Golf hatchback to a near-vertical position, to let auto-show visitors get a good look at its underside.

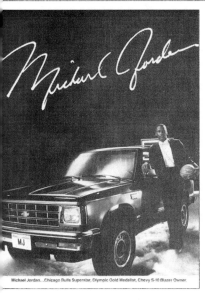

asketball legend Michael Jordan tarted as a spokesman for the hevrolet Blazer even before his career it full stride. This ad appeared in the hicago Auto Show program.

Chevrolet launched a high-performance IROC-Z version of its Camaro for 1985, joining the familiar Z28. A high-output V-8 engine was exclusive to the IROC (which stood for International Race of Champions).

Even Ferrari had something new at the Chicago Auto Show in 1985: a sleek Testarossa, easily identified by the six long horizontal strakes along its bodysides. The Testarossa first appeared at the Paris auto show, late in 1984.

Taking a different path toward promoting its products, Volvo displayed a crashed sedan at the auto show. The Swedish automaker was well-known for its emphasis on safety, including crashworthiness.

Oldsmobile exhibited a convertible version of its Cutlass Ciera at the 1985 auto show; but alas, this Olds never would see production.

Workers at McCormick Place generally managed to get the show floor ready before opening day. Once in a while, though, some last-minute touch-ups were needed.

From 1983-86, Chrysler offered a Town & Country convertible—basically an open LeBaron with simulated wood all the wa along the bodysides. At the rear is the Chrysler/Maserati "C coupe," a joint venture between the companies, planned to g into production.

1986
78th annual Chicago Automobile Show
(February 8–16, 1986)

- 973,917 visitors see 1986 auto show
- Redesigned Toyota Supra is unveiled
- Mazda displays turbocharged version of RX-7 sports car—seen first in Chicago
- Volkswagen shows new Scirocco 16V
- Lincoln-Mercury previews Merkur Skorpio, to go on sale in fall 1986
- Concept Pontiac Trans Sport suggests shape of 1990 GM minivans to come
- "Discover Dodge Dakota" exhibit uses robotics to promote compact pickup truck
- Chrysler previews luxury "Q" coupe—a joint venture with Maserati
- Bertone-styled Volvo 780 debuts
- Chevrolet displays mid-1986 Corvette convertible—first ragtop since 1975
- Concept vehicles include Nissan Mid-4 sportster, Toyota FX-V mid-engine sedan, Mazda MX-03, and Buick Wildcat
- Pontiac exhibits GT version of Fiero
- Nissan has restyled 300ZX sports car
- Chrysler stand has mini-stage revue and tuxedoed salespeople ... AMC's salespeople don western garb
- Chicago Bears players and Oprah Winfrey appear at auto show
- GMC has "Return to the Future" revue

Pontiac launched a 2+2 "aero" limited edition of its Grand Prix for mid-seaso, featuring a huge back window. Only 200 were built. Chevrolet had a similar ide with its Monte Carlo SS Aerocoupe.

Displays of stock-car victors always drew attention. This Ford Thunderbird ha been piloted by NASCAR champion Bill Elliott.

Cadillac shrunk its Eldorado personal-luxury coupe for 1986, chopping off the back end. Buick and Oldsmobile did the same thing with the Riviera and Toronado, respectively, and sales suffered.

Vanden Plas was the poshest version of the Jaguar XJ6 saloon (sedan) in 1986. British-built Jaguars had been seen at the auto show since the Fifties.

Starting in 1985, Lincoln-Mercury dealers offered the European-built Merkur Skorpio. Many displays still relied on female presenters, while others turned to robots to draw attention.

Not many Chicagoans had an opportunity to take a close look at an exotic Lamborghini Countach—except at the auto show. Built in Italy, the cramped-inside Countach had scissors-style doors and a sticker price that topped $100,000.

Marketers for the new Yugo (left) tried in vain to equate the low-budget, Yugoslavian-built minicar with the Volkswagen Beetle and Model T Ford. Although the Yugo's price was tempting, reliability problems cropped up quickly.

1987
79th annual Chicago Automobile Show
(February 7–15, 1987)

- Auto-show attendance totals 964,627
- More than 800 vehicles displayed, in two halls ... 17 concept cars shown
- Korean-built Ford Festiva makes its public debut at Chicago Auto Show
- Porsche displays new slant-nose body for its 911 Turbo
- Buick displays 1988 front-drive Regal, plus convertible version of Riviera—which will not go into production
- Buick announces availability of rear-drive Regal GMX, built by ASC Corp.
- New-for-1987 cars include Dodge Shadow and Plymouth Sundance, sleekly restyled Chrysler LeBaron convertible, mini Subaru Justy, Cadillac Allante, and Brazilian-built Volkswagen Fox
- Chrysler exhibits convertible version of Plymouth Sundance at Chicago show
- American Motors' Premier sedan debuts at Chicago show ... company head Joseph Cappy predicts new Premier and Medallion will "spark a financial recovery at AMC"
- Walter Payton and Michael Jordan are among sports celebrities at auto show
- Magician Arnie Kolodner levitates and saws his assistant at Chrysler stand
- Chevrolet shows concept Express—vision of transportation in 21st century

Crowds lined up early to get into the 1987 Chicago Auto Show at McCormick Place—just as they did every year, especially on weekends.

Long after the original Studebaker Avanti disappeared, and its Avanti II successor had gone through several changes in ownership, yet another version of the shapely Avanti appeared at the auto show—this time in convertible form.

Making its second appearance at the auto show was the Chrysler/Maserati joint-venture coupe (above), now called the TC by Maserati—but still not ready to go on sale. That wouldn't happen until late 1988, as an '89 model.

Left: *Buick had a series of performance cars in the Eighties, based the old rear-drive Regal coupe. In addition to the Grand National, this hotter-yet limited-edition GNX went on sale 1987, built by ASC Inc. with a $30,000 price tag. Only 500 were produced.*

Cadillac had a fresh idea in 1987, turning out the two-passenger Allante convertible as rival to the Mercedes-Benz 560SL. Riding a shortened Eldorado chassis, it wore bodywork designed and built by Pininfarina in Italy.

Racing legend Carroll Shelby's name gave the modest Dodge Lancer a more vibrant image as the Shelby Lancer, first seen as a show car. Shelby's company turned out special editions of several Dodge models, notably the sporty Daytona coupe.

Britain's Austin Rover company had been producing Acura Legends for sale in the United Kingdom. So, why not try the same thing for the U.S. market? Result: the Sterling 825, which never managed to attract many buyers during its 1987-90 run.

Ford continued to promote its rear-drive Aerostar minivan at the truck exhibit on the lower level of McCormick Place. Not until 1995 would Ford have a front-drive minivan to match Chrysler's. At left is a "body-in-white" display of the Aerostar, to give viewers an idea of the manufacturing process.

Year after year, Chevrolet's workaday full-size C/K pickup trucks racked up hefty sales totals—but Ford's F-Series wound up the victor when the final figures were counted.

1988
80th annual Chicago Automobile Show
(February 13–21, 1988)

- 974,432 visitors see auto show at McCormick Place
- Auto-show program includes Jim Mateja on anti-lock braking, and Dan Jedlicka giving tips for better service
- American Motors workers stage protest prior to show, in reaction to Chrysler's announced plan to close the Kenosha, Wisconsin, plant after taking over AMC
- Chrysler's new Jeep-Eagle division unveils Eagle Summit at show ... Eagle Premier also is new this year, while old 4WD Eagle is in its final season
- Ford introduces Probe sport coupe, to go on sale in May as a 1989 model
- Ford displays 1988-1/2 Escort, scheduled for sale in May
- Honda introduces new Accord coupe at Chicago show—to be built only in U.S.
- Mercury previews Australian-built Capri roadster, scheduled for production—based on Ghia-designed Barchetta
- Mazda introduces 10th-anniversary RX-7 Turbo special edition
- Toyota announces addition of All-Trac four-wheel-drive to Corolla station wagon
- Jeep shows Cherokee Sport
- Cadillac exhibits Voyage concept—actual production is considered
- Oldsmobile displays Cutlass Supreme pace-car replica, with heads-up display
- Mercedes-Benz introduces 300SE
- Vehicles at show include Range Rover, Sterling, Zimmer, Yugo, Excalibur
- Dodge Intrepid show car foretells 1991 Stealth coupe

Following the lead of Cadillac, Buick turned out a two-seat model for 1988, named Reatta. Built at a special "Reatta Craft Centre," the sport coupe was related to the larger Riviera. Customers failed to flock to this new breed of Buick.

Ford exhibited something new at the 1988 Chicago Auto Show: a stylish sport coupe to be produced in Michigan, named the Probe and on sale as a 1990 model. The same plant would turn out Mazda MX-6 coupes.

Looks like this young lady was ready to drive home a kiddie Corvette. Actually, someone did win the miniature sports car during the 1988 auto show.

A transparent hood showcased the workings of a Chevrolet Cavalier Z24 convertible—a new model for 1988. Cavaliers earned a substantial facelift this year, markedly more rounded than before. Note the add-on panels along the lower body of the sporty Z24.

Displayed in concept form as the Plymouth X2S, this sport coupe would later go on sale as the Laser—a close cousin to the Mitsubishi Eclipse, to be introduced as an early 1990 model.

Why was this Volkswagen Jetta pictured in front of a jet plane? Because an '88 GLI had circled the globe in under 37 hours, stored aboard a record-setting Boeing 747.

Alfa Romeos always were shapely, and the Italian company's subtly elegant display showed off the Milano sedan to best advantage.

No, that's not a Hummer; it's a Lamborghini LM002, of all things. Beneath the hood of this monstrous 4x4, which weighed nearly three tons and had a foot of ground clearance, sat a V-12 engine. The 73-gallon fuel tank was a virtual necessity, since gas mileage hovered around 8 mpg.

A convertible pickup truck? That's exactly what Dodge had in mind for its compact Dakota—an idea that no other automaker chose to duplicate.

When Dodge displayed its concept Viper at the Chicago Auto Show, hinting at the old Shelby Cobra, few imagined it would ever go into production. Overwhelming public reaction helped convince Chrysler Corporation to plan a "real" Viper.

1989
81st annual Chicago Automobile Show
(February 11–19, 1989)

- Auto-show attendance sets another record: 990,858 visitors during 9-day run
- Mazda Miata sports car makes official debut—to go on sale as early '90 model ... Mazda also exhibits new MPV minivan
- Nissan unveils restyled 300ZX at Chicago show, plus new Axxess minivan
- Acura displays concept NSX two-seat sports car for first time, at Chicago show
- Subaru chooses Chicago show to unveil new Legacy sedan—first U.S.-built model
- Audi Coupe Quattro and Sterling 827 make their North American debuts
- New Volkswagen Corrado and Isuzu Amigo seen for first time
- Showgoers see Corvette ZR-1, Dodge Dakota convertible, prototype of AWD Eagle Talon, five Ford concept vehicles, and Cadillac Solitaire concept sedan
- Dodge Viper RT/10 is one of favorite dream cars—will go into production ... Plymouth Speedster concept also seen
- In auto-show program, Jim Mateja compares Chicago Auto Show to Tokyo's ... historian Duane Mackie compares 1959 and 1989 automobiles

Amazing as it sounds, some folks weren't satisfied with the performance of everyday Corvettes. Chevrolet had an answer waiting for the 1990 model year: a ZR-1 edition, with a completely different high-output engine and special body features.

A supercharged engine went into the new Ford Thunderbird SC, named "Car of the Year" by Motor Trend *magazine.*

Nissan flamboyantly reshaped its 300ZX sports car, packing in a far more potent powertrain. The next-generation Z-car went on sale as an early '90 model.

Highlight of the 1989 Chicago Auto Show had to be the first public viewing of the new Mazda Miata—a traditional-type roadster, loosely based on the old Lotus Elan. Thousands of folks who loved the roadster slapped down cash to get one of the first examples, eagerly paying far above sticker price.

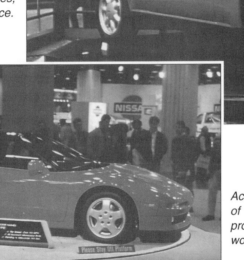

Acura, Honda's luxury division, exhibited a prototype of the NSX sports car at the auto show. Soon, a production version of the aluminum-bodied coupe would go on sale.

Suzuki's Sidekick was a larger sport-utility companion to the company's Samurai. Built in Canada, the Sidekick also was sold by Chevrolet dealers as the Geo Tracker.

1990

82nd annual Chicago Automobile Show

(February 10–18, 1990)

- 981,343 visitors see auto show
- For the first time, *Motor Trend* magazine announces "Import Car of the Year" award at Chicago show—19 cars nominated
- Five models make their North American or world debuts at Chicago show
- Mazda introduces Ford-built Navajo sport-utility at Chicago Auto Show
- Toyota introduces Previa minivan to U.S. market at Chicago Auto Show
- Lincoln-Mercury unveils subcompact Tracer, companion to Ford Escort ... Escort GT is new this year
- Lamborghini Diablo exoticar makes its world debut in Chicago
- Pontiac shows Sunfire concept coupe with unique rear half-doors ... Toyota Sera features gullwing doors
- Eagle Optima concept predicts "cab-forward" LH sedans of 1993
- Concept vehicles include supercharged Buick Bolero, Cadillac Aurora, Dodge Daytona R/T, Mercury Cyclone, Geo Tracker Hugger, Nissan Gobi, Hyundai Scoupe, Ford Ghia Via, and GM Impact (which will evolve into electric EV1)
- Experimental Chrysler Voyager III holds smaller vehicle inside
- Two booths demonstrate airbags
- Jeep/Eagle stand has video game race

General Motors launched a trio of futuristic-looking minivans for 1990 including the Pontiac Trans Sport (shown). The far-reaching snout failed to appeal to consumers, even though the minivan's plastic body gave it a practical edge on the Dodge/Plymouth competition.

Ford exhibited its Explorer sport-utility vehicle, successor to the Bronco II and on sale early in 1990, as a '91 model. Mazda, which shared several vehicle designs with Ford, launched a Ford-built Explorer-like Navajo sport-utility at the Chicago show.

Mayor Richard M. Daley (center) tours McCormick Place with a group of past CATA board chairmen. Pictured are (l-to-r) Edward Mize, CATA President Jerry H. Cizek III, Mayor Daley, Ronnie Colosimo, and Jerry Schiele.

When a Beretta convertible was selected to pace the 1990 Indianapolis 500 race, Chevrolet intended to produce the car. Development problems, however, kept the car from going on sale.

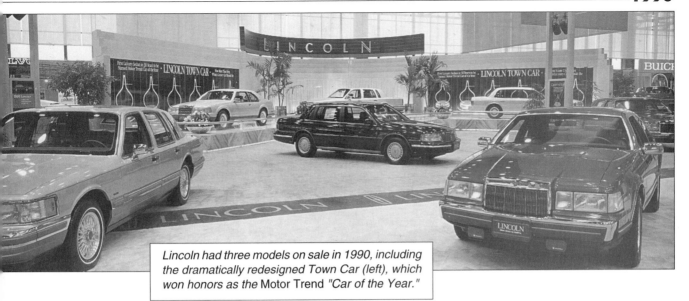

Lincoln had three models on sale in 1990, including the dramatically redesigned Town Car (left), which won honors as the Motor Trend *"Car of the Year."*

exus, Toyota's new luxury division, introduced its LS400 *agship"* sedan this year, packed with just about every comfort *d* convenience feature that affluent consumers were likely to *vor*. A 4.0-liter V-8 engine provided the power. Main rival: the *finiti* Q45, from Nissan's new luxury division.

Alfa Romeo exhibited this stubby-shaped Zagato ES30 prototype, with a 3.0-liter engine, at the Chicago Auto Show. Only three were built.

lkswagen had a full-fledged sports car ready for sale in 1990, *med* Corrado. Equipped with a supercharged "G-Charger" *gine*, the four-passenger replacement for the Scirocco *atured* an "active" rear spoiler that extended automatically *ove* 45 mph.

Those who couldn't afford a Rolls-Royce could always order a Bentley instead. Produced by the same British manufacturer, the Bentley saloon (sedan) cost a mere $114,100 in 1990.

1991

83rd annual Chicago Automobile Show

(February 9–17, 1991)

- 954,785 visitors see 1991 auto show, despite concerns that American entry into Persian Gulf War could hamper car sales
- Three 1992 production cars are unveiled: Buick LeSabre, Olds 88, and Pontiac Bonneville—plus reworked Ford Econoline
- Oldsmobile exhibits Achieva concept
- Lincoln-Mercury unveils Mystique minivan concept ... Ford has Contour sedan
- Environmentally-focused Neon concept car has two-stroke engine—not much kinship to Neon that will arrive for '95
- Concept vehicles include Mercedes-Benz F100 with solar roof panels, four-door Pontiac ProtoSport sports car, Ford Zig (roadster) and Zag (minivan), Chrysler 300 with V-10 engine, Chevrolet Monte Carlo, GMC Sagebrush and Rio Grande
- Cadillac shows off restyled '92 Seville
- Buick displays '92 Roadmaster sedan
- Ford flaunts redone '92 Crown Victoria and Mercury Grand Marquis

Official Pace Car for the Indianapolis 500 race this year was supposed to [a Dodge Stealth—a variant of the Mitsubishi 3000GT. Upheaval over havir a Japanese-built car do the honors resulted in "disqualification," so a Dodg Viper actually paced the race.

Right: Motor Trend *magazine named the curvaceously restyled Chevrolet Caprice Classic its "Car of the Year" for 1991. Only GM and Ford continued to offer traditional full-size rear-wheel-drive sedans.*

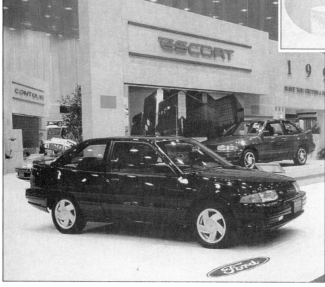

Ford's subcompact Escort got a revamping for 1991, as did its Mercury Tracer counterpart, resulting from joint efforts by Ford and Mazda. Escorts had a lot of competition in the "entry-level" field, including Ford's own imported Festiva. The Escort GT used a 127-horsepower Mazda engine, while others carried an 88-horsepower four-cylinder.

A brand-new model debuted for 1991: Saturn, a division General Motors but maintaining a separate identity. Saturr were produced in Tennessee, as coupes and sedans. Eig years in the making, Saturns sold for "no-haggle" prices ar soon became known for a customer-friendly buying experienc

252

Left: *After seven years on the market, the Dodge Caravan (shown) and its Plymouth Voyager counterpart earned a reworking for '91, adding an all-wheel-drive model. Despite only modest appearance change, nearly all body panels were new.*

Right: *Exotic sports cars inevitably occupied a corner of the lower-level exhibit area. Maserati still had several models available, including the $80,000 Shamal, but sales were modest. Chicagoland had only two authorized Maserati dealers.*

Right: *Ford exhibited the 1992 version of its Econoline full-size van at the '91 auto show—on the lower level, along with other "trucks." Econolines had been a part of Ford's lineup for three decades.*

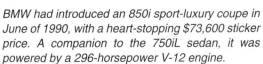

BMW had introduced an 850i sport-luxury coupe in June of 1990, with a heart-stopping $73,600 sticker price. A companion to the 750iL sedan, it was powered by a 296-horsepower V-12 engine.

1992
84th annual Chicago Automobile Show
(February 8–16, 1992)

- 981,963 people visit the auto show at McCormick Place
- More than 1,000 vehicles are exhibited, from 40 manufacturers
- Eight new models debut in Chicago
- World debuts at Chicago Auto Show include 1993 Ford Escort and Mercury Tracer, 1992 Toyota Camry station wagon, and 1992 Subaru Touring Sports LE wagon
- Ford unveils Mustang Cobra in Chicago, plus high-performance F-150 pickup truck
- New Mazda 626 sedan is seen for first time in U.S.
- Audi shows new 90 sedan for first time
- Ford exhibits Bronco "Boss" concept
- Infiniti J30 with four-wheel-steering makes U.S. debut ... so do Saab 9000CD Turbo flex-fuel concept, and Toyota Avalon four-door convertible concept
- Chrysler exhibits Concorde and New Yorker concepts
- Buick Skylark is given away at Charity Preview on Friday night
- Cadillac Seville and Eldorado are redesigned for 1992
- Two new lobby displays lure visitors: NASCAR vehicles, plus concept artwork from The Center for Creative Studies
- In auto-show program, Jim Mateja writes about battery-powered cars, Dan Jedlicka advises how to keep car clean, and Phil Arendt gives maintenance tips

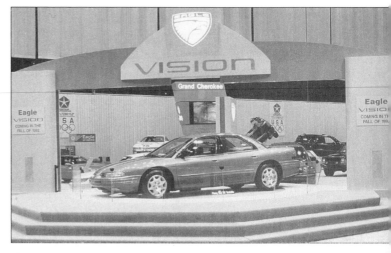

Chrysler Corporation displayed its coming-soon "LH" sedans: the Dodge Intrepid, Chrysler Concorde, and Eagle Vision (shown). The trio featured a new "cab-forward" profile.

Ford was preparing to introduce a more curvaceous Probe sport coupe as a 1993 model—but auto-show visitors got to see it early.

Pontiac's most popular model, the Grand Am, earned a fresh look for 1992. Produced as a coupe or sedan, the compact Grand Am had a choice of four engines.

ficial automobile of the 1992 Chicago Auto
ow was a compact Buick Skylark, introduced
a redesigned '92 model. Skylark was related
the Pontiac Grand Am and Oldsmobile
hieva, also reworked for 1992.

MC exhibited a GT edition of its full-size Yukon sport-utility
icle—though the notion of "Gran Turismo" and big SUVs
n't seem to mix. A GT sport package later became available
Yukons.

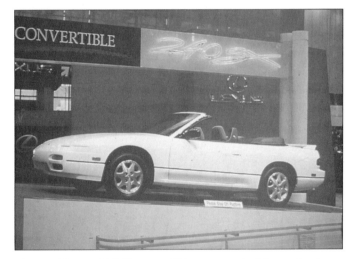

A new Nissan 240SX convertible appeared at the auto show,
and went on sale in the spring to join the coupe and hatchback.

designed for 1992, the Toyota Camry gained an
bag. Longer and heavier in this third generation, the
d-size model came in coupe and sedan form—with a
tion wagon added later.

Introduced in 1991, Toyota's seven-passenger Previa minivan got an
airbag this year. The four-cylinder engine sat below front seats.

1993

85th annual Chicago Automobile Show

(February 6–14, 1993)

- 977,847 visitors attend auto show
- Toyota introduces redesigned Supra sports car, as well as a "Sidewinder" concept pickup (based on new T100)
- Toyota's exhibit includes AXV-III advanced concept car
- GMC debuts redesigned Sonoma compact pickup truck
- Pontiac flaunts eagerly-awaited GTO coupe concept, based on Grand Am, plus Grand Prix GTP
- Hyundai shows sporty SunScoupe convertible concept, along with HCD-II concept coupe
- Mazda unveils new B-Series pickup
- Mercedes-Benz introduces AMC accessory package for 300E sedan
- Jaguar's 6.0-liter V-12 sedan makes its North American debut
- Chrysler displays bold new full-size Ram pickup truck, plus a batch of concept vehicles including classic-themed Thunderbolt and retro-look Prowler ... Chrysler also announces prices for new LHS and New Yorker
- Charity Preview raises $350,000
- Concept vehicles include Ford Mustang Mach II
- Chrysler has new "LH" sedans on sale this year: Chrysler Concorde, Dodge Intrepid, and Eagle Vision
- Buick announces 90th anniversary edition of LeSabre sedan

Lincoln launched a new Mark VIII coupe for 1993, replacing the old Mark V which had been around since '84. Again rear-wheel drive, the luxury coupe got dual airbags and a new aluminum V-8 engine.

Almost two years before an Oldsmobile Aurora would go on sale, a concept sedan by that name appeared at the Chicago Auto Show. A Cadillac Aurora concept had been seen earlier yet—at the 1990 auto show—as the company's "vision of an international high performance sedan."

Porsche flaunted a sleek, low-slung prototype Speedster, borrowing a designation from the company's legendary heritage. The first Speedsters had been sold in the mid-Fifties.

After introducing its "LH" sedans, Chrysler followed up with a lengthened LHS and New Yorker that promised greater rear-seat room. The pair went on sale in spring of 1993, as '94 models.

...dge earned both praise and criticism for its boldly redesigned ...-size Ram pickup truck, available with everything from a ...dest V-6 engine to an awesome V-10 when it went on sale as ...4 model.

Auto-show visitors got to see a prototype of the reworked Toyota Supra, which went on sale in summer '93—much more costly than before, with a turbocharged engine available.

...di exhibited its sleek new Cabriolet, based on the Series ... sedan platform, to be introduced as a 1994 model. The ...dded power top stored beneath a hard cover.

Above: Yes, that's a Hummer—the go-anywhere vehicle that gained a worldwide reputation during the Persian Gulf War and became a favorite of such celebrities as Arnold Schwarzenegger.

...nda replaced its little two-seat CRX coupe with a new Civic del ...l. The two-passenger semi-convertible had a lift-off roof panel ...d a motorized drop-down back window, to let the breezes ...ough. This was Honda's first open car in the U.S. market.

In addition to all the full-size automobiles, show visitors could take a look at this scale model of the Presidential limousine, a stretch of the current Cadillac.

1994

86th annual Chicago Automobile Show

(February 5–13, 1994)

- 954,389 people visit auto show at McCormick Place
- Nearly 1,000 vehicles are displayed
- Debuts at Chicago Auto Show include redesigned Mitsubishi Eclipse and Eagle Talon, Chevrolet Blazer, Toyota Avalon, and Mercury Mystique
- Hyundai introduces Accent show car, which will be Excel replacement ... market researcher Suzi Chauvel gives rundown on attitudes of "Generation X"
- Ford shows Mustang Cobra convertible that will pace Indianapolis 500 race
- Dodge Ram VTS concept pickup is painted like Viper, packs V-10 engine
- Pontiac displays Firebird convertible for first time, including 25th anniversary Trans Am
- GMC shows S15 Extended Cab HiRide 4x4 pickup
- Subaru has two front-drive SVX coupes and launches Impreza Outback Sport
- Mazda exhibits special M-Edition Mazda Miata roadster, plus Miatas powered by hydrogen and batteries
- Jeep-Eagle shows Vision Aerie concept
- CATA marks its 90th anniversary
- Chevrolet Camaro convertible is grand prize at Charity Preview
- Media preview includes 50 Little Tikes Cozy Coupes, "driven" onto show floor by a bevy of youngsters
- Former NHTSA chiefs, Joan Claybrook and Diane Steed, debate at media dinner
- Concept vehicles include brawny Ford Power Stroke F-Series pickup, Lincoln Contempra, Isuzu XU-1

A small number of Mustang Cobras went on sale, after a Cobra converti? paced the Indianapolis 500 race in 1994. Each was equipped with a 2? horsepower V-8 engine and manual shift.

Not only was the '95 Buick Riviera far different from earlier Rivieras, it look? like nothing else on the road—inside and out. Auto-show visitors could ta? a close look before the Riviera went on sale in spring 1994.

Dodge launched the subcompact Neon as an early '95 model. Only a few would be equipped with the ACR racing package.

Despite its appearance at the 1994 Chicago Auto Show, the Mitsubis? 3000GT Spyder—with a retractable solid top—would not go on sale u? early in 1995. Carrying hefty price stickers, the Spyders were converted fr? 3000GT coupes by ASC Inc.

e Bugatti badge had not been seen since 1951, but here was an ticar of that name at the 1994 Chicago Auto Show. Brought to show by John Weinberger of Continental Motors, this EB110 med for Ettore Bugatti) was the only one in the country, ended to sell for $235,000. Five were ordered, but before U.S. sions could be built, the Bugatti company fell into receivership.

Cadillac dealers wouldn't be getting a Catera for quite a while yet, but auto-show visitors could take a peek at the car in concept form, under another name: LSE. Cadillac announced in 1994 that the platform for a production version would be engineered and built in Russelsheim, Germany.

ab redesigned its 900-series for the first time in 15 years. Built Finland, this new convertible went on sale in summer of 1994, h a power top and glass rear window. The Swedish company s now half-owned by General Motors.

Mazda displayed its new Millenia luxury sedan, to go on sale in spring of 1994. The top "S" model got an innovative Miller-cycle engine.

BMW's 3-Series came in coupe, sedan, and convertible form. The 325is coupe (left) held an inline six-cylinder engine; the 318is (right) had a four-cylinder. A passenger airbag was new for '94.

1995

87th annual Chicago Automobile Show

(February 10–19, 1995)

- Auto-show attendance totals 987,768 visitors
- Mazda M-Speedster concept features cutdown windshield—but no plan to go into production
- Redesigned Ford Taurus and Mercury Sable station wagons are unveiled in Chicago, accompanied by pair of old "woodie" wagons
- Infiniti I30 debuts—slotted between G20 and J30 sedans
- Acura TL sedan makes first appearance—replacement for Vigor
- Pontiac Sunfire convertible and GT coupe debut at Chicago Auto Show ... so does Chevrolet Cavalier convertible
- Toyota launches 1995-1/2 Tacoma compact pickup truck
- Four-door Geo Tracker debuts at Chicago show
- GMC displays Sierra pickup truck with "side access panel" for rear entry
- Chrysler displays new Sebring coupe, but journalists see only a drawing of forthcoming Sebring convertible
- Mitsubishi exhibits Eclipse convertible, but only in concept form
- Volvo promotes new turbocharged T-5R edition of its 850 sedan
- Oldsmobile reintroduces Bravada sport-utility and shows concept version of Aurora sedan
- Oscar Mayer's "Wienermobile" makes appearance at auto show

A Corvette paced the Indianapolis 500 race, but the design of Chevrole legendary sports car was getting old—dating back to 1984. This year's ZF held a 405-horsepower V-8 engine, but other Corvette owners made do w a mere 300.

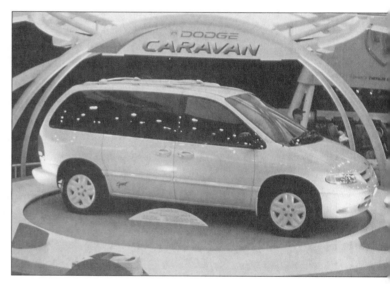

On sale in spring of 1995, as a '96 model, the restyled Dodge Caravan h a more aerodynamic look and a newly optional driver-side sliding do Removable seats had built-in rollers. The Plymouth Voyager and Chrys Town & Country were similar.

Once again, Mercury's Sable was structurally similar to the Ford Taurus, if a little less radical in appearance. Sedans and station wagons made up the Taurus/Sable model line.

Bigger and more rounded than its predecessor, the redesigned Ford Taur produced a variety of reactions from consumers. Many applauded t dramatically fresh design, but others preferred the old model, produced fro 1986-95 and ranking as the top U.S. seller.

Saturn elected to demonstrate the versatility of its station wagon by mounting a bicycle up top.

...rysler launched the Sebring coupe after the 1995 model year ...gan, following the similar Dodge Avenger, which debuted in ...l of '94. Both were built in the same Illinois plant as the smaller ...tsubishi Eclipse/Eagle Talon.

...guar sedans were redesigned for 1995, topped by the high-...erformance XJR with a 322-horsepower supercharged engine. ...yling cues brought back memories of earlier (pre-1988) Jags.

Nissan exhibited a special 25th-anniversary SMZ edition of its 300ZX sports car, built by IMSA champion Steve Miller. The SMZ went on sale at Nissan dealerships in spring 1995, priced near $55,000.

Al Unser won the 1994 Indianapolis 500 race in a Marlboro-Penske Mercedes-Benz-powered racer. Therefore, Mercedes-Benz displayed the Borg-Warner trophy at its stand at the auto show.

Jeep wagons came in two sizes: Cherokee and the larger, posher Grand Cherokee, available with a V-8 engine. Technically-minded auto-show visitors could get a good look at the four-wheel-drive system.

10

Dream Cars—the Later Years
(1974-98)

As the overall excitement within the auto industry diminished during the Seventies, so too did the flamboyance of the "dream cars" that manufacturers brought to the Chicago Auto Show. Eye-pleasing they might be, but few echoed the vitality of the Fifties: the Exner/Ghia show cars, the GM Motorama cars, the futuristic and fantastic Ford concepts.

Dream cars underwent a transformation. Gone, to an extent, were the fanciful renderings of possible automotive futures. Gone, too, were some of the more daring designs from the pens of the most innovative stylists—designs that made the onlooker think, and dream, and imagine.

In their place stood cars that often weren't far removed from the production models displayed nearby. Partly because the "muscle car" era was gone, too, and gas mileage was replacing performance in consumers' "must have" lists, vibrant colors and assertive graphics often took the place of more ambitious creations.

Oh sure, a succession of futuristic machines trickled into the mix over the years, just as they had in the Fifties and Sixties—sometimes from the Japanese companies rather than the Americans. Echoing the trends of the time, though, concept vehicles turned more ordinary for a while: mild offshoots of production cars to draw sales as "spring specials," experimental "safety" cars, plus the occasional predictor of a coming-soon model.

Concepts of minimalist commuter cars made people think about an automotive future that seemed considerably bleaker than had ever been imagined. Environmentally-focused cars, "safety" cars, conveyed a more sober foretelling of the motoring prospects that lay ahead. No wonder, then, that car-buyers fell for the gaudy decals, colorful striping jobs, and tricky gadgetry of the time. Silly as some of that artificial excitement might seem today, looking backward, that was what drew the crowds in the Seventies, and into the Eighties.

Even if automobiles grew duller in the Seventies, "idea cars" continued to proliferate. Stylists and engineers stayed busy coming up with fresh ideas, even if few—other than the most obvious, even trivial, innovations—were destined to see the light of day at American dealerships.

Innovation, part of American tradition long before the first automobiles went on sale, took fresh forms. Ford's Prima of 1978, for instance, was actually four vehicles in one, altered by changing its roof. General Motors took its performance-oriented Pontiac Firebird and transformed it into a utility vehicle for auto-show display. Plenty of conce cars—some developed by import manufacturers—continu to suggest possible modes of future family travel. Advanc powertrain ideas often appeared first in concept vehicles.

Of course, no one bothered to tell the public that thir were getting dull in the industry. Even as the auto wo darkened, hundreds of thousands of Midwesterners ke coming to the show each winter. They came to see the tone down production cars, but also to gaze upon drea machines—just as they had in more stimulating seasons.

As excitement made a comeback among production c by the mid-Eighties, so too did hot concepts. Even more th before, some of them actually foretold coming-so products—if not necessarily in the same form. Chrysle "cab-forward" styling, which highlighted the LH sedans 1993, had first appeared on a series of concept cars, from t Portofino to the Millenium to the Eagle Optima. Chrysle Neon appeared first as a show car, far more imaginative form than the actual subcompact.

Dodge's Viper, too, arrived first as an RT/10 concept, the 1989 auto show. Partly because of vigorous put response to the basic premise, as well as the car's muscu details—including the prospect of a V-10 engine—Dod decided to find a way to produce such a sports car.

By the Nineties, Chrysler Corporation was emerging the leader in concept-car creation. Each year, the media a the general public alike awaited the latest group imaginative machines from Chrysler stylists.

Volkswagen's Beetle-like Concept One appeared strictly a show car in 1994. VW executives insisted at the tir that they had no plans whatsoever to produce such a vehic Fantastic response from the media and consumers ali triggered a change of the corporate mind, and—*voila*, fc years later the New Beetle debuted.

Unlike many show cars that eventually go ir production, too, the New Beetle and the Viper made without sacrificing their most appealing characteristics—t ones that made them special in the first place.

Showgoers continue to contribute to decisions on futu products. Manufacturers reveal concepts to observe reactio whether given in interviews or questionnaires, or watching. Who knows? Your smile when gazing upon t latest dream car just might help determine whether that c becomes real one day soon.

Ford displayed an experimental Sportiva, a roadster version of the new Mustang II, at the 1974 Chicago Auto Show. A Ghia-designed Mustella also appeared that year.

Making its U.S. debut at the 1976 show was this cute little AD-1, an experimental mid-engine sports car. Features included a fuel-injected engine, five-speed gearbox, and four-wheel disc brakes. The fiberglass body stood only 46.8 inches tall. A removable sunroof stowed in the front compartment.

panese automakers did not yet develop too many concept nicles, but Toyota brought this futuristic F101 to the 1974 auto ow. Billed as a styling exercise, the fastback coupe featured aerodynamic nose and sleek rear-quarter lines. Powered by ordinary Toyota Corona engine and automatic transmission, car featured four-wheel disc brakes and a fully independent spension.

Chevrolet's Monza Super Spyder II, seen at the 1976 auto show, combined elements from several Chevy lines, new and old. Painted gold metalflake, the Monza-based 2+2 hatchback had a Cosworth engine (borrowed from the Vega) in competition tune, plus a five-speed gearbox, wheel flares, and a rear spoiler. Fluorescent lighting in the nose was supposed to suggest the future.

Exploring styling possibilities of the 1976 Dodge Charger SE was the duty of the XS-22, which appeared at the 1976 auto show. Starting with the basic body, it featured glass panels over front seats, a padded vinyl roof with stainless steel surround trim, and blocked rear-quarter windows. Cast aluminum wheels and a small wood steering wheel provided the finishing touches.

Ford's concept Prima, seen at the 1978 auto show, was actually four vehicles in one. Removable tops interchanged to convert the vehicle from pickup truck to wagon, to two-seat coupe, to 2+2 fastback. Dimensions were similar to the mini-size Fiesta.

Pontiac unveiled this Trans Am Type K van wagon hybrid prototype at the Chicago Auto Show in 1977. Based on the Firebird Trans Am, it seated four in the rear compartment, beneath lift-up side glass.

AMC's AM VAN, seen at the 1978 Chicago Auto Show, was a van conversion of the Pacer. Note the porthole—not too practical, perhaps, but an eye-catcher.

Five occupants would be surrounded by glass in the Ford Megastar, touted as a possible family car for the future. Ghia design studios collaborated on the four-door wedge-shaped aluminum body. The Megastar appeared at the 1978 auto show, with a 3.0-liter V-6 under its hood.

convertible landau soft-top fit over the rear compartment of this ecial Pontiac Grand Prix coupe. Rose-colored glass hatches uld be removed. The car appeared at the 1979 auto show.

"Big Red," seen at Dodge's area of the 1979 auto show, was a light-duty pickup truck version of an over-the-road hauler—complete with chrome exhaust stacks, dual air horns, wind foil, and a fifth wheel.

es, that's a rumble seat in the back of this Mercury XM concept r, displayed in 1979. Ordinarily a two-seater, it converted into four-passenger model by popping open the decklid to reveal e external seat, far to the rear.

Dodge developed the silver-colored Mirada Magnum, seen in 1980, to have the look of a European sports coupe. Features included concealed headlights, a T-bar roof, and closed-off quarter windows.

Bertone created the body for this concept Ferrari, named "Rainbow," which appeared at the 1980 auto show. Built on a 308GT chassis, but different in appearance from any Ferrari, the two-seater was an attempt at a new sports car design style. The detachable top could be stood on its end, behind the seats. Part of the top was transparent, so it would not obstruct the driver's view when stored upright.

AMX TURBO

The AMX Turbo Pace Car is an exclusive — the personal design of Richard A. Teague, American Motors' Vice President of Automotive Design. It was constructed by Autodynamics of Troy, Michigan under contract from PPG Industries. This two-passenger, aerodynamically efficient vehicle will be one of four official pace cars in the PPG Indy Car World Series during the 1981 auto racing season.

The AMX Turbo is powered by a turbo-charged fuel-injected 258 CID 6-cylinder AMC engine delivering 450 horsepower, built by Turbo-Systems Inc. The AMX Turbo measures 50 inches in overall height, 164 inches long and is 72 inches in overall width. The car is equipped with Goodyear Eagle GT low profile 245x50x16 tires on 16" x 8" Gotti aluminum alloy wheels on a 96" wheelbase.

Richard A. Teague, vice-president of design at AMC, penned this bold AMX Turbo, which served as one of four PPG Official Pace Cars at the Indy Car World Series. Displayed at the 1981 Chicago Auto Show, the AMX Turbo seated two and stood 50 inches tall. Its fuel-injected 258-cid six-cylinder engine developed a whopping 450 horsepower.

Developed with the cooperation of Ghia, Ford's Mustang RSX of 1981 was described as a "one-of-a-kind rallye sport two-seater." Molded rear skirts and a rear airfoil were supposed to improve stability.

Based on the Bronco, Ford's Montana Lobo 4x4 featured tint bubble doors that could be removed and replaced by webbir A plexiglass T-bar roof also could be removed. Lobo was collection of ideas and designs that may be used in future For vehicles, said William Cramer, manager of advanced a international design at the 1981 auto show.

lints of the Ford Aerostar minivan, to be issued several years *ater*, could be seen in this Ford Ghia Aerovan, which appeared t the 1982 Chicago Auto Show.

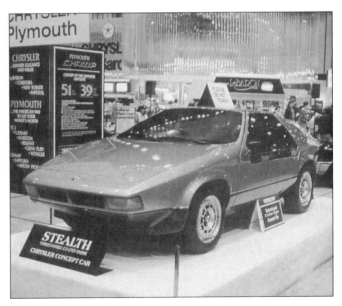

Designed to respond to potential future fuel crises, the three-wheeled Ford Ghia Cockpit appeared at the 1982 auto show. With a hinged canopy and tandem seating, it resembled a jet fighter. A tiny 12-horsepower engine sat inside the rear wheel. Projected mileage: 75 mpg.

"Styled for the future" was Lincoln's description of the Continental Concept 90, which hinted at future aerodynamic styling and the shape of the 1984 Mark VII. Its front-end profile also suggested the forthcoming Ford Thunderbird, due to be restyled for '83.

opearing at the 1982 Chicago Auto Show was one of the '81 ace cars from the PPG Indy Car World Series: the 024 Dodge urbo Charger. At a low point in domestic performance-car story, it demonstrated what could be accomplished. Put gether by Chrysler's Product Design Office, it featured a rbocharged 2.2-liter four, extensive body flaring and odification, and a rear wing—a hint of the old Dodge Daytona.

At the 1982 auto show, Chrysler provided a peek at its forthcoming sports coupe, planned for '84, in the form of a Stealth concept. The front-drive 2+2 coupe evolved from the Plymouth TC3 platform, powered by a turbocharged 2.2-liter engine.

Ford claimed that its Probe IV research car, exhibited at the 1983 Chicago Auto Show, was the world's most aerodynamic sedan—comparable to the slipperiness of a jet fighter.

Not only did Pontiac launch its new mid-engined Fiero spo[rt] coupe for 1984, but it displayed a convertible concept of that ca[r] with a rakish cut-down windshield. No open Fieros ever we[nt] into production, however.

Mazda's experimental MX-02 concept hatchback, shown in 1984, featured four-wheel steering for improved maneuverability as well as a glass hatch and a rear tailgate.

Later in the decade, the Mercury Capri would borrow more th[an] a few styling touches from this Ford Ghia Barchetta two-seat[er] seen at the 1984 Chicago Auto Show. In Italian, Barchetta mea[ns] "little boat."

Scissors-style doors permitted entry into th[e] Peugeot Quasar, a concept two-seater with [a] transparent dome and twin-turbocharg[ed] four-cylinder engine, which developed 6[00] horsepower. A video screen in the conso[le] could display warnings and maps. Auto-sho[w] visitors got to see the Quasar in '85.

splayed at the 1985 Chicago Auto Show, Toyota's FX-1 sport
upe served as a prototype for the coming-soon replacement
r the Supra.

The Corvette Indy, seen at the 1986 auto show, was a mid-engine research vehicle. All four wheels on a running prototype were to be powered by Chevrolet's new Indy V-8 engine. An "active" suspension adjusted electronically to match road conditions.

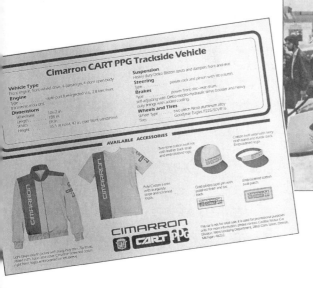

Cadillac, Triad Series, and PPG created a dual-cowl convertible version of its subcompact Cimarron for the 1986 auto show—and to serve as trackside courtesy car for the CART/PPG Indy Car World Series. Riding a stretched Cimarron platform, the convertible was filled with safety, control, and communications devices.

minous in countenance, only 43.2 inches tall, the Dodge M4S
as a pace car for the CART/Indy Car World Series. Its mid-
ounted 2.2-liter engine developed 440 horsepower.
howgoers got to see it in 1986. Note the scissors-style doors.

Pontiac's Trans Sport concept of 1986, a blend of minivan and station wagon, foretold the GM minivans to come four years later. Built on a stretched Pontiac 6000 sedan platform, the experimental Trans Sport had front-wheel drive, a plastic body, and 2.9-liter V-6 engine.

Raising the acrylic canopy of the Buick Wildcat, seen at the 1986 auto show, revealed a 230-horsepower V-6 engine. The two-seater had a plastic body and four-wheel drive.

Pontiac stylists created the ground-hugging, aerodynamic Pursuit for display in 1987, adding that name to suggest the company's pursuit of the future. The four-seat coupe had four-wheel drive and a light bar in its nose.

For its Jeep-division display in 1987, AMC created the Comanche Thunderchief pickup truck. Chrysler Corporation was about to take over AMC, tempted mainly by its Jeeps.

Designed by Ford's North American Design Center and built by Ghia in Italy, the Lincoln Vignale convertible included a removable hardtop with large glass area. An air suspension and all-wheel drive were installed in the car, seen at the 1987 auto show.

Oldsmobile's Aerotech was created in long-tail (shown) and short-tail form, serving as a test bed for the high-performance turbocharged 2.3-liter Quad 4 engine.

ne of the more unusual cars at the 1988 auto show was 'ymouth's Slingshot concept, which almost looked like that item childhood weaponry. Designed to appeal to the youth market, grew out of a collaboration between college students and hrysler designers. Measuring less than 150 inches overall, on wheelbase close to 103 inches, the two-seater had a carbon er chassis and rear-mounted four-cylinder engine.

Many observers thought the Pontiac Banshee concept would be the next Firebird, when it appeared at the 1988 auto show. In fact, a variant of its pointy front end did wind up on production Firebirds. No outside mirrors or door handles spoiled the Banshee's lush contours.

een at the 1989 Chicago Auto Show, Chrysler's Lamborghini rtofino predicted the "cab-forward" styling that Chrysler would dopt in the Nineties. Scissors-style doors were strictly for the oncept sedan.

Visitors to the 1989 auto show got to see the experimental bubble-topped Mitsubishi HSR (High Speed Research), claimed to be capable of speeds beyond 200 mph, using computers for navigation.

eviewing features of its coming-later range of full-size "LH" sedans, hich would arrive for '93, the Chrysler Millenium was seen in 1989. ab-forward" styling blended with low, swoopy lines.

Futuristic was the word for the Millenium's four-passenger interior. The safety-focused sedan was loaded with technical features, including traction control, active suspension, voice activation, infrared forward vision, and radar.

Subaru referred to its SRD-1, seen at the 1990 auto show, as a "dream wagon." With a short nose and long passenger compartment, it was designed for maximum utility.

Nissan Design International in San Diego styled the Go concept for the 1990 auto show. Meant to suggest an entry-level vehicle, it featured a "helicopter-style" cab and a cargo bed with folding sides.

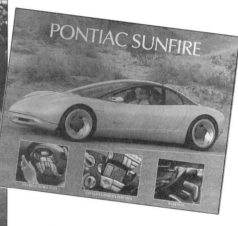

Half doors permitted entry into the 1990 Pontiac Sunfire, with a body made of carbon-fiber. Those doors opened outward, and rear seats angled outward.

Pontiac's concept Sunfire was designed to ride on 20- and 21-inch tires. A 190-horsepower engine provided the power.

Released at the auto show, Plymouth's Voyager III amounted to two vehicles in one—and foretold the basic shape of the 1996 minivans. The 104-inch front portion seated three, with a propane engine for propulsion. When attached, the separate rear portion added its 2.2-liter engine, forming an eight-passenger, eight-wheeled vehicle. Chrysler called it a "possible solution" to traffic congestion and pollution.

Mercury's 1990 Cyclone demonstrated "cab-forward" styling generally considered the province of Chrysler. An electrochromic roof allowed the driver to adjust for changes in sunlight conditions.

ubbed HSR-II, the second edition of Mitsubishi's High Speed esearch vehicle included all-wheel drive and four-wheel eering. It was part of Mitsubishi's 1991 exhibit.

"Suicide" doors at the rear marked Pontiac's ProtoSport 4, shown in 1991. Considered a true four-door sports car, the ProtoSport had color video monitors in front seatbacks, camera-operated mirrors, and ultraviolet headlights.

Left: Chrysler borrowed the old "300" designation for its sleekly futuristic concept sedan, borrowing various touches from the past and seen at the 1991 auto show. Underpinnings actually came from the Dodge Viper. Note the rear-hinged "suicide" back doors.

ight: Austin Rover of England created the MG E-XE concept for a ebut at the Frankfurt (Germany) auto show in 1985. Chicagoans ot to see it in 1991. Aerodynamically shaped, the sports car rode n an aluminum chassis with all-wheel drive. A mid-mounted all-luminum V-6 engine developed 250 horsepower. Three uniformed uards from London's Buckingham Palace presided over the resentation.

A multi-purpose vehicle, the Jeep Wagoneer 2000 (exhibited in 1991) was filled with entertainment extras, including a TV and VCR. Pulling down the ailgate revealed removable stadium-type seats.

One of the highlights of the 1992 auto show appeared at the Oldsmobile exhibit: General Motors' futuristic four-passenger Ultralite. Powered by a rear-mounted two-stroke, three-cylinder engine, it was said to be capable of nearly 100-mpg fuel economy at a constant 50 mph, yet able to accelerate to 60 mph in 7.8 seconds. The body was made of composite carbon fiber.

Before the all-new 1993 Lincoln Mark VIII coupe went on sale, visitors to the '92 auto show got to see a teaser preview, in the form of the Marque X concept. This was a Mark VIII, customized into convertible form by ASC. Painted bright orange pearl, it featured a custom interior, passenger entertainment centers, ID-card starting, and arc discharge headlights.

Zero-emissions vehicles were a hot topic at the 1992 auto show. BMW's entry in the experimental realm was this E2, which featured a rear-mounted electric motor and was claimed to be able to go 75 mph. Following a prior E1, it had a steel space frame and aluminum floor, and a body said to be recyclable.

Tandem seating and ultra-high fuel efficiency were the distinctive features of Honda's EP-X (Efficient Personal Experimental) concept vehicle, seen at the 1992 auto show. The egg-shaped body was aluminum monocoque. Power came from a 1.0-liter three-cylinder engine. Occupants could enter via two side doors and an opening canopy.

Reminiscent of Mustangs of the distant past, the two-passenger 1993 Mach III featured a low windshield, body air scoops, cat's-eye headlights, and 19-inch tires.

Traditional Volvo buyers, used to squared-off styling, must have been shocked by the ECC (Environmental Concept Car) at the 1993 Chicago Auto Show. Styled at Volvo's California design center and built in Sweden, it combined a gas turbine engine and electric motor/battery propulsion, to meet low/zero emissions requirements of the future. Based on the 850, the ECC featured aluminum bodywork.

While exhibiting its HCD-II concept coupe at the 1993 Chicago Auto Show, Hyundai vowed that a real-life version would go on sale around 1997.

California provided the inspiration for the Ford Ranger Jukebox concept pickup. Flashing its neon lights, the topless low-rider/cruiser was displayed in 1993, to demonstrate the potential for customizing a compact Ranger. A cut-down windshield and side windows created a wraparound effect, and occupants could "enjoy" a 2,500-watt stereo system.

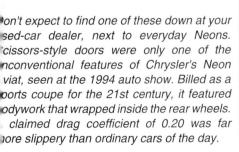

Don't expect to find one of these down at your used-car dealer, next to everyday Neons. Scissors-style doors were only one of the unconventional features of Chrysler's Neon Aviat, seen at the 1994 auto show. Billed as a sports coupe for the 21st century, it featured bodywork that wrapped inside the rear wheels. A claimed drag coefficient of 0.20 was far more slippery than ordinary cars of the day.

Right: *"Yesterday's power, today's sophistication." That was the theme for the Dodge Venom, exhibited in 1994. Because Dodge's Viper had gone from concept to production, many predicted the same fate for the rear-drive Venom coupe, but it faded away instead. Though emulating old-time muscle cars, it featured contemporary "cab-forward" design and an overhead-cam V-6 engine, on a modified Neon floor pan.*

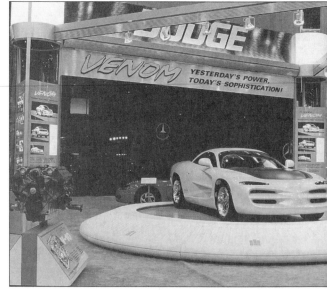

Whimsical? Goofy? Or just plain fun? Visitors to the 1994 auto show might have used any of these terms to describe this bright yellow pearl Neon Expresso at the Chrysler-Plymouth display. Styling might be considered cartoonish, but the family-oriented four-door featured chair-high seating and "sightseeing" windows.

Plymouth called this stubby little 1995 two-passenger conce the Backpack. Note the tiny open space for camping or bea gear—whatever the young folks might want to carry.

Ford's Power Stroke Turbo Diesel pickup truck, featured at the 1994 auto show, was thought to be a predictor of the 1996 F-Series pickups. Naturally, the "real thing" was toned down considerably when it finally arrived.

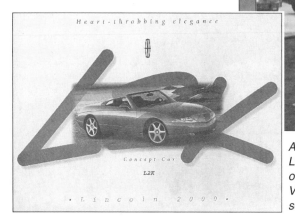

A pleasant surprise turned up at the Lincoln-Mercury display in 1995: the Linco L2K (which, as spokespersons quickly explained, meant "Lincoln 2000"). Ridir on a short 93-inch wheelbase and weighing about 2,900 pounds, with a 3.4-lit V-8 under its hood, the two-passenger L2K qualified as a "hot rod Lincoln" sorts. The behind-the-seats spoiler was said to reduce wind noise.

Inspired by the luscious Bugatti Type 57 coupe of the late Thirties, Chrysler's Atlantic sedan of 1995 blended flowing futuristic lines with plenty of hints out of the past. Beneath the hood sat an operative straight-eight engine.

For the 1995 Chicago Auto Show, Mazda cut down the windshield of its Miata roadster and faired-in the headrests to create the M Speedster. Journalists and showgoers loved it, but no Speedsters went into production.

tended to suggest family-transportation odes for the next century, Ford's ynergy 2010 flaunted the company's Jew Edge" design theme and held a vbrid (gasoline/electric) engine. Note the nclosed back wheels.

A V-12 engine, displayed on a separate stand at the 1996 Chicago Auto Show, was ready to power the Ford Indigo. This blending of Ford and Indy Car technologies was thought to predict a possible street-legal sports car.

Though shaped like a coupe, Mercury's MC4 had four doors—the back pair narrower and rear-hinged, echoing the pattern of 1930s cars. Twin trunk lids, one on each side, opened outward in "gullwing" style.

Dual-cowl phaetons hadn't been marketed for decades, b[] Chrysler borrowed that idea in 1997, developing a mode[] interpretation and naming it the Phaeton. Note the massive ve[] style grille. The rear windshield slid up and down.

Showgoers in 1997 went wild over the Dodge Copperhead roadster—especially when they learned that the potent machine was being targeted as a candidate for possible production at some later date. Snakeskin upholstery was strictly for the concept car.

Pontiac issued a Trans Sport Montana minivan in 1998, but als[] exhibited this boldly-augmented "Thunder" concept version [] the auto show that year.

Buick borrowed from the past and added ideas for the future to create this Signia station wagon, seen at the press dinner prior to the 1998 Chicago Auto Show. Instruments and decorative touches—including "portholes"—rekindled memories of Buicks of the distant past.

Mitsubishi had another version of its research vehicle on tap for the 1998 Chicago Auto Show, dubbed the SST Targa and flaunting "geo-mechanical styling." Along with the redesigned 1999 Galant, the SST was unveiled on Saturday (opening day), as part of a lavish fashion show. Most cars—concept and production—are first shown to the media, and later to the general public.

Chrysler borrowed the Jeepster name from an open model produced in 1948-51, for its concept Jeep of 1998, considered a sports-car/sport-utility hybrid. An electronic suspension could raise or lower the Jeepster by four inches. Its 4.7-liter V-8 was scheduled to go into the 1999 Grand Cherokee.

Honda developed the JV-X coupe, seen in 1998, as a "socially responsible sports car." Its Integrated Motor Assist System combined electric power with a gasoline engine.

Chrysler had yet another updating of ideas from sedans of the past at the 1998 auto show. Evoking memories of the Virgil Exner show cars of the Fifties, the Chrysler Chronos carried a unique V-10 engine and rode on 20-/21-inch tires. A humidor inside acknowledged the revived popularity of cigars.

11
The Chicago Automobile Trade Association
(CATA, Then and Now)

When the first Chicago Auto Show opened its doors, near the beginning of the 20th century, there was little need for a dealers' association. After all, no one was entirely sure who was going to sell those newfangled machines. About 250 automobiles might be seen in the Chicago area, initially sold by former bicycle retailers and repair shops.

Because cars were considered a "rich man's plaything," competition for the few likely customers was fierce, and cooperation deemed inappropriate. By 1904, however, car sales in the Chicago area were beginning to blossom. A Chicago newspaper already had observed that early "prejudice against the automobile [was] slowly but surely wearing away." Retailers had begun to meet informally—often at the Metropole Hotel, sitting over the 25-cent businessmen's lunch.

A.C. Faeh—showman extraordinaire in the Thirties

Dealers quickly recognized the benefits of joining forces. On April 20, 1904, a dozen of them formed the Chicago Automobile Trade Association, chartered as a non-profit corporation by the State of Illinois. Howard Tucker (a Winton dealer) was named its first president. Although they had no office at first, the New Southern Hotel soon donated free use of its banquet rooms for CATA meetings.

Early accomplishments included blocking a bill that would have instituted a 6-mph speed limit, and halting a state resolution that would have required that cars be geared to a maximum speed of 20 mph. In 1906, the CATA sponsored three major events: a 100-mile Chicago, Elgin and Aurora reliability run; the Algonquin Hill Climb; and a Cedar Lake Economy Test. Organizers also conducted a "gymkhana," in which drivers demonstrated precision in such events as a high-gear slow race and "sabreing" the enemy (spearing lemons strung over the course).

Because many automobiles were driven by chauffeurs in the early years, the CATA opened a labor registration office in 1908, to bring chauffeurs and employers together

Executives plan the November 1935 auto show (l-to-r): O.F Larson (chairman, style show committee), K.K. Kenderdin (CATA president), A.C. Faeh (show manager), H.T Hollingshead (chairman, show committee), H.F. Malo (executive secretary, Associated Fur Industries), L.E. Himme (president, Associated Fur Industries), and Miss Kathryn Wilso (style show producer).

Safety-slogan winners from Chicago schools show off the handiwork in time for the 1940 auto show (November 1939).

After World War II, the CATA sought to assist war veterans in their quest for employment in the auto trade.

In 1918, as the automakers were occupied with wartime concerns, the CATA sponsored Chicago's auto show for the first time. Organizing the show was accomplished in just 35 days, under President George H. Bird, which helped earn the CATA a national reputation for administrative skills. Even so, control of the show reverted to the manufacturers after that single wartime venture.

As the war ended in 1919, the CATA helped promote Good Roads Bond issues. Now located at 22nd and Michigan, the CATA had 261 members and a staff of 28. Treasurer Henry Paulman wrote that statistically, Chicago was "the largest motor car market in the world."

and investigate worker qualifications. Members voted unanimously to close on Saturday afternoons and Sundays. Chicago now had 11,000 automobiles, and the total was rising rapidly. Ralph Temple, a dealer in electric cars, had followed Howard Tucker as president. He was succeeded by Rambler dealer Joseph Gunther; W.L. Githens (Oldsmobile); and Thomas T. Hay (a Ford branch manager).

Chicago's "automobile row," a conglomeration of dealerships, had developed along South Michigan Avenue (south of 12th Street). That area became the focal point mainly because of its proximity to Prairie Avenue, where many of the wealthiest Chicagoans lived.

Although an auto show took place every year at Chicago's Coliseum, the CATA played no role in organizing or operating that event. That was the province of the Automobile Manufacturers Association. By mid-1911, when N.H. Van Sicklen served as CATA president, the organization employed an assistant secretary and opened an office on Michigan Avenue. Thirty members made up the group (eleven of whom were behind in their dues).

Safety has been emphasized at the auto show for decades. Here, two young ladies at the auto show study a safety poster. Note the poster promoting actor Robert Young's Good Drivers Club.

Charitable work was one of the many CATA activities over the years, highlighted by the annual Orphans' Day Outing, launched way back in 1906. In 1919, more than 4,000 orphans enjoyed their day of fun as a result of the CATA's efforts, joined by the Chicago Automobile Club and Chicago Garage Owners Association.

Through the Twenties, the CATA continued its activities as a valuable ally to Chicagoland dealers, but management of the auto show remained with the automakers. They also were responsible for New York's annual show.

General Manager Edward Cleary, past-President Max Evans, and Show Chairman Don Mullery study the proposed design theme for the 1961 auto show—the first to be held at McCormick Place.

Used cars got considerable attention in the teens. In 1912, the CATA issued to its members a book that gave allowance values for used automobiles. That evolved into the *Great Central Market Used Car Report*, first published in 1914 and issued to dealers. A year later, the *National Used Car Market Report* covered the entire country.

During World War I, which the United States entered in late 1917, CATA members conducted a variety of patriotic activities, selling bonds and mobilizing motor vehicles for the government. In May of that year, the CATA held its first Used Automobile Show at the Coliseum, selling 369 cars worth a total of $275,000.

CATA board members study the floor plan for the 1957 Chicago Auto Show. Manufacturers participate in a drawing for space allocations.

Official auto-show car in 1956 was an Imperial. Pictured on the right is Jerry H. Cizek, then serving as a CATA director and the grandfather of the association's current president, Jerry H. Cizek III.

By 1931, under President J.R. Histed, CATA membership had passed the thousand mark. R.G. Tiffany, the next president, explained that as a bonus, "employment will be given during auto show week to hundreds of extra waiters, porters and others." Furthermore, "hundreds of tradesman are given jobs decorating the Coliseum and hotels." That was good news to some of the work-starved Americans, suffering the pains of the Great Depression. For a change, the CATA sponsored the 1932 Salon of custom automobiles at the Drake Hotel.

Assisting with the auto exhibits at Chicago's Century of Progress, in 1933–34, put another feather in the CATA's cap. As unemployment hit its peak, people needed diversion. That's exactly what they found at Chicago's lakefront exposition. Several years previous, CATA President O.G. Heffinger had written that this would be "the greatest fair the world has ever seen."

By 1935, the CATA had been instrumental in eliminating the auxiliary hotel shows that had been part of the automotive picture each winter. From that point forward, Chicago would have only one auto show. The exotic machines could have their displays at the Coliseum, just like everyone else.

In an attempt to stabilize employment, President Roosevelt directed that manufacturers should introduce their new models in the fall, not in the spring. For that reason, Chicago had two auto shows in 1935: one early in the year, showcasing 1935 models; and another in the fall, heralding the '36 cars.

CATA executives had a sudden shock, however. The automakers and their

An annual food drive lets visitors into the show for a reduced price if they bring food items for distribution to the needy.

organization, the Automobile Manufacturers Association, decided to stop sponsoring auto shows in both Chicago and New York. For a while, it looked like there might be no 1935 show at all. But the CATA stepped in and took over the show's management after the 1934 event—and has remained in charge ever since. Harry T. Hollingshead led the CATA show committee for their initial effort.

Another big change took place in 1935. That fall, the auto show moved from the castle-like Coliseum on South Wabash Avenue, its home since 1901, to the recently-completed International Amphitheatre, at 43rd and Halsted. Though more prosaic in appearance, the Amphitheatre offered four times the space.

That move also ushered in a new age of showmanship, directed by A.C. Faeh, the show manager. Taking over after the death of Samuel Miles, who had operated Chicago auto shows since 1901, Faeh believed that people wanted to be entertained as well as informed. Faeh started in 1935 with a pageant of cars, highlighted by models wearing furs. At each auto show during the late Thirties, he gave the public precisely what they appeared to want, in the form of twice-daily stage revues. The CATA explained that the show was "a non-profit venture, conducted and planned and managed by business men with no outside promotional organization needed."

Show Manager Edward Cleary and "Sheriff" Joe Higgins look over attendance figures during the 1970 auto show.

Managing the auto show was just one of the association's activities, even though it drew the most attention. Among other things, CATA executives had to answer a variety of questions put forth by member dealers. On a given day, there might be questions about sales tax, flat-rate repair figures, wage surveys, dealer liability when a wrecked car is taken in for repairs, questionable finance companies, misrepresentation in advertising, legality of contracts with minors, and much more. All along, the CATA worked closely with Chicago's Better Business Bureau and the daily papers, to control advertising and business practices by its member dealers. A committee on highway safety sought "to improve

Above: *Groundbreaking for the new CATA headquarters took place in autumn 1996.* **Below:** *Manufacturer representatives meet to draw space for the 1999 auto show. Meeting rooms at the new headquarters also are used regularly by members of the association, as well as by other groups.*

driving practices." The CATA became a model for trade associations nationwide, even in other industries.

Even before the United States entered World War II, the CATA decided not to hold an auto show in the fall of 1941. Although the CATA remained active through the war years, headed by Presidents Ben T. Wright and Paul B. Smithson, its activities were limited since no cars were produced for civilian use. During the economic "boom" period that followed the war, cars were on sale, but it was a "seller's" market and there was little need to promote the new models. Not when every automobile to arrive at the showroom had a customer waiting eagerly.

By 1950, the early postwar automotive euphoria was dying down. Manufacturers and dealers knew they would have to begin to "sell" cars again, as they had before the war, rather than merely write up orders from consumers practically waving money in their faces.

Fortunately, the industry had been busy creating brand-new products, most of which had been issued in 1949. Even if most of the 1950 cars were essentially facelifts, however, Chicagoans responded eagerly to the announcement that the Amphitheatre would again host an auto show. Thousands of them had attended the Railroad Fair along the lakefront, in the late Forties. But with the newfound prosperity that had emerged since the war, Americans were even more eager to own private transportation. They wanted cars, and the CATA was ready to put on a show again. A real show, complete with entertainers, lights,

action—and plenty of automobiles to delight the eyes of Midwesterners.

Close to 500 dealers and other firms belonged to the CATA in 1951, when Frank H. Yarnall served as president and Edward L. Cleary was the auto-show manager. In cooperation with the Chicago Safety Information Committee, the CATA sponsored a safety-slogan contest for students, with winners given prizes at the auto show.

Since the late Thirties, the CATA had promoted a used-car warranty for its member dealers. They also monitored relevant activities in Chicago's city council and the Illinois state legislature in Springfield, issued a weekly news bulletin, and formulated a model group insurance plan. Staffers also offered tax and legal information to members. Safe-driving campaigns were promoted, and the CATA worked with state legislators on issues of dealer ethics. They also worked to protect dealers against "red tape" and "excessive tax burdens."

Moving the auto show into McCormick Place in 1961 was a highlight in CATA history. But that success was dashed six years later, when the lakefront exposition center caught fire—mere weeks before the show was scheduled to open. Executives had their hands full, scrambling to arrange an auto show against awesome odds. Fortunately, the old Amphitheatre was still usable, though plenty of work was needed to make it habitable. Four years later, a new McCormick Place was constructed. And in 1997, another new McCormick Place put the show on a single huge floor.

Under the stewardship of Jerry H. Cizek III, today's CATA is a blend of administrative, planning, and managerial duties, coupled with charitable activities. Solving the problems of member dealers remains their first priority, and the auto show ranks high on the list of duties. In addition to organizing the show and arranging the drawing for manufacturer space, the CATA sets up a schedule of news conferences prior to each show's opening. For years, a formal gathering for VIPs and invited guests was held on the

At each year's formal preview, officials present an oversize check to a group of charitable organizations. Pictured at the 1998 First Look for Charity are (l-to-r): Illinois Secretary of State George Ryan, TV personality Janet Davies, Vice-Chairman Patrick Fitzgibbon, Chevrolet General Manager John Middlebrook, and Show Chairman Raymond Scarpelli.

The CATA staff in 1998 (l-to-r): Erik Higgins, Tom Hunt, Maxine Sinda, Jack Gallagher, Jerry H. Cizek III, David Sloan, Rose Hansen, Dennis Buckley, Stacey Cizek, and Paul Brian.

night before the show opened. That evolved into First Look for Charity, which has raised several million dollars for a dozen worthy causes.

CATA members include not only auto dealers, but also finance companies, insurance firms, banks, and the like. A biweekly *CATA Bulletin* goes to members. The CATA provides license information to members, holds a schedule of seminars, and works with journalists to communicate a positive image of the business. They also provide essential forms to member dealers, and conduct CATPAC (a political action committee). Serving as a dealer advocate, the CATA monitors activities at the State Legislature in Springfield, as well as the Chicago City Council, to unearth and fight legislation that might be unfair to dealers. The CATA has been involved in such issues as Chicago's transaction tax, the Sunday Closing law, and Illinois Franchise Act.

Scholarships to Northwood University for the study of automotive marketing are awarded regularly, to dealership employees and their children. The CATA also operates two Internet sites: dealerlocator.com (which helps consumers locate a dealership) and chicago-autoshow.com (with information on the auto show).

Truth in advertising remains a high priority. The group is vigilant about watching the ads. Their weekly "Drive Time" radio program, hosted by Communications Director Paul Brian, helps get the CATA's message out to the public.

Most of all, "we're looking for ways to bring value to the CATA members," says Executive Vice-President David Sloan. "We also want to bolster our lobbying," and develop a "stronger training aspect." Operating the auto show "enables us not to be a traditional association."

Jack Gallagher—a long career with the auto show

JACK GALLAGHER

No one at the CATA has a history with the auto show like Jack Gallagher's. Now the show's exhibit coordinator, he began in 1949 (see page 9) as an usher.

"McCormick Place started out with a bang," Jack says. The fact that it "faced the lake" was a big bonus, but "nobody knew where to go....

"In the first two years, there were no chairs in the Arie Crown [Theatre]. So you'd get more people in there." Four or five cars went onstage, followed by a musical interlude. They proceeded alphabetically, and a "guy had a spiel about each one." Among the entertain-

ers who appeared, Gallagher particularly remembers Wes Harrison, who did imitations (including motorcycles).

Officially, Jack served as sales manager for the Andy Frain organization. Each year, he was the auto show's "official driver." In those days, they had one official car (today, four). "I was a trusted individual," he admits, and "had the run of the office." A "jack of all trades," he did everything from running an Addressograph to answering questions at the show.

At McCormick Place, he recalls, "the weekend would be like a nightmare. The radio guys would say, 'Don't come near the automobile show. There's no room.' The outer drive was a sea of traffic." People even "used to walk across the ice, to take a shortcut."

Jack left Andy Frain in 1988 and came to the CATA as a field representative. At that time, the CATA was "bombarded" with calls from consumers. Today, he barely gets two a week. Bumper-to-bumper warranties account for the difference, he believes.

12
Aftermarket Memories

Tires and lights. Horns and bumpers. Tools and gadgets. Those were the kinds of items a visitor to early auto shows was likely to find, tucked among the motorcars. For many years, the show floor even featured shop equipment, destined not for car owners but for garage operators.

By the 1950s, a great contingent of aftermarket firms were becoming "regulars" at the Chicago Auto Show. They were joined each year by a batch of first-timers who hoped to lure passersby into their booths, and then induce them to part with a few dollars. A visitor in the Fifties could find seatbelts and Continental kits. The Sixties brought promoters of high-performance accessories into

the fold: multiple carburetor setups, electronic ignitions, and more.

Not all of the exhibitors had anything at all to do with cars, however. Some of the popular booths were held by vendors hawking everything from cutlery to kitchen gadgets, homemade fudge to encyclopedias. Off in a corner of the Amphitheatre, or occupying the far walls of McCormick Place's lower level, the auxiliary vendors were an integral part of the festivities. When the show moved to its newest facility, the vendors came right along.

Through the next few pages, we've assembled photos of just a few of the popular aftermarket exhibits, from the early days to the present time.

Tires were popular products in the early years, when even the shortest trip was likely to result in one or more "flats." Ads in 1906 promoted the fact that a product could be seen at the Coliseum.

Not every automobile came equipped with a horn in 1910, and some owners liked to replace the original horn with a different sound. The Jericho company came to the rescue.

In the teens and before, service and trade equipment was exhibited at the auto show, along with vehicles. These portable gasoline pumps were promoted at the 1911 show.

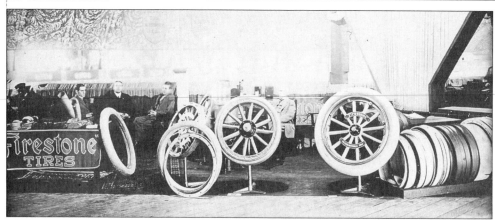

Firestone had a full line of replacement tires at the 1911 auto show.

Early motorists had to be do-it-yourselfers, so replacing a carburetor was a common task. Stromberg exhibited its wares at the 1911 auto show.

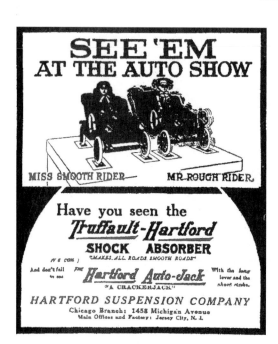

Believe it or not, many early automobiles had no shock absorbers at all. Aftermarket companies soon developed accessories that the automakers omitted, or offered only in primitive form. These shocks were promoted at the 1911 auto show.

Most automobiles in 1916 had no heater for front-seat occupants, much less those in the rear. The floor-mounted outlet for this Perfection rear-seat heater looks like it belongs in a home, not a car.

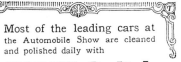

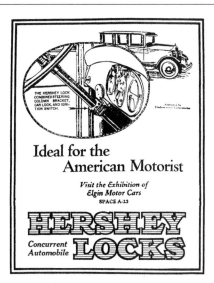

Thieves began to look at stray automobiles early in the century, but automakers provided little in the way of protection. A Hershey ignition lock just might have made that 1924 automobile a bit tougher to steal.

No, that isn't "moonshine" liquor in the jug; it's auto body polish, marketed at the 1916 auto show. Car care products arrived on the scene early, as motorists were induced to shine their "motors" on weekends.

At the 1932 Chicago Auto Show, two young women dubbed Miss Stewart and Miss Warner helped promote Stewart-Warner accessories.

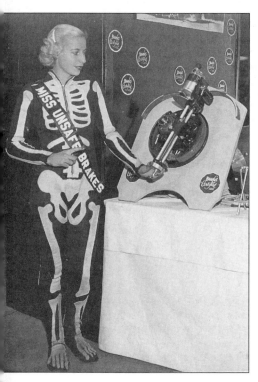

This woman donned a deathly skeleton outfit at the 1939 Chicago Auto Show to publicize the dangers of unsafe brakes. Ford was among the last automakers to adopt hydraulic brakes—not until 1939.

Simoniz was one of the best known car waxes in the 1930s and '40s. Promoting relevant products at the auto show generally resulted in substantial sales.

Lincoln mounted an external spare tire on its Continental in 1940-48. In the early Fifties, "continental" kits became popular on custom cars, and were installed by ordinary motorists who wanted to give their cars a distinctive look.

Below: *Makers of the Chicagoan, a build-it-yourself "kit car," promised at the 1954 Chicago Auto Show that the fiberglass-bodied sports car would be "easy to assemble." As a rule, some buyers of kit cars discovered otherwise.*

Sweetest Part of the Show

Pictured behind the Ryba's Fudge counter at the 1968 auto show are (l-to-r) Noreen Riley, founder Harry Ryba, and Ethel Ryba.

Right: *Victor Callewaert makes fudge while "walking the slab."*

Beyond the lure of viewing the new cars lies an attraction of another sort. Each year, the public flocks to the annual auto show in Chicago not only to survey the automotive scene, but also to purchase their half-pound of confectionery heaven from Ryba's Fudge. This love affair between Ryba and the Chicago show crowd has been going on since 1955.

The simple fact that owner Victor Callewaert and his crew sell two tons—that's right, four thousand pounds—of their delicious fudge during the nine-day auto show is proof positive of its popularity.

Each loaf of fudge is made fresh at the show. The process takes about 45 minutes, from the mixing of the ingredients to the final stage of "walking the slab."

Right in front of the show crowd, the cooked fudge is poured out onto a marble slab. Then, the candy maker takes special tools and walks around the large slab for several minutes, folding the fudge into a hardened loaf. The loaf is then cut into individual wedges for retail sale.

What's the most popular of the six luscious fudge flavors offered at the Chicago Auto Show? It's chocolate with pecans.

Victor Callewaert has been connected with Ryba's Fudge since 1951, when, as a high school student, he started working part-time for founder Harry Ryba in Detroit, Michigan. Six years later, Victor married Rena Ryba, the boss' daughter. In 1959, following his military service, he became a full-time employee.

Victor's five children—Mary, Todd, Amy, Ann, and Gregg—are all involved with the family's growing business. Their fudge empire includes the Island House Hotel on Mackinac Island, Michigan, plus many retail fudge and ice cream shops (including one at Navy Pier in Chicago), and a mail-order candy division. The Ryba's crew also follows a yearly schedule of 40 shows to sell their fudge.

Ryba's Fudge has been a Chicago tradition for decades. Let's hope they continue to put smiles on the faces and fill the sweet tooth of future auto-show generations.

Right: When everyone used fold-out maps, calculating mileage between points could be a hassle. The Rolla company had an answer with their Map Ruler, promoted at the 1956 auto show.

Left: Not too many motorists were interested in safety belts in 1956, but they were available at the 1955 auto show—marketed by a parachute company, no less. These two gentlemen appear to be happily belted, but safety did not sell cars in the Fifties.

Ingenuity knew no bounds when it came to car accessories. Who could have dreamed that there might be a demand for a hat carrier—even in 1956, when plenty of men wore fedoras and the like? For only a buck, though, it might be worth a try.

Children always seemed to enjoy the auto show—but probably not as much as these youthful gentlemen, tucked behind the wheel of the Junior (Pontiac) Star Chief at the 1956 event.

Pocket transistor radios had been developed in the Fifties. When the 1960 auto show opened, transistors were displacing the old vacuum tubes in aftermarket auto radios. Produced by Motorola, these radios came in different mounting styles, depending on the car. The $39.95 minimum price wasn't exactly cheap, considering that a new Ford Falcon sold for as little as $1,912.

Cars didn't have cupholders in 1961, and takeaway restaurants weren't yet pervasive on American streets. Motorists who craved their morning coffee might go for a "coffee break" kit that used an immersion heater to warm up the brew.

Members of the Junior Association of Commerce (Chicagoland region) promoted the use of amber lights at the 1963 auto show.

Leaving a convertible parked with the top down was taking a chance, even in 1962. With a Bedol unit installed, the roof allegedly raised automatically when rain began, or the outside temperature reached 110 degrees.

What model-car collector today wouldn't like to grab a stack of these AMT, Johan, and Monogram kits— for just 98 cents each? Sorry, that was the price at the 1964 Chicago Auto Show.

Roland H. Prince Sr.: a master pitchman

Anyone who's been to the Chicago Auto Show over the past four decades has seen and heard one of the premier after-market product pitchmen in the industry: Roland Prince.

Starting in 1959, Roland began selling all kinds of popular merchandise from the small retail booths that circled the perimeter of the auto show. Roland and his crew of professional demonstrators have become an integral part of the festive atmosphere. And with good reason. First, they can masterfully develop a crowd around their display. Secondly, they demonstrate interesting products, through highly entertaining and crowd-pleasing sales pitches.

Most of the products are auto-related: waxes and polishes, chamois and speed-socket wrenches. But these "pitchmen" (as Roland calls them) also are famous for the no-stick cookware and knives. For kids, they might demonstrate and sell color-changing marker pens.

One non-automotive item that Roland sold was a liquefying food blender for health drinks, aptly called "Vitamix." He sold this item for 25 straight years at the auto show. His famous line to the crowd was: "Look, folks, I'm still here. I've been drinking this liquid for years and I'm still here." Skeptics in the crowd who were holding their kids' hands would be reminded by Roland that he remembered them as kids coming to the auto show, holding their *own* dad's hand.

"This type of sales is a dying art," says Mr. Prince today, "at least on the traveling show circuit—though you see some of our people branching out onto the home shopping TV networks. Our people love to talk for hours and travel around the country. They have developed ways to save their voices for long-running events like the Chicago Auto Show.

"We have made many friends and customers over the years. I've had people say to me, after our pitch, that they were going to buy what we're selling—but that the show we put on is worth ten times the price."

Looks like a satisfied customer, hustling away from Mr. Prince's booth in 1966 with a seatbelt and a Vitamix device.

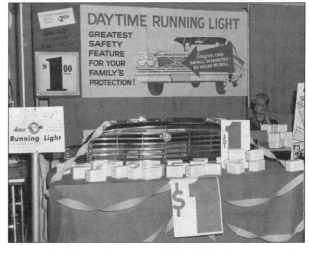

Daytime running lights? In 1965? They weren't quite the same as the DRL units installed on cars today, but the special auto-show price was only a buck.

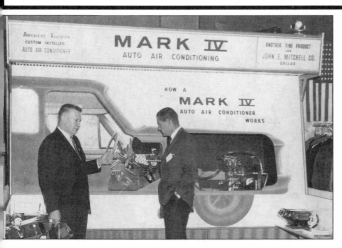

Above: *Marketers of Mark IV air conditioners, ready for under-dash installation, had a modest display at the 1964 Chicago Auto Show.*

Go-karting was popular in Chicagoland in 1965, as it was elsewhere in the nation. Visitors to this booth could see the vehicles and a few karting magazines. Then, they might move one space left to see what Mr. Norm's Grand-Spaulding Dodge had to offer in the way of race-ready equipment.

Transistor ignitions were still something new in 1966, offered by aftermarket companies. A Chevrolet with its hood off demonstrated the installation for technically-minded visitors.

Above: Warshawsky's was a Chicago institution long before 1968, when this photo was taken. Known as J.C. Whitney elsewhere in the country, the company issued a 25-cent catalog that listed thousands upon thousands of auto parts and accessories: fender skirts, headrests, air fresheners, carburetors—just about everything a motorist or do-it-yourselfer might need.

Van conversions were popular by 1971—and continued to attract customers for years afterward. This Beachcomber conversion, billed as a multi-purpose vehicle, cost $7,360.

A pitchman for the Monte Cristo company hawks his fog-proof products for car windows at the 1971 auto show.

Looks like the European Parts company brought a section of its store to the 1971 auto show. Volkswagen Beetle accessories and hop-up kits were particularly popular.

Yes, those are 8-track tapes for sale at $3 in 1972 ($6 for the special "Bangladesh" concert). A few years later, 8-tracks would be gone, displaced by smaller cassettes.

This Dodge doesn't look too rusty. Were its "22 critical rust areas" treated with Ziebart? Many companies marketed rust-protection products, but Ziebart was probably the best-known in 1976.

All you had to do was supply a wrecked Ford Pinto. For $4,495 in 1978, this company supplied everything else needed to create a "kit" sports car, named Bearcat. The finished product is shown at left; parts required at right.

Motor scooters had been popular back in the Fifties. Vespa's booth still attracted visitors at the 1982 Chicago Auto Show.

Moloney was one of the best-known makers of stretch limousines in 1988. One of these biggies could be leased for $789 a month, for 48 months.

Displays of replacement and custom wheels always drew plenty of potential customers. This display by Lucas was set up at the 1998 auto show.

Left: *By the time the 1997 auto show rolled around, custom T-shirt sales and special airbrushing had a long history.*

Wouldn't it be fun to ride around the 1997 Chicago Auto Show in one of these uncommonly-shaped golf carts?

Stan Hegberg—a popular vendor of books

Programs weren't the only printed items that could be purchased at the Chicago Auto Show. Anyone who took an interest in older cars was likely to stop at the book stand operated by the late Stanley W. Hegberg.

Through four decades, starting in 1950, Hegberg turned up each year to display his wares. Instead of a conventional, fixed space at the Amphitheatre or McCormick Place, he was simply issued a "spot" on which to place his rolling cart.

Hegberg's specialty was the highly popular series of books by Floyd Clymer, first published in the early years of motoring but then reissued after World War II for a more "modern" audience. Clymer books not only told the story of automotive history, but they offered practical instructions on repair and maintenance. As the years went by, Stan Hegberg added other books for enthusiasts to savor. For many, who did not ordinarily attend antique-vehicle events, Hegberg's display at the auto show would be the only opportunity to see—and buy—car books of this nature.

13
Modern Times
(1996 and beyond)

Chicago's auto show opened in McCormick Place East, right at the lakefront, for the last time in February 1996. Instead of holding the customary news conferences prior to the show's opening, three manufacturers introduced their latest products on Saturday, the first public day of the show. Acura exhibited its RL sedan, Mitsubishi trotted out its Eclipse Spyder convertible, and Oldsmobile had a new Cutlass sedan on tap.

Honda displayed a CR-V that was already on sale in Japan, looking for customer reaction before deciding whether to bring it to the United States. Mazda launched a mid-season Miata M Edition, and Pontiac exhibited its Grand Prix coupe for the first time. Toyota debuted a Paseo convertible, expected to go on sale that fall.

A brand-new McCormick Place (South) was ready in time for the 89th Chicago Auto Show, in February 1997. Instead of having exhibits on two floors, as had been the case for many years, they could now all fit on a single massive floor—the size of half a dozen football fields.

Dodge displayed its 1998 Ram trucks. Ford flaunted a redesigned Ranger pickup and performance-focused SVT Contour. Chevrolet's entry was the facelifted Camaro. Chrysler had its usual array of concept vehicles, including a bright orange Dodge Sidewinder pickup, decked out like a street rod with a Viper V-10 engine. GMC showed its Envoy concept, a spin-off of the Jimmy, for the first time. Lexus had an unnamed Sport Luxury Vehicle concept (which evolved into the RX 300). Mercedes-Benz debuted its F200 concept coupe, driven by "side stick" controls. Toyota introduced a Solara concept convertible.

For the 1998 auto show, Nissan introduced a redesigned Quest minivan, Acura showed a concept TL-X, Ford unveiled a Libre concept convertible and SVT F-150 Lightning pickup, and GMC debuted a Sierra DEUCE Sportside show truck. Kia unveiled a minivan for future production. Mitsubishi waited until Saturday, the first public day, to officially introduce the redesigned Galant. Toyota showed its latest Land Cruiser for the first time.

The 91st annual Chicago Auto Show again takes place at the new McCormick Place, from February 12–21, 1999. For the first time, the show will open on Friday, following a two-day media preview. Formally-attired guests will attend the 1999 First Look for Charity on Thursday night.

What's next for the auto show? CATA President Jerry Cizek (see page 302), has blazed a strong trail forward during his tenure and is optimistic about the future. So are the member dealers, and the manufacturers that participate.

Whether in small, medium, or large size, sport-utility vehicles continued to attract auto-show visitors—and buyers—in the late 1990s. Lexus displayed a stylish new luxury compact RX 300 at the 1998 show, on sale as a '99 model.

Ford favors Chicago for SVT debuts

Since 1992, Ford's Special Vehicle Team has chosen Chicago to introduce their exciting new products to the world. Here, they've unveiled such vehicles as the Mustang Cobra, F-150 Lightning, and SVT Contour to the press and the buying public.

"Chicago is picked year after year because it offers manufacturers some specific advantages in gaining recognition for their vehicles," says Jim Sawyer, former SVT public relations manager. "This includes high show attendance and excellent coverage received during the show.

"SVT's goal is to produce limited-edition, high-performance machines aimed at dedicated driving enthusiasts." The Chicago show "best represents this buyer who appreciates our enhanced vehicles."

Among the intriguing new entrants at the 1996 auto show was BMW's Z3 roadster, ready to go on sale in the spring. Front-end styling was reminiscent of the 1950s BMW 507 roadster.

Developed by Ford's Special Vehicle Team, the Cobra convertible debuted as a mid-1996 model, joining the already available coupe. Cobras benefited from a 305-horsepower engine, versus 215 horses under regular Mustang V-8 hoods.

Chevrolet's Impala SS (left) a performance-oriented offs' of the full-size Caprice sec Both were in their final seaso' the market. Chevrolet planne' build a thousand Corvette G' Sport coupes (right), taking c' as performance leader after demise of the ZR-1.

Not many V-12 engines could be found anymore, except for the 5.7-liter example used in the exotic Lamborghini Diablo, developing 485 horsepower.

1996
88th annual Chicago Automobile Show
(February 10–18, 1996)

- This is last auto show at McCormick Place East ... new facility is under construction nearby
- Record-setting 993,646 visitors attend this year's auto show
- Three official debuts are held on Saturday, for general public, rather than earlier in the week for media only: 1997 Oldsmobile Cutlass sedan, Acura RL sedan, and Mitsubishi Eclipse convertible
- Toyota introduces Paseo convertible and shows special-trim versions of Tercel, Camry, and Celica ... also exhibits new Indycar engine
- Mercedes-Benz introduces Sport packages for C280, E420, and SL
- Honda displays Civic-based CR-V, plus SSM concept roadster
- Cadillac promotes GM's OnStar driver assistance system
- Lincoln introduces RESCU assistance system and SecuriTire run-flat system
- Ford's Triton V-10 engine is showcased in Chicago concept van ... SVT division unveils Mustang Cobra convertible
- Chevrolet unveils sporty Lumina LTZ, with engine from Monte Carlo Z34
- Pontiac launches coupe version of redesigned Grand Prix
- Charity Preview raises $850,000
- Saab announces new sales program to bypass dealer for initial test-drives
- Infiniti announces name for new sport-utility (QX4), but vehicle is not shown

A special "Indy 500" edition of the formidable Dodge Ram pickup appeared at the auto show.

After seven seasons on the market, Infiniti was ready to launch a modified version of its rear-drive Q45 "flagship" sedan. Instead of the former 4.5-liter V-8, the '97 model would get a 4.1-liter engine.

Land Rover's display took the form of a rain forest, complete with misty air. The lineup of British-built sport-utilities included the Land Rover Discovery and Defender 90, as well as two versions of the Range Rover.

Toyota launched a mini-size sport-utility vehicle for 1996, dubbed RAV4 (Recreational Activity Vehicle with 4WD). The auto-show display even included a battery-powered version.

Suzuki tried something different for 1996: a two-passenger X-90, targeting younger buyers by mixing the benefits of a sport-utility vehicle with a sporty subcompact coupe.

1997

89th annual Chicago Automobile Show

(February 8–16, 1997)

- Auto show moves to brand-new site: McCormick Place South, a short distance west of prior facility on Chicago's lakefront
- All exhibits are now on one floor: 840,000 square feet—one of the largest rooms in the world
- Attendance tops the million mark for first time: 1,021,981 visitors in all
- Chevrolet displays facelifted 1998 Camaro, offered with Corvette-based V-8
- Dodge exhibits group of concept vehicles including Sidewinder pickup, plus new Ram Quad Cab pickup truck, redesigned Ram van, and Dakota R/T
- Ford focuses on 1998 SVT Contour, a high-performance rendition of compact sedan ... redesigned Ranger pickup also is seen, along with electric-powered Ranger and brawny PowerForce concept truck
- GMC exhibits concept version of the Jimmy sport-utility, named Envoy
- Lexus shows forthcoming sport-utility vehicle, based on ES 300 sedan
- Lincoln-Mercury exhibits L'Attitude concept "family adventure" vehicle
- Futuristic Mercedes-Benz F200 concept coupe appears for first time in U.S.
- Mitsubishi has special Eclipse Spyder Speedster—not to be produced
- Subaru promotes new sport-utility vehicle, to be named Forester
- Toyota shows Solara convertible concept
- Volvo displays C70 coupe and convertible
- First Look for Charity raises more than $1 million ... Dodge Viper GTS coupe is grand prize

PATRICK FITZGIBBON

Patrick Fitzgibbon was chairman of the auto show as it moved into the new facility. "It was an honor to serve as the chairman of the Chicago Auto Show during 1997," he recalls, "the inaugural year of McCormick Place South. The transition into this mammoth 840,000-square-foot exhibit hall was intense, but done with ease. I credit this accomplishment to the talented team from the Chicago Automobile Trade Association, along with the dedication of the show committee. The automobile manufacturers' cooperation was also tremendous. Major exhibitors brought new displays, created especially to maximize the openness of this modern building. McCormick Place South demonstrates the commitment that the city of Chicago and the dealers' associations bring to continue the World's Greatest Auto Show tradition into the next century."

No longer situated directly along the lakefront, the new McCormick Place s&
a block to the west, along Martin Luther King Drive. The lavish entryway wa
more inviting than that of the old McCormick Place, which was intended i
remain in use for certain events.

Left: A lucky attendee at the Charity Preview got to drive home this Dodge Viper GTS coupe. Each year, the formal preview raises a considerable sum for various charitable organizations.

Above: Moving to the new McCormick Place permitted th display of all vehicles—and auxiliary exhibitors—on single floor. Previously, trucks and specialty displays ha been on the lower level.

verwhelming praise after its appearance in concept form rompted Chrysler Corporation to put the Plymouth Prowler into roduction, as a mid-1997 model. Eliciting memories of Fifties hot ds, the Prowler used a V-6 engine with AutoStick transmission.

Brand manager Ken Stewart describes the Oldsmobile Intrigue sedan, scheduled for debut as an early '98 model, to journalists. Media people attend news conferences at the show for several days prior to its opening to the general public.

uccess of the full-size Ford Expedition led to development of a osh Lincoln Navigator (shown), on sale as a mid-1997 model.

After exhibiting a battery-powered Impact several years earlier, General Motors put an electric car on sale. The sporty two-passenger EV1 was marketed by Saturn dealers in the southwest.

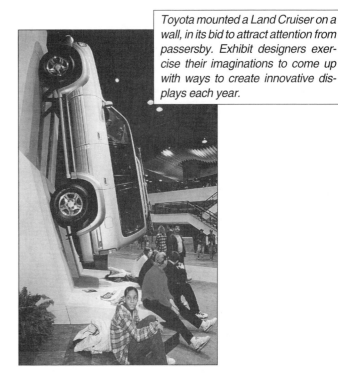

Toyota mounted a Land Cruiser on a wall, in its bid to attract attention from passersby. Exhibit designers exercise their imaginations to come up with ways to create innovative displays each year.

ercedes-Benz planned to get its new SLK roadster to dealerships ound the time of the Chicago Auto Show. Wearing a retractable el roof, the '98 SLK carried a supercharged engine.

1998
90th annual Chicago Automobile Show
(February 7–15, 1998)

- Record-breaker: 1,080,637 visitors see auto show at McCormick Place South
- Mitsubishi makes its announcement of new Galant on Saturday, the first public day of the auto show
- Nissan exhibits redesigned Quest minivan and four-door concept pickup truck
- Toyota shows redesigned Land Cruiser for first time, plus T150 concept truck
- Biggest attraction at the Chicago show might be Volkswagen's New Beetle, seen first in Detroit a month earlier
- Chevrolet shows Tahoe Z71, to go on sale as '99 model, plus TrailBlazer edition of Blazer LT, also expected in 1999
- Chrysler stand flaunts coming-soon Chrysler 300M and LHS, as well as batch of concept vehicles ... Town & Country Limited minivan is announced
- Ford introduces bright red Libre concept convertible with four doors (but no top)
- Oldsmobile promotes tie-in between Intrigue sedan and "X Files" TV show
- Successor to Ford's SVT F-150 Lightning pickup debuts at Chicago show ... NASCAR edition of F-150 also seen
- Despite corporate problems, Kia unveils new minivan, expected late in 1999 ... also shows Sportage convertible and tiny two-seat Elan (not for sale in U.S.)
- GMC has DEUCE concept Sierra Sportside show truck at its display
- Concept vehicles include Acura TL-X, Mercedes-Benz Maybach, Honda JVX, Mazda MV-X, Isuzu VX-2 and Zaccar
- Dozen charities get more than $1 million from black-tie benefit preview—raffle winner gets Corvette convertible

Among the coming-soon models available for inspection at the 1998 auto show were the redesigned Chrysler LHS (shown), a luxury sedan, along with its sportier 300M mate.

Introduced as a 1997 model, the Pontiac Grand Prix came in coupe and sedan form. Pontiacs of every size were known for their sporty appearance.

Below: *More than any vehicle in modern times, Volkswagen's New Beetle drew hordes of auto-show patrons who were eager to ask questions and look inside the uniquely-styled sedan.*

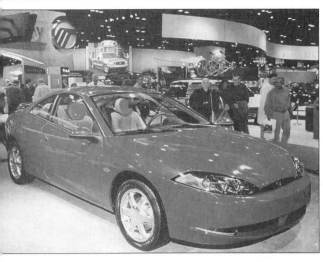

ercury exhibited its new-for-1999 Cougar, borrowing a name sed previously—but this Cougar bore no resemblance to its ncestor.

Mazda's Miata roadster had been a phenomenal success when introduced at the Chicago show early in 1989. At the '98 show, Mazda displayed its redesigned 1999 Miata: more powerful, wearing newly-exposed headlamps, and promising more luggage space.

ord marked the 50th anniversary of its F-Series pickup truck in 998. Seen at the auto show was this Lightning pickup from ord's SVT group, packing a load of bold performance extras.

Cutaways of cars had been displayed at the auto show for decades, and continued to attract interested shoppers who wondered about construction details. Buick sliced away a segment of its Century sedan for the 1998 show.

rior to the opening of the 1998 auto show to the public, ousands of people attended the formal "First Look for Charity" ent. Here, a formally-attired couple looks over the Shelby eries I, a limited-edition street-racer with a $100,000 price tag d a modified Oldsmobile Aurora-based engine.

Volkswagen wasn't the only automaker to look back at the past for ideas. Two Japanese-brand companies, Infiniti and Lexus, displayed modern updates of old "hot rod" roadsters in 1998, in concept form. The Infiniti Q29 (shown) borrowed its powertrain from the big Q45 sedan.

Jerry H. Cizek III: steering the Auto Show into the 21st century

Jerry H. Cizek III, the president of the Chicago Automobile Trade Association, grew up in an auto-dealer family in the Chicago area. Cizek joined the CATA in 1973, and has been president since 1988.

Jerry Cizek's ties to the auto business date back to childhood. His grandfather, Jerry H. Cizek I, had a Chrysler dealership at 2505 N. Milwaukee Avenue, in Chicago's Logan Square neighborhood. While attending Riverside-Brookfield High School, the young Cizek "worked summers," he recalls, "in service, chasing parts.... This was before I could drive. I took the bus."

Attending the auto show started early, too. "It was always a lot of fun," he remembers. "I went with my grandpa and father. We would go to the director's hospitality room [and] always went to the Saddle & Sirloin Room [nearby] for dinner."

Long before entering the business, Cizek "actually worked the auto shows." In his memory, the Amphitheatre, was a rather dark place, with "passageways and ramps." The show occupied two floors, and "big trucks were at the end of the arena." At the 1969 show, he won the $25 Mystery Shopper Award.

In the early Seventies, though armed with a Business Administration degree, Cizek considered becoming a teacher and coach. Instead, he worked for a while for his father, but "saw where Chrysler was going. And the dealership was having a tough time." After it closed, Cizek turned to F&I (finance and insurance).

For a time, he worked at Bill Tomczak Dodge. Then, Don McAuliffe called. He'd just opened a Volkswagen dealership. Cizek moved there for a while, but notes that "I knew I would never have my name" on the building. Next came a stint at Shamrock Oldsmobile.

Early in 1973, Cizek "answered a blind ad in the *Tribune*, from AMC in Franklin Park." He went to work in the distribution office. Then, "Gil Gillaspy came through one day," he recalls. Dawson Gillaspy was a "field guy" for CATA. Gil called a week later, inviting Cizek to have lunch with Ross Kelsey and Ben Orloff. "Ross offered me a job at CATA," as a field representative. "They had to create that position."

"I really enjoyed the face time with the dealers.... Gil and I split up the city. He did everything north of Madison, I did everything south of Madison." The two men "visited dealers in November or December, which was the busy time for the auto show."

At that time, dealers had strong opinions on the CATA: "some good, some very bluntly critical." Cizek eventually took over Gil's job—essentially, doing the job of three. Cizek attended his first auto show as a CATA employee in 1974.

When the time came for a new head of the association to be named, Cizek says he "was hoping the board wouldn't go outside." He took the job, and has been at it for ten years.

"We have made a lot of changes" in that decade, he says, "going in different directions. Today, the Board of Directors is a lot more responsive to the dealers." Cizek is particularly proud of the new headquarters building in Oakbrook Terrace.

"We have a good relationship with NADA [the National Automobile Dealers Association]." The CATA is a "much more active organization" now than in the past, and that has "paid off handsomely for us."

Cizek takes pride in the "responsiveness not only of our staff, but our directors." Even though "you can't fight [a dealer's] individual battle," he likes to take on those that benefit everyone. He's also proud of the First Look for Charity program, and the change in show hours (formerly 11 to 11, now 10 to 10).

Coming to the aid of member dealers is his foremost responsibility, but the CATA also focuses on improving the image of the dealer community with the media and the public. Cizek decries the "stereotype image" of car dealers that persists, arguing that "anytime you can get facts in front of the media," the quest for understanding moves forward. He sees a need for true professionalism in sales and service.

At the auto show, Cizek would like to see displays of medium and heavy-duty trucks. Motorcycles too, and "do it the right way." Better parking is needed, starting with a new four-story garage on Martin Luther King Drive. He'd like to see more women attend.

"Working with the show, with the association, there are no two days the same. It may be legislation; it may be a dealer with a problem. I like the day-to-day challenges. It's never drudgery."

Cizek gets high marks from the experts. "I think the leadership under Jerry Cizek has been phenomenal," says Jim Mateja of the *Chicago Tribune*. Cizek has "met some resistance" from certain dealers, but he has "put his neck on the line."

The Chicago Automobile Trade Association moved into its striking new headquarters building, in Oakbrook Terrace, Illinois, in 1997.

ABOUT THE AUTHORS

To create this unique commemorative book, noted automotive journalist and historian James M. Flammang joined forces with auto historian/ researcher/artist Mitchel J. Frumkin. More than just another history book, this has been a labor of love for the authors, who, between them, bring more than 35 years of professional automotive editorial experience to the project.

A full-time professional writer and editor for nearly all his adult life, Jim Flammang has been writing about cars since the mid-Seventies. In addition to producing a steady flow of automotive articles and reviews of current models, he contributes regularly to consumer buying guides for new and secondhand vehicles. Tirekicking Today—his compact, informative consumer newsletter—is now in its fifth year of publication. Material from Tirekicking Today has appeared on the Internet since mid-1995. His work may be seen at www.tirekick.com.

Flammang also has written more than a dozen books on automotive history, including: Volkswagen: Beetles, Buses & Beyond, the Corvette Chronicle, Standard Catalog of Imported Cars 1946-1990, Cars of the Fabulous Fifties, and Chronicle of the American Automobile. He brings the knowledge of an enthusiast, the concern of a consume advocate, the technical expertise of a mechanic, and th thoroughness of a dedicated journalist to every report and review.

Mitchel J. Frumkin is the author of three books: Muscle Car Mania, Son of Muscle Car Mania, and The Great Aut Trivia Book. Mitch served as Director of Research & Development for nearly 14 years at Publications Internationa Ltd. He was responsible for the development and photographic acquisition of more than 300 Consumer Guid books and issues of Collectible Automobile magazine.

Before getting into publishing, Mitch designed toys and holds several design patents. Mitch is the founder of Driv Communications, which provides new-car evaluation report and photography to buyers' guides and web sites, develop new book projects, and organizes automotive archives. H also brings first-hand personal experiences of attending th Chicago Automobile Show beginning in the early Fifties, and as a press representative and manager of an exhibitor's booth since the mid-Eighties. Mitch's original automotive painting and computer-enhanced photographs have appeared in many recent books and magazines.